T0344388

After the Flood

After the Flood

How the Great Recession Changed Economic Thought

EDWARD L. GLAESER, TANO SANTOS, AND E. GLEN WEYL

THE UNIVERSITY OF CHICAGO PRESS   CHICAGO AND LONDON

The University of Chicago Press, Chicago 60637
The University of Chicago Press, Ltd., London
© 2017 by The University of Chicago
All rights reserved. No part of this book may be used or reproduced in any manner
whatsoever without written permission, except in the case of brief quotations in critical
articles and reviews. For more information, contact the University of Chicago Press,
1427 E. 60th St., Chicago, IL 60637.
Published 2017.
Printed in the United States of America
26 25 24 23 22 21 20 19 18 17   1 2 3 4 5

ISBN-13: 978-0-226-44354-6 (cloth)
ISBN-13: 978-0-226-44368-3 (e-book)
DOI: 10.7208/chicago/9780226443683.001.0001

Library of Congress Cataloging-in-Publication Data

Names: Scheinkman, José Alexandre, honouree. | Glaeser, Edward L. (Edward Ludwig),
    1967- editor, author. | Santos, Tano, editor, author. | Weyl, E. Glen (Eric Glen),
    1985- editor, author. | Columbia University. Graduate School of Business, host institution.
Title: After the flood : how the Great Recession changed economic thought / Edward L.
    Glaeser, Tano Santos, and E. Glen Weyl [editors].
Description: Chicago : the University of Chicago Press, 2017. | Includes papers presented at
    a conference held at the Columbia Business School in the spring of 2013 in honor of José
    Scheinkman's 65th birthday. | Includes index.
Identifiers: LCCN 2016044854 | ISBN 9780226443546 (cloth : alk. paper) |
    ISBN 9780226443683 (e-book)
Subjects: LCSH: Financial crises—Congresses. | Financial crises—Prevention—Congresses. |
    Banks and banking—Congresses. | Capital assets pricing model—Congresses.
Classification: LCC HB3722 .A3225 2017 | DDC 332—dc23 LC record available at
    https://lccn.loc.gov/2016044854

♾ This paper meets the requirements of ANSI/NISO Z39.48-1992 (Permanence of Paper).

FOR JOSÉ AND MICHELE

Contents

CHAPTER ONE

Introduction

Edward L. Glaeser, Tano Santos, and E. Glen Weyl

The past three decades have been characterized by phenomenal up-heavals in financial markets: the United States has witnessed two remarkable cycles both in the stock market during the late 1990s and in real estate during the first decade of the 21st century, followed by the Great Recession, the Japanese banking crisis that itself followed two equally impressive cycles in that country's stock and real estate markets, the larger Asian crisis of 1997, and the Eurozone banking crisis that still is ongoing at the time of this writing. These crises have occurred not in politically unstable countries without sound governance institutions and stable contractual environments, but at the heart of the developed world: the United States, Japan, and the Eurozone. The fact that all these events have led to a flurry of books, papers, journal special issues, and so on exploring the causes of, consequences of, and remedies for large systemic financial crises, which some had thought a thing of the past, is therefore not surprising. What are the origins of these speculative cycles? Are modern financial systems inherently prone to bubbles and instabilities? What are the effects on the real economy?

This volume follows in this tradition but takes a distinct perspective. The chapters in this book consist of papers presented at a conference held at the Columbia Business School in the spring of 2013 in honor of José Scheinkman's 65th birthday. These papers are centered on the lessons learned from the recent financial crisis, issues that have been high in José's agenda for some time now. They are all written by José's coauthors and former students during his remarkable and ongoing career as an economist. José's contributions span many different fields in economics,

from growth to finance and pretty much everything in between. In this
volume, we sought to use this diversity to bring new ideas to bear on the
events of the past three decades. In doing so, we recruited José's closest
colleagues from a variety of fields to speak to his most recent interests,
in financial economics, which he has pursued for the past decade and
a half.

We begin this introduction by focusing on the core financial contributions contained in the volume and gradually connect the papers outward
from there, returning in our discussion of the final chapter to the core
themes we take away from this collection.

1 Asset Pricing

Asset pricing not only lies at the core of finance, but also the core of
José's intellectual interests. His first contribution to the field is an un-
published manuscript from 1977, *Notes on Asset Pricing*. Starting this volume with the contribution that fits squarely in this field is therefore only
appropriate.

The law of one price implies prices can always be expressed as the
inner product of the asset's payoff and another payoff that we term the
stochastic discount factor.[1] The stochastic discount factor is of interest
to economists because, in the context of general equilibrium models, it
encodes information about investors' intertemporal preferences as well
as their attitudes toward risk. Information about these preferences is
important because, for example, they determine the benefits of additional
business-cycle smoothing through economic policy. A long literature in
macroeconomics and finance derives specific models for the stochastic
discount factors from first principles and tests the asset-pricing implications of these models. Since Hansen and Singleton's (1982) seminal
paper that rejected the canonical consumption-based model, we have
learned much about what is required from models that purport to explain
asset prices. But our current models, such as those based on habits or
long-run risks, have difficulty explaining the kind of cycles described in
the opening lines of this introduction. Still, we have sound reasons to
believe elements of those models have to eventually be part of "true"
stochastic discount factor, because not even the most devoted behavioral
finance researcher believes asset prices are completely delinked from
macroeconomic magnitudes at all frequencies.

In sum, our current models for the stochastic discount factors are misspecified. Lars Hansen and José himself contribute the most recent product of their remarkable collaboration with a paper that explores a powerful representation of the stochastic discount factors, one outside standard parametric specifications. By a felicitous coincidence, Lars received the 2013 Nobel Prize, together with Eugene Fama and Robert Shiller, partially for his work on asset pricing. The inclusion of his work in this volume is thus doubly warranted.

In their paper, José and Lars explore the possibility that some components of that representation may be errors arising from an imperfectly specified model that may provide an accurate description of risk-return trade-offs at some frequencies but not others. This decomposition is important, because it will allow the econometrician to focus on particular frequencies of interest, say, business-cycle frequencies, while properly taking into account that the model may not be able to accommodate high-frequency events, such as fast-moving financial crises or even short-term deviations of prices from their fundamental values. This flexible representation of the stochastic discount factor thus captures our partial knowledge regarding its proper parameterization while maintaining our ability to conduct econometric analysis.[2]

In addition, this approach opens the way for further specialization in the field of asset pricing. Some financial economists may focus on those components of the stochastic discount factor with strong mean-reverting components and explore interpretations of these components as liquidity and credit events or periods of missvaluation, for example. Others may focus on those business-cycle frequencies to uncover fundamental preference parameters that should be key in guiding the construction of macroeconomic models geared toward policy evaluation. What arises from the type of representations José and Lars advance in their work is a modular vision of asset pricing—one that emphasizes different economic forces determining risk-return trade-offs at different frequencies.

2 Financial Intermediation

Although the asset-pricing approach of this paper by José and Lars largely abstracts away from financial intermediation and financial institutions, José's research has always attended to the importance of financial institutions. The crises mentioned at the beginning of this introduction all feature financial intermediaries, such as banks, investment banks, or insurance companies, in starring roles. These entities hold vast portfolios of securities. Conflicts of interest within these intermediaries may affect their portfolio decisions and potentially, prices. The study of these agency problems, and of the compensation schemes designed to address them, may then be a critical component in our understanding of these crises. Many commentators have in fact placed the speculative activities of these large financial institutions (including AIG Financial Products and Lehman Brothers) at the center of the crisis and have argued that financial deregulation is to blame for these institutions drifting away from their traditional activities. This volume includes three papers specifically concerned with the issue of banking and what banks did before and during the present crisis.

Patrick Bolton's paper takes issue with the view that restricting what bankers can do is the appropriate regulatory response and instead places compensation inside banks at the heart of the current crisis. In particular, he emphasizes that compensation schemes typically focused on the wrong performance benchmarks, rewarding short-term revenue maximization at the expense of longer-term objectives. Bolton et al. (2006) show how, indeed, privately optimal compensation contracts may overweight (from a social perspective) short-term stock performance as an incentive to encourage managers to take risky actions that increase the speculative components of the stock price. Compensation issues and speculation thus go hand in hand and may offer clues as to why prices deviate from fundamentals. Patrick's paper argues the problem thus is not the broad bundling of tasks inside these new large financial institutions, but rather the adoption of compensation practices that encouraged inefficient risk-taking behavior precisely to induce speculation.[3]

Bolton argues that a significant upside exists to providing clients with a wide range of financial services. Banks acquire information about their clients, and by pursuing many activities, they further expand their expertise. Restricting bankers' activities, in Bolton's view, would reduce the quality of services their clients receive and would hinder the ability of banks to direct resources efficiently throughout the real economy.

One standard argument is that the advantages of providing multiple services must be weighed against the potential conflict of interest that occurs if commercial banks attempt to raise money for firms in equity or bond markets in order to enable them to pay back existing loans. Bolton cites the Drucker and Puri (2007, 210) survey, noting that securities issued by "universal banks, who have a lending relationship with the issuer have lower yields (or less underpricing) and also lower fees." If these "conflicted" relationships were producing particularly risky loans, buttressed by the banks' reputations, fees and yields would presumably be higher, not lower.

Bolton also notes the banks that experienced the most difficulty during the downturn were not universal banks, but rather banks that specialized in investment banking, such as Bear Stearns and Lehman Brothers, or residential mortgages, such as New Century. Moreover, the troubles universal banks, such as Bank of America or JP Morgan Chase, experienced were often associated with their acquisitions of more specialized entities, such as Merrill Lynch, Bear Sterns, Countrywide, and Washington Mutual.

These empirical facts suggest to Bolton that restricting the range of banking services is unlikely to produce more "good bankers." Instead, he advocates better regulation of bankers' compensation. If banks reward their employees for taking on highly risky activities with large upside bonuses and limited downside punishment, those employees will push the bank to take on too much risk. Some studies, including Cheng et al. (2015), find those banks that provided the strongest incentives fared the worst during the crisis. Given the implicit insurance that governments provide to banks that are deemed "too big to fail," this risk-taking is likely to generally inflict larger social costs. In some cases, excess risk-taking by employees may not even be in the interests of the banks' own shareholders.

Bolton considers a number of possible schemes to regulate bankers' compensation, although he accepts that gaming almost any conceivable regulation will be possible. Attempts to ban bonuses altogether or to limit bankers' pay to some multiple of the lowest-paid employee at the bank seem like crude approaches. Surely, many bonuses deliver social value by inducing higher levels of effort. Restricting pay to a multiple of the least well-paid employee may induce banks to fire their least well-compensated workers and use subcontractors to provide their services.

Bolton finds subtler approaches to be more appealing, such as requiring employees whose compensation is tied to stock price to also pay a penalty when the bank's own credit default swap spread increases, essentially punishing the bankers for taking on more risk. Bolton also suggests changing corporate governance in ways that enhance the powers of the chief risk officer might be beneficial. Although outside regulators cannot perfectly enforce a new culture of more limited incentives, Bolton sees more upside in incentive reforms than he does is restricting the range of banking activities.

Albert Kyle's paper concerns a second tool for reducing the externalities from bank default—increased capital requirements. Regulations, especially those associated with the Basel Accords, have often required banks to hold minimum levels of risk-adjusted equity, which reduces the chances that a market fall will lead to a bank default, because the drop wipes out the value of equity before it reduces the value of more senior debt. In the wake of the crash, many economists have called for increasing the minimum capital requirements, perhaps from 8% to 20%.

Kyle's essay takes a somewhat stronger line than Bolton's—and one stronger than our instincts—by arguing that the primary externality stems from the government's inability to commit to refrain from bailing out insolvent banks. We have taken a more agnostic approach, arguing bank insolvency may create social costs whether or not the public sector bails them out. Moreover, whether the social costs come from failures or bailouts, a good case remains for regulatory actions that decrease the probability of bank failure, such as increased capital requirements.

Yet Kyle's remedy does not depend sensitively on the precise reasons for attempting to limit risk. Kyle supports those who want to raise equity requirements but favors a somewhat novel manner of increasing capital stability. Instead of merely issuing more equity, his proposal calls for an increase in the level of contingent capital, which represents debt that is converted into equity in the event of a crisis. This contingent capital offers the same capital cushion (20%) to protect debtholders and the public that an increase in equity capital creates, but Kyle's proposal creates stronger incentives, especially if the owners of contingent capital have difficulty colluding with the owners of equity.

Kyle echoes Kashyap et al. (2008), who argue that an excess of equity may insulate management from market pressures. Because abundant equity makes default less likely, bondholders are less likely to take steps to protect their investment from default. In principle, equity holders can monitor themselves, but in many historical examples, management appears to have subverted boards. Moreover, the equity holders also benefit from certain types of risk taking, because bondholders and the government bear the extreme downside risk. This fact makes equity holders poorly equipped to provide a strong counterweight to activities with large downside risks.

Therefore, like Kashyap et al. (2008), Kyle argues for contingent capital that increases only during downturns, but the structure of Kyle's proposal is radically different. Kashyap et al. (2008) suggest capital insurance, in which banks would pay a fee to an insurer who would provide extra capital in the event of a downturn. Kyle proposes the bank issue reverse preferred stock that naturally converts itself into equity in the event of a bust. Although the capital insurance structure has an attractive simplicity, Kyle's proposal also has advantages. Most notably, it eliminates the incentive to regulate the insurer, because bank insurers seem likely to pose significant downside risk themselves in the event of a market crash. Moreover, he argues that widespread owners of the preferred stock instruments seem likely to be better positioned than a single insurer to advocate for their interests. Obviously, this claim depends on the details of the political economy, because in some cases, more concentrated interests have greater influence, but his observation about the political implications of asset structures is provocative and interesting.

In its simplest formulation, banks would have a 20% capital cushion, but 10% of that cushion would come from equity and 10% would come from convertible preferred stock. During good times, the preferred stock would be treated like standard debt. During a conversion event, which would be declared by a regulator, banks would have the option of either converting the preferred stock to equity or buying back the preferred stock at par, using funds received from a recent issue of equity. Conversion events would have multiple possible triggers, including those created by external market events, such as a rapid decrease in the value of equity, or regulatory events, such as a low estimated value of the bank's capital.

In the event of a conversion, the preferred stock would become equity, and $1 of preferred stock, at par, would become $4 of equity. If the original capital structure were 10% equity and 10% preferred stock, then, after a complete conversion, the former owners of the preferred stock would hold 80% of the equity. In this way, the bank would suddenly get an infusion of capital without the difficulties of having to raise new equity in the middle of a crisis.

This contingent-capital plan creates pre-crisis incentives through two mechanisms. First, because the holders of the contingent capital would have an incentive to avoid conversion, they would push to reduce the bank's exposure to downside risks. This push could take the form of lobbying or lawsuits. Second, the bank would have incentives to avoid a conversion event that would highly dilute the value of the shares held by its equity owners. Raising equity before the crisis would be one way to avoid a conversion event.

Although Kyle recognizes that no capital requirement is without costs, contingent capital, like capital insurance, creates the possibility of a mechanism that automatically increases banks' capital during a downturn without the downsides of issuing too much equity. Extra equity carries capital costs for the bank and may reduce some attractive incentives to avoid default. The plan provides a relatively flexible means of making banks less vulnerable to extreme downside risk.

The paper by Aloisio Araujo, Rafael Ferreira, and Bruno Funchal concerns the regulation of collateral and bankruptcy. The paper is applied to the Brazilian economy, but its insights are also relevant to the United States and the optimal design of a bankruptcy code in general. These authors work in the class of general equilibrium with incomplete markets and default that José has also exploited in some of his work. Specifically, whereas Araujo, Ferreira, and Funchal are concerned with regulatory issues, Santos and Scheinkman (2001) focus on the level of collateral that one should expect in competitive security-design environments, such as over-the-counter markets.

In the wake of the foreclosure crisis, a widespread call went out for foreclosure moratoria that many states adopted. A foreclosure moratorium essentially reduces the ability of housing to serve as collateral for loans. Economists have typically argued that reducing the ability to pledge housing will effectively reduce the supply of lending. Araujo, Ferreira, and Funchal suggest the situation is more complicated than the simplest economics would suggest.

If no extra costs were associated with foreclosing or imposing other harsh penalties on delinquent borrowers, the conventional pro-creditor logic of economics would be correct. By ensuring lenders can extract collateral quickly, lenders will more aggressively advance resources to borrowers. The ultimate beneficiary of strong collateral laws may end up being the borrowers who can access capital at a lower rate than if lenders were uncertain about their ability to collect.

This logic holds outside the realm of home mortgages and includes general consumer loans or even corporate debt. As creditor rights become stronger, creditors will be more willing to lend. Borrowers will obtain loans more easily, and interest rates will be lower.

But this rosy picture of creditor rights becomes muddied when protecting creditor rights leads to social costs. For example, if a homeowner values a house considerably more than any alternative owner, reallocating a foreclosed home destroys social value. If companies are destroyed inefficiently to allocate assets to creditors, or if consumer debt defaults lead to an inability to work, pro-creditor policies may be counterproductive.

Dobbie and Song (2015) examine the impact of consumers receiving Chapter 13 protection, which protects more assets than the more draconian Chapter 7 bankruptcy. Dobbie and Song use the random assignment of bankruptcy judges as a natural experiment, and find an individual who receives Chapter 13 protection increases annual earnings in the first five post-filing years by $5,012, increases employment over the same time period by 3.5 percentage points, and decreases five-year mortality by 1.9 percentage points. These results suggest that a substantial trade-off exists between providing lenders with better ex ante protection and reducing ex post social costs.

This trade-off is the focus of the paper by Araujo, Ferreira, and Funchal. This essay first reviews the work of Araujo et al. (2012) on consumer lending with collateral. Regulating collateral cannot lead to a Pareto improvement, but it can sometimes lead to reallocations of welfare across agents. Somewhat surprisingly, restrictions on subprime lending are particularly harmful, because the gains from trade are the highest for the borrowers with the least collateral. This result would be weakened if default for subprime borrowers were more socially costly, but these authors' basic conclusion does stand as a warning to those who are most enthusiastic about restricting subprime borrowing.

Their paper also reviews the results of Araujo and Funchal (2015) on corporate bankruptcy. In this case, pro-creditor policies essentially ease banks' ability to seize physical assets in the event of a default. The cost of taking those assets is that the productive viability of the firm is destroyed. Because a trade-off exists, their results typically suggest an intermediate level of creditor rights that trades the benefit of attracting creditor supply with the benefit of reducing ex post damage. Credit demand also falls when defaults lead to quick liquidation.

They find the optimal strength of creditor rights depends on the nature of the production process. When output is primarily dependent on alienable physical assets, the costs of liquidating the firm are small, and creditor rights should be strong. When output is primarily dependent on nonseizable assets that complement the physical goods, liquidations costs are high and optimal creditor rights are somewhat weaker.

The last theoretical section of their paper turns to personal bankruptcy rules. These rules seem particularly relevant to the mortgage crisis, because some authors have argued that increased stringency of personal bankruptcy rules enacted in 2005 subsequently led to more mortgage defaults. In this case, the impact of a change in rules might be quite different on the current stock of debtors, who would obviously have fewer resources to repay their mortgage debt if bankruptcy protection were reduced, and on any potential future stock of debtors, who might have to pay lower interest rates if bankruptcy options were reduced.

In their structure, enhancing creditor rights during bankruptcy reduces the incentives to invest in a second asset that would be taken in the event of a default. Strengthening creditor rights does enhance the supply of credit, but it also decreases the demand for credit, because borrowers risk losing the value that can come from the second asset. As in the case of corporate bankruptcy, the optimal amount of creditor rights lies between extremes, depending on the relative importance of encouraging the investment in the second asset and encouraging lending.

The paper by Araujo, Ferreira, and Funchal ends with a discussion of Brazilian bankruptcy law, which serves as a bridge to the last pair of papers that deal with international aspects of the crisis. The authors note that a strengthening of the bankruptcy procedure led to a significant increase in the total flow of corporate credit in Brazil, suggesting the important impact bankruptcy rules have on credit markets.

3 Global Perspective

Financial institutions and monitoring rules played a crucial role in the euro crisis. This is particularly clear in the case of Spain, as Santos highlights in his contribution. His paper provides a sketch of the history of Spanish finance, cataloguing the periods of crisis and reform that preceded the current downturn. The great banking boom in Spain, before 2007, was particularly dominated by real estate loans, both to homebuyers and real estate developers. A crucial difference between home purchase loans and developer loans is that loans to homeowners were generally securitized, whereas loans to developers were not.

Much has been made of the downsides of securitization in the United States following the crisis. Securitization may have reduced the tendency to fully screen borrowers and introduced difficulties into the renegotiation of loans that have gone into default. However, securitization also has a considerable upside—banks are no longer as vulnerable to the twists of the real estate cycle. Because Spanish banks held an enormous amount of real estate developer debt, they were particularly vulnerable when that sector lurched into crisis.

The Spanish real estate bubble appears to have had its roots in real causes. The Spanish economy was surging prior to 2007, and the country proved to be a particularly attractive locale for immigrants. Sunshine attracted migrants from the United States, and January temperatures were was a strong correlate of the U.S. real estate boom between 1996 and 2006 (Glaeser 2013). Thus, unsurprisingly, within the European Union, Spain was particularly appealing to real estate investors. Moreover, for institutional reasons, Spain has a particularly underdeveloped rental sector, so any demand for real estate was going to directly influence housing prices. Easy credit, created both by expansionist policies by the Bank of Spain and the global credit supply, also supported the boom.

Moreover, one major part of the Spanish banking sector—the *cajas* (viz., savings and loans)—were particularly poorly governed. These non-profit, politically run institutions faced little discipline, at least in the short run, and often had relatively inexperienced management that was more interested in expansion than in sound financial management. The *cajas*, especially the poorly run ones, were especially aggressive in real estate during the boom and were particularly prone to collapse during the bust. Unsurprisingly, a number of significant accounting issues appeared after 2007 when regulators attempted to merge these entities. Indeed, Santos argues the mergers themselves may have contributed to a lack of transparency.

The increase in Spanish real estate values between 2000 and 2007 was enormous, and Spain likely would have experienced a major correction without any influence from the outside world. Still, the unraveling of the subprime market in the United States was the first source of external pressure on Spanish banks. Once again, the integration of global markets enabled downturns to spread.

As banks lurched into crisis, the country proved unable to handle its troubles on its own. Ultimately, Spain had to turn to the EU for support, which provided a 100 billion euro credit line in exchange for strict supervision. Ultimately, Spain's travails caused it to surrender its independent economic sovereignty. With EU aid, the Spanish banking crisis seems to have turned a corner, but its magnitude serves as a reminder of the ability of real estate crashes to undo an entire economy. As the world contemplates reform, it would do well to remember that the stakes are enormous.

The paper on the Spanish financial crisis emphasizes what happened before the crisis. Indeed, researchers have spilled much ink describing the many twists and turns of banking crises. But much less has been written on the lead-up to the crisis: a lot of research on the flood and on after the flood and less on before the flood. If we are to understand financial crises, we need to better understand the path followed up to the crisis and the different actions taken by the many actors needed to support these long speculative cycles. As mentioned, the Spanish banking crisis is interesting, because a real estate boom like no other accompanied it; supply increased dramatically during the period of real estate appreciation and still was not enough to put a significant dent in this appreciation. Spanish banks originated and distributed huge real estate portfolios, including to foreign banks hungry for exposure to the booming Spanish economy. Spain became the largest securitization market in Europe after the United Kingdom, thereby facilitating the trading of Spanish real estate through both domestic and international portfolios. Therefore, when the crisis hit, many were exposed.

This theme permeates much of José's recent work on bubbles, which has stressed the importance of understanding prices and trading volumes jointly (see, e.g., Scheinkman and Xiong 2003; Hong et al. 2006; Scheinkman 2014). As José emphasizes in his Arrow Lectures, what distinguishes rational bubbles from the speculative bubbles experienced over the past few years is precisely the fact that in a rational bubble, agents are content to hold the asset because the price appreciation is a compensation for the risk that the bubble may burst at any point in time. Thus, rational bubbles have a hard time accounting for the exaggerated volumes that characterize speculative cycles. In these cycles, assets trade hands: they require finding another agent with different beliefs ready to hold what the selling agent is no longer willing to. In all these stories, restrictions on short-selling are a critical ingredient for sustaining the speculative cycle. Indeed, shorting the Spanish real estate market appears to have been difficult.

Yet the international connections in the financial crisis were not just within regions but also across them. Indeed, nothing illustrates the global integration of financial markets better than the events of the past six years. Financial markets are now global, and financial events in one part of the world have the capacity to shape markets across the globe. Many observers have argued that a global glut of savings, especially due to China, helped increase the price of assets before the booms. The crisis that began in U.S. mortgage markets caused pain elsewhere, and the world may still not have experienced the full implications of the financial problems that plague the Eurozone. To consider these global considerations, the next two papers in the volume focus on U.S.-Asian connection and on the unfolding of the financial crisis in Spain.

The paper by Conghui Hu and Wei Xiong concerns the information role of commodities traded in U.S. markets on subsequent events in Asia. Their basic approach is to look at the correlation between stock price changes in Asia and changes in commodity prices during the previous day in the United States. They are also able to control for changes in overall U.S. stock prices, and their results are typically robust to that control.

The basic finding is a striking sign of the increasing integration of global markets. Prior to 2005, little correlation existed between U.S. commodity prices and subsequent changes in Asian stock prices. After 2005, the correlation rose substantially for copper and soybeans and has stayed relatively flat for crude oil. An increase in Asian imports of copper and soybeans also mirrors the rise, illustrating a general pattern of rising global connectivity that would seem to also increase the capacity of crises to spread from nation to nation.

Why do lagged U.S. commodity price changes predict changes in Asian stock prices? For those Asian firms that actually sell these commodities, the interpretation would seem obvious. Higher prices for these goods mean that those companies can sell their output for more money. A question remains as to whether the commodity prices are revealing that information directly, or whether the Asian stock prices are responding to other information flows that are merely reflected in the U.S. markets. Still, the strong empirical connection between the stock prices of Asian commodity suppliers and U.S. commodity prices is easy to understand.

Yet making sense of the positive connection between commodity prices and stock prices is somewhat harder for companies that use those commodities, or for companies that neither use nor supply those goods. If global prices for downstream products were fixed, an increase in commodity prices would be a negative shock to the profits of the users of those products. As such, the most likely explanation for the correlation Hu and Xiong observe is that prices are not being held constant. Indeed, the rising commodity prices seem likely to reflect an increase in demand for the product, perhaps because of increased demand for the downstream product itself. An increase in supply costs, on its own, might even cause the profitability of a downstream firm to rise if the input price increase causes marginal costs and prices to rise more than average costs.

Perhaps the most puzzling correlation is between commodity prices and stock prices for firms that have nothing to do with that commodity. Why should Chinese auto part companies see their share prices rise after the price of American soybeans increases? One possibility is that these commodity prices are proxying for the overall state of the global economy, but the regressions also control for the lagged returns on the Standard and Poor's 500 Index. Perhaps commodity prices carry information beyond that carried in the overall stock index about the state of economic conditions that is relevant to these Asian firms. This issue remains an important one for future research.

The connection between American commodity prices and Chinese stock prices may seem arcane, but it provides a helpful barometer to measure the integration of global markets. This integration seems to have increased dramatically after 2005, and this rising interconnection in turn further augments the possibility that a crisis can spread across oceans. When Wall Street catches a cold, all of Asia may start to sneeze.

4   Social Interactions and Beliefs

José's interest in bubbles and speculative behavior builds on an older interest of his in the study of social interactions.[4] This progression is natural, because many of the speculative cycles have a social dimension that helps explain the widespread effects associated with the boom and bust.

Ed Glaeser and Bruce Sacerdote's paper fits squarely with this side of José's interest. It concerns anomalies that occasionally appear where aggregate relationships take an opposite sign from individual relationships. For example, religious attendance rises with education at the individual level but declines with education at the state level. Richer people are more likely to vote Republican, but richer states are more likely to vote Democratic.

But the explanation given for these phenomena is crucially important to finance—the social formation of beliefs. The paper argues these reversals can be understood if a causal variable has two effects on an outcome—a direct effect that works through incentives and an indirect effect that works through beliefs. For example, income may both increase the direct benefits from the lower taxes anticipated under Republican leadership and decrease the social beliefs that are compatible with recent Republican platforms, such as opposition to abortion. If beliefs are partially formed through social interactions, the belief effect—but not the incentive effect—gets magnified at higher levels of aggregation. This magnification, or social multiplier, as Scheinkman discussed (along with Glaeser and Sacerdote) in an earlier paper (Glaeser et al. 2003), causes the belief effect to overwhelm the direct effect at the aggregate but not the individual level, and an aggregation reversal results.

This paper comes out of a longstanding Scheinkman agenda to better understand social interactions and to import tools—like so-called Voter Models—from physics into economics. For example, Scheinkman (again along with Glaeser and Sacerdote) wrote a paper 20 years ago (Glaeser et al. 1996) trying to use these physics-based models to understand the high variance of crime rates over time and across space. The general result is that positive social interactions, which might come from beliefs diffusing across individuals, can lead to excess variation.

These arguments are relevant to the asset-pricing concerns with which we began. Keynes's beauty contest analogy is essentially an argument for complementarity between investors; each speculator seeks to match the investments of the crowd. This complementarity is only strengthened if the investors' beliefs are in turn shaped by the beliefs of other investors. If the complementarity is sufficiently strong, we can understand why great waves of optimism, perhaps about the value of mortgage-backed securities, are followed by great waves of pessimism: booms and busts are then the product of these waves.

5   The Economist as an Economic Agent

José's view on financial markets is informed not only by his work as an academic but also by his contact with the financial services industry, a trait he shares with many other financial economists of his generation. José enjoys a phenomenal reputation among practitioners for his unique ability to bridge theory and practice and to articulate complex ideas in the language that matches the knowledge and skills of the other side. José, once again, is unique in that, to his engagement with the financial services industry, one has to add his extensive policy work in Brazil, his native country. Combining these two different forms of engagement outside academia is rare, but yet again, few can match José's breadth of knowledge. Still, his feet have always been solidly planted in academia, and his commitment to the highest standards of research has been uncompromising. José is an academic through and through.

This engagement of academic economists with the outside world is the topic of Glen Weyl's paper. Financial economists, perhaps more so than economists from other fields, are frequently exposed to the possibility of leveraging their knowledge in pursuits outside academia. Indeed, advances in financial economics, both in asset pricing and corporate finance, over the past 40 years have had a profound influence in practice, from the development of financial markets as illustrated in Donald MacKenzie's (2006) remarkable book, to managerial compensation practices.

In addition, academics developed core practical tools, such as portfolio theory and derivatives pricing. These tools were of obvious practical use, but knowledge of these matters was to a large extent concentrated in academia. Therefore, unsurprisingly, many academic financial economists were asked to join this or that financial services company as a way of importing that knowledge into those organizations, at least until universities and business schools were able to produce enough students trained in the new methods and techniques. Obviously, these contacts with the industry serve also as a cross-pollination device: knowledge flows in both directions.[5] A voluminous literature developed in some areas of financial economics, such as portfolio theory or derivatives pricing, that was closely aligned with the problems facing these financial intermediaries and potentially may have stimulated profitable speculation.

Glen's paper offers a provocative thesis about the effect of this relation on the nature of research in finance compared to other fields. In particular, Glen focuses on two fields: industrial organization (IO) and finance. He notes that, compared to finance, IO has three times as many articles published in the top journals in the profession concerned with normative issues. He argues that the nature of the demand for the services that economists can provide may partially explain this difference. Indeed, as Kovacic and Shapiro (2000) note, Congress enlisted the courts in the development of the Sherman Act, perhaps, among the statutes that regulate trade, the one that suffers (or benefits) from the broadest generality. As these authors emphasize, this openness to economic evidence in turn gave economists a unique opportunity to shape competition policy, as both regulators and firms called on them to argue for or against the plaintiff in the myriad cases brought before the courts for elucidation. Law and economic thinking on IO co-evolved, thereby affecting the tradition and focus of the literature.

Clearly, finance researchers have also reacted to regulatory developments. For instance, a literature has arisen on the Glass-Steagall Act or the effects of the different incarnations of Basel on the structure of banking. But unlike the IO experience, this literature is not driven by the consulting opportunities of the economists involved or their role as expert witnesses, but mostly by standard academic incentives. Note that research on financial regulatory developments is, to a considerable extent, conducted by the remarkable group of economists in the central banks around the world and by international organizations, such as the Bank for International Settlements or the International Monetary Fund. Their work may sometimes not be published in top journals, but, of course, this fact doesn't make the research less relevant.

In sum, IO researchers were in heavy demand to inform competition policy and thus were concerned early on with normative issues, whereas financial economists in academia faced a different demand for their services. Recent reforms in finance may cause demand profiles across fields to converge. Understanding that economists are economic agents, subject to the same incentives that they have tried to put at the center of policy debates, will in turn help inform policy, as policy changes may change economics itself and thus what regulators are able to draw on in formulating policy. Modeling these relations requires taking the sort of outside perspective José's real-world engagement inspires us to see while grasping an economist's incentive-based perspective. Glen's contribution is a tribute to José in its attempt to combine these perspectives and thereby helps tie together the wide-ranging themes of the volume.

Notes

1. *Notes on Asset Pricing* was concerned precisely with the seemingly obvious question of when the price of a share can be represented as the discounted value of the infinite stream of future profits in a certainty environment. It shows that

general equilibrium restrictions imply the standard transversality condition and thus that the standard Euler equation obtains under very general conditions.

2. José's concern with econometrics and asset pricing dates back to 1989, when he published a simple and remarkable example illustrating the biased inferences the econometrician may draw about fundamental parameters when his or her information set differs from that of the agents.

3. Note that Bolton et al. (2006) was written well before the current financial crisis. It used the corporate crisis that followed the bursting of the NASDAQ bubble as a motivation, but the message of that paper seems even more pertinent for the current crisis.

4. His survey (Scheinkman 2008) on the matter in the *New Palgrave* is a wonderful summary of the main questions in the literature. See also his lectures on the topic.

5. José's brief stint at Goldman Sachs in the mid-1980s produced a classic in the fixed-income literature (Litterman and Scheinkman 1991).

References

Araujo, A., and B. Funchal (2015). How much should debtors be punished in case of default? *Journal of Financial Services Research 47*(2), 229–245.

Araujo, A., F. Kubler, and S. Schommer (2012). Regulating collateral requirements when markets are incomplete. *Journal of Economic Theory 147*(2), 450–476.

Bolton, P., J. Scheinkman, and W. Xiong (2006). Executive compensation and short-termist behavior in speculative markets. *Review of Economic Studies 73*(3), 577–610.

Cheng, I.-H., H. Hong, and J. Scheinkman (2015). Yesterday's heroes: Compensation and risk at financial firms. *Journal of Finance 70*(2), 839–879.

Dobbie, W., and J. Song (2015). Debt relief and debtor outcomes: Measuring the effects of consumer bankruptcy protection. *American Economic Review 105*(3), 1272–1311.

Drucker, S., and M. Puri (2007). Banks in capital markets. In B. E. Eckbo (Ed.), *Handbook of Empirical Corporate Finance*, Volume 1, pp. 190–232. Amsterdam: North Holland.

Glaeser, E. L. (2013). A nation of gamblers: Real estate speculation and American history. *American Economic Review 103*(3), 1–42.

Glaeser, E. L., G. Ponzetto, and J. M. Shapiro (2005). Strategic Extremism: Why Republicans and Democrats Divide on Religious Values. *Quarterly Journal of Economics 120*(4), 1283–1330.

Glaeser, E. L., B. Sacerdote, and J. A. Scheinkman (1996). Crime and social interactions. *Quarterly Journal of Economics 111*(2), 507–548.

Hansen, L. P., and K. J. Singleton (1982). Generalized instrumental variables estimation of nonlinear rational expectations models. *Econometrica 50*(5), 1269–1286.

Hong, H., J. Scheinkman, and W. Xiong (2006). Asset float and speculative bubbles. *Journal of Finance 61*(3), 1073–1117.

Kashyap, A., R. Rajan, and J. Stein (2008). Rethinking capital regulation. In *Maintaining Stability in a Changing Financial System*. Symposium at Jackson Hole. Kansas City: Federal Reserve Bank of Kansas City.

Kovacic, W. E., and C. Shapiro (2000). Antitrust policy: A century of economic and legal thinking. *Journal of Economic Perspectives 14*(1), 43–60.

Litterman, R. B., and J. A. Scheinkman (1991). Common factors affecting bond returns. *Journal of Fixed Income 1*(1), 54–61.

MacKenzie, D. A. (2006). *An Engine Not a Camera: How Financial Models Shape Markets*. Cambridge, MA: MIT Press.

Santos, T., and J. A. Scheinkman (2001). Competition among exchanges. *Quarterly Journal of Economics 116*(3), 1027–1061.

Scheinkman, J. A. (2008). Social interactions. In S. Durlauf and L. Blume (Eds.), *New Palgrave Dictionary of Economics* (2nd ed.). London: Palgrave Macmillan.

——— (2014). *Speculation, Trading and Bubbles*. New York: Columbia University Press.

Scheinkman, J. A., and W. Xiong (2003). Overconfidence and speculative bubbles. *Journal of Political Economy 111*(6), 1183–1219.

CHAPTER TWO

Stochastic Compounding and Uncertain Valuation

Lars Peter Hansen and José A. Scheinkman

1 Introduction

To build structural models of asset valuation and the macroeconomy, empirical researchers use asset market data to learn about investors' preferences, including their beliefs and aversion to risk. When studying assets with stochastic cash flows, empirical analyses often focus on the implied risk-return trade-off over short—say, one-period—investment horizons. (See van Binsbergen et al. (2012) for a recent exception.) In contrast, we describe methods that feature the interplay between stochastic discounting and growth over alternative horizons. We apply these methods to understand how compounding stochastic growth and discounting alter valuation and thus provide new perspectives on the information content of asset prices. Our characterizations allow for non-linear stochastic specifications outside the realm of log-normal models or approximations often used in asset pricing models. The methods we describe give characterizations of the components of valuation that become more prominent over longer investment horizons. Specifically, we consider three related substantive problems.

First, we address the question of identifying investor's beliefs and stochastic discounting from asset prices observed at a point in time. To frame this question, we use the mathematically convenient construct of a stochastic discount factor process. Stochastic discount factors represent market valuations of risky cash flows. They are stochastic in order to adjust for risk as they discount the future. Multiperiod risk adjustments reflect the impact of compounding single-period risk adjustments. Stochastic discount factors are only well defined relative to a given probability distribution. As is well known, when markets are complete and market prices are observed by an econometrician, for a given probability measure there is a unique stochastic discount factor process that is revealed from financial market data. Ross (2015) extends this claim to argue that the probability measure itself can also be recovered. By studying a class of stochastic economies with growth, we show that the recovery approach of Ross (2013) typically does not recover the underlying probability measure but instead recovers a long-term counterpart to a forward measure. See Section 3.

Second, we explore misspecification of parametric models of valuation. It is common to identify stochastic discount factor processes through parametric restrictions. Parametric models, while tractable, are typically misspecified. By studying how the consequences of the misspecification are related to the payoff or investment horizon, we motivate and catalog different forms of misspecification. For instance, economic fundamentals as specified in a parametric model could dominate over longer investment horizons. Thus econometric identification should reflect this possibility. Alternatively, statistically small forms of model misspecification might become more evident over longer time periods if the source is the misspecification of the underlying stochastic evolution as perceived by investors. See Section 4.

Third, recursive specifications of preferences of the type first suggested by Kreps and Porteus (1978) are known to have nontrivial implications for economies with stochastic growth and volatility. By looking at long-term stochastic characterizations of consumption, we obtain tractable mathematical characterizations of the limiting specifications and in turn general characterizations of when solutions exist for the infinite horizon version of Kreps and Porteus's (1978) preferences. In effect, we isolate long-term contributions to the risk adjustments embedded in recursive utility. For specifications in which the impact of the future on the continuation values is particularly prominent, we show what aspects of the riskiness of the consumption process dominate valuation from the perspective of investor preferences. See Section 5.

We study these three problems using a common analytical approach. This approach starts by characterizing the limiting impact of compounding in a stochastic environment. It applies a generalized version of

Perron-Frobenius theory for Markov processes and has much in common with large deviation theory as developed by Donsker and Varadhan
(1976). In Section 2 we describe the stochastic environment that under-
lies our analysis. We show how to use Perron-Frobenius theory to identify
a state-invariant growth or discount rate and an associated martingale.
This martingale induces an alternative probability measure that helps
reveal the long-term contributions to growth and valuation. Thus Section
2 lays out the mathematical tools that facilitate our study in subsequent
sections.

2   A Factorization Result

Many examples in economics and finance feature a Markov environment and stochastic processes that display stochastic growth. The implied
equilibrium stochastic discount processes display stochastic decay as the
investment horizon increases. To capture this behavior, the logarithms
of the stochastic growth or discount factor processes are modeled conve-
niently as having stationary increments. In this section, we show how to
use Perron-Frobenius theory to decompose such processes as the product of three positive processes: A deterministic trend, a martingale with
stationary increments in logarithms, and a stationary process. Unless the
martingale component is trivial, it makes a stochastic contribution to
the growth or discounting embedded in the original process. As is familiar
from mathematical finance, there is a change of measure associated with
the positive martingale component. When we use the martingale component to change measures, we preserve the Markov property but produce a
different transition density for the Markov state. We exploit implications
of this factorization in the remainder of the paper.

We begin with a Markov representation of stochastic growth or discounting. This representation is convenient for analyzing the impact of
compounding in a stochastic environment. Here we use a discrete-time
formulation as in Hansen and Scheinkman (2012a). Continuous-time
counterparts have been developed in Hansen and Scheinkman (2009) and
Hansen (2012). We apply a general version of Perron-Frobenius theory in
this investigation. Recall that in the case of a matrix A, such that A^k has
all strictly positive entries for some positive integer k, Perron-Frobenius
theory implies that A has a positive eigenvalue that is associated with a
positive eigenvector. This positive eigenvalue dominates in absolute value

all other eigenvalues of A and thus dominates the exponential growth rate of A^k as $k \to \infty$. Perron-Frobenius theory generalizes to a class of non-negative linear operators. By applying this approach, we isolate components of growth and valuation that become much more prominent over longer horizons.

We start with a joint Markov process (X, Y).

Assumption 1 *The joint Markov process (X, Y) is stationary.*

We could weaken this by imposing some form of stochastic stability, while not initializing the process using the stationary distribution.

Assumption 2 *The joint distribution of (X_{t+1}, Y_{t+1}) conditioned on (X_t, Y_t) depends only on X_t.*

In light of this restriction, we may view X alone as a Markov process, and Y does not "cause" X in the sense of Granger (1969). Moreover, the process Y can be viewed as an independent sequence conditioned on the entire process X, where the conditional distribution of Y_t depends only on X_t and X_{t-1}. The role of Y is as a device to introduce an additional source of randomness, but it allows us to focus on the intertemporal impact using a smaller state vector process X.

Construct a process M of the form

$$\log M_{t+1} - \log M_t = \kappa(X_{t+1}, Y_{t+1}, X_t).$$

This process has stationary increments. As a result of this construction, the process M will grow or decay stochastically over time, and it is convenient to have methods to characterize this stochastic evolution. Examples of M include stochastic growth processes. These processes could be macro time series expressed in levels that inherit stochastic growth along some balanced growth path or stochastic discount factor processes used to represent equilibrium asset values. In what follows, we will also have use for

$$\bar{\kappa}(X_{t+1}, X_t) = \log E\left(\exp\left[\kappa(X_{t+1}, Y_{t+1}, X_t)\right] | X_{t+1}, X_t\right).$$

The following example illustrates this construction.

Example 1 *Consider a dynamic mixture-of-normals model. Suppose that X evolves as an n-state Markov chain and that Y is an iid sequence of standard normally distributed random vectors in $\mathbb{R}^m$. Let the realized values of the state vector X_t be the coordinate vectors u_i for $i = 1, 2, \ldots, n$, where u_i is a vector of zeros except in entry i, where it equals 1. Suppose $\bar{\beta} \in \mathbb{R}^n$ and $\bar{\alpha}$ is a m × n matrix. Let*

$$\log M_{t+1} - \log M_t = \kappa(X_{t+1}, Y_{t+1}, X_t) = \bar{\beta} \cdot X_t + (X_{t+1})'\bar{\alpha}'Y_{t+1}.$$

The current state X_t affects the growth in M in two ways. First, if the state at time t is i, the average growth of (log) M between t and $t + 1$ is $\bar{\beta}_i$. In addition, the state at t determines the distribution of X_{t+1} and thus the variance of the growth of (log) M. In a more elaborate model, the state could also affect the distribution of Y_{t+1}, but in this example, we assume that Y is iid.

Since $\kappa(X_{t+1}, Y_{t+1}, X_t)$, conditioned on X_t and X_{t+1}, is normally distributed, we have

$$\bar{\kappa}(X_{t+1}, X_t) = \bar{\beta} \cdot X_t + \frac{1}{2}(X_{t+1})'\bar{\alpha}'\bar{\alpha}X_{t+1}.$$

Next we develop the discrete-time counterpart to an approach from Hansen and Scheinkman (2009) and Hansen (2012). This approach extends a log-normal formulation in Hansen et al. (2008). While log-normal specifications are commonly used because of their convenience, they limit the channels by which locally subtle statistical components can become prominent. We use the process M to construct one-period operators and then explore the impact of applying these operators in succession multiple times. This sequential application reflects the impact of compounding. The first operator $\mathbb{M}$ maps functions $g(x, y)$ into functions of the state variable x, $\mathbb{M}g$ via

(1)
$$[\mathbb{M}g](x) = E\left(\exp[\kappa(X_{t+1}, Y_{t+1}, X_t)]g(X_{t+1}, Y_{t+1})|X_t = x\right)$$
$$= E\left(\frac{M_t + 1}{M_t}g(X_{t+1}, Y_{t+1})|X_t = x\right).$$

Notice that the stationarity of (X, Y) makes the right-hand side independent of t. The second operator $\overline{\mathbb{M}}$ maps functions $f(x)$ of the state variable x into functions of the state variable x, $\overline{\mathbb{M}}f$ via:

$$[\overline{\mathbb{M}}f](x) = E\left(\exp[\bar{\kappa}(X_{t+1}, X_t)]f(X_{t+1})|X_t = x\right).$$

The function $g(x, y)$ may be independent of y, that is, $g(x, y) = f(x)$. In this case, the two operators are consistent. The law of iterated expectations ensures that

$$\begin{aligned}
[\mathbb{M}f](x) &= E\left(\exp\left[\kappa(X_{t+1}, Y_{t+1}, X_t)\right]f(X_{t+1})|X_t = x\right) \\
&= E\left(\exp\left[\bar{\kappa}(X_{t+1}, X_t)\right]f(X_{t+1})|X_t = x\right) \\
&= [\overline{\mathbb{M}}f](x).
\end{aligned}$$

Thus $\overline{\mathbb{M}}$ and $\mathbb{M}$ agree when they are both well defined. For now we will be vague about the collection of functions g or f that are in the domain of the operators $\mathbb{M}$ and $\overline{\mathbb{M}}$.

Since $\mathbb{M}g$ is only a function of the state x, for any $j \geq 1$, we have

$$[\mathbb{M}^j g](x) = \overline{\mathbb{M}}^{j-1}[\mathbb{M}g](x).$$

This relation shows that, when we look across multiple horizons, we can concentrate our attention on the operator $\overline{\mathbb{M}}$ and its iterates featuring X dependence.

In addition, again applying the law of iterated expectations, we obtain

$$[\mathbb{M}^j g](x) = E\left[\left(\frac{M_{t+j}}{M_t}\right)g(X_{t+j}, Y_{t+j})|X_t = x\right].$$

Finally, since M is a positive process, the operators $\mathbb{M}$ and $\overline{\mathbb{M}}$ map positive functions into positive functions.

Example 2   *It is straightforward to compute the operator $\overline{\mathbb{M}}$ in Example 1. Since X is an n-state Markov chain, functions of x can be identified with vectors in $\mathbb{R}^n$, and the linear operator $\overline{\mathbb{M}}$ can be identified with its matrix representation $A = [a_{ij}]$. Applying $\overline{\mathbb{M}}$ to u_j amounts to computing Au_j and reveals the jth column of A. Let $P = [p_{ij}]$ be the transition matrix for X. Then it is easy to show that*

(2) $a_{ij} = p_{ij}\xi_{ij},$

where

$$\xi_{ij} \doteq \exp\left[\bar{\beta} \cdot u_i + \frac{1}{2}(u_j)'\bar{\alpha}'\bar{\alpha}u_j\right].$$

Thus the probabilities are adjusted by growth or decay factors, ξ_{ij}, but all entries remain positive. If A^{j_0} has strictly positive entries for some j_0, then the Perron-Frobenius theorem states that there exists a unique (up to scale) eigenvector e *satisfying:*

$$A\mathbf{e} = \exp(\eta)\mathbf{e}$$

with strictly positive entries. The eigenvalue associated with this positive eigenvector is positive and has the largest magnitude among all of the eigenvalues. As a consequence, this eigenvalue and associated eigenvector dominate as we apply $\overline{\mathbb{M}}$ j times, for j large.

For general state spaces, we consider the analogous Perron-Frobenius problem, namely, find a stricly positive function $e(x)$ such that there exists an η with

$$[\mathbb{M}e](x) = [\overline{\mathbb{M}}e](x) = \exp(\eta)e(x).$$

Existence and uniqueness are more complicated in the case of general state spaces. Hansen and Scheinkman (2009) presents sufficient conditions for the existence of a solution, but even in examples commonly used in applied work, multiple (scaled) positive solutions are a possibility. See Hansen and Scheinkman (2009) and Hansen (2012) for such examples. However, when we have a solution of the Perron-Frobenius problem, we follow Hansen and Scheinkman (2009), and define a process $\tilde{M}$ that satisfies

$$(3) \qquad \frac{\tilde{M}_t}{\tilde{M}_0} = \exp(-\eta t)\left(\frac{M_t}{M_0}\right)\frac{e(X_t)}{e(X_0)}.$$

While this leaves open the question of how to initialize $\tilde{M}_0$, the initialization is inconsequential to much of what follows, as long as $\tilde{M}_0$ is strictly positive. Notice that by construction, we have

$$E\left(\frac{\tilde{M}_{t+1}}{\tilde{M}_t}|\mathcal{F}_t\right) = E\left(\frac{\tilde{M}_{t+1}}{\tilde{M}_t}|X_t\right) = 1,$$

implying that $\tilde{M}$ is a positive $\{\mathcal{F}_t : t = 0, 1, ...\}$-martingale, when $\mathcal{F}_t$ is the sigma algebra of events generated by $X_0, X_1, ..., X_t$ and $Y_1, Y_2, ..., Y_t$. Moreover, we have

$$\log \widetilde{M}_{t+1} - \log \widetilde{M}_t = -\eta + \kappa(X_{t+1}, Y_{t+1}, X_t) + \log e(X_{t+1}) - \log e(X_t)$$

$$\doteq \tilde{\kappa}(X_{t+1}, Y_{t+1}, X_t).$$

Thus the process $\widetilde{M}$ has the same mathematical structure as the original process M. In logarithms, this constructed process has stationary increments represented as a function of X_{t+1}, Y_{t+1}, and X_t.

An outcome of this construction is the factorization that helps us understand how compounding works in this Markov environment. Inverting (3) results in

(4)
$$\frac{M_t}{M_0} = \exp(\eta t) \left(\frac{\widetilde{M}_t}{\widetilde{M}_0} \right) \left[\frac{\tilde{e}(X_t)}{\tilde{e}(X_0)} \right],$$

where $\tilde{e} = \frac{1}{e}$. The first term in this factorization determines a deterministic growth (when $\eta > 0$) or decay (when $\eta < 0$) of the M process. The last term is a fixed function of the (stationary) process X_t. Except when the martingale is degenerate, the middle term is a stochastic contribution to compounding. The positive martingale term can be used for a "change of measure." Specifically,

$$[\widetilde{\mathbb{M}}f](x) = E \left(\exp[\tilde{\kappa}(X_{t+1}, Y_{t+1}, X_t)] f(X_{t+1}) | X_t = x \right)$$

defines the conditional expectation operator implied by the transition distribution for a Markov process. The term $\exp[\tilde{\kappa}(X_{t+1}, Y_{t+1}, X_t)]$ is the relative density or Radon-Nykodym derivative or a new transition distribution relative to the original transition distribution. In what follows, we suppose that the following stochastic stability condition is satisfied:

(5)
$$\lim_{j \to \infty} [\widetilde{\mathbb{M}}^j f](x) = \int f(x) \widetilde{Q}(dx),$$

where $\widetilde{Q}$ is a stationary distribution for the transformed Markov process. When there are distinct solutions to the Perron-Frobenius problem, at most one solution will satisfy this stochastic stability requirement (see Hansen and Scheinkman 2009). This stochastic stability is what permits the change of probability measure to be valuable for characterizing long-horizon limits. The change-of-measure captures the long-term impact of the stochastic component to compounding.

In fact, we can write

$$\exp(-\eta j)[\mathbb{M}^j f](x) = e(x)E\left[\frac{\widetilde{M}_j}{\widetilde{M}_0}f(X_j)\tilde{e}(X_j)|X_0 = x\right] = e(x)[\widetilde{\mathbb{M}}^j(f\tilde{e})](x).$$

The stability condition (5) allows us to interpret η as the asymptotic rate of growth.

We next explore some applications of this factorization.

3 Stochastic Discount Factors

In dynamic economic models, stochastic discount factors are used to map future payoffs into current prices. As in Hansen and Richard (1987), we use stochastic discount factors both to discount the future and to adjust for risk. They serve as "kernels" for pricing operators that assign current-period prices to future payoffs. Standard price-theoretic reasoning connects these discount factors to intertemporal marginal rates of substitution of investors. We presume that the stochastic discount factor S has the mathematical structure described in the previous section for a generic process M, and we use the process S to construct a family of valuation operators indexed by the investment horizon. Recall that the positive martingale constructed in Section 2 defines a probability measure. We show how this alternative probability measure can be revealed by financial market data. When the martingale that induces the alternative probability measure is a constant, the alternative measure is identical to the actual probability measure, and thus we obtain the "recovery" result of Ross (2013). In an equilibrium model, however, the martingale of interest is unlikely to be a constant unless utility is time separable and consumption is stationary (up to a deterministic rate of growth), as in examples discussed in Ross (2013).[1] In the more general stochastic environment used in this paper, the probability measure recovered using Perron-Frobenius is typically not the one-period transition distribution, but it is an altered measure that can be used to characterize value implications for long investment horizons.

Let $\mathbb{S}$ be the valuation operator that corresponds to the stochastic discount factor, assigning date t prices to date $t+1$ payoffs that are functions of a Markov state, as in equation (2).[2]

We apply factorization (4) to the stochastic factor process:[3]

$$(6) \qquad \frac{S_t}{S_0} = \exp(\eta t)\left(\frac{\widetilde{S}_t}{\widetilde{S}_0}\right)\left[\frac{\tilde{e}(X_t)}{\tilde{e}(X_0)}\right],$$

where $\tilde{e} = \frac{1}{e}$, and e, η are solutions to the Perron-Frobenius problem associated with $\mathbb{S}$:

$$\mathbb{S}e = \overline{\mathbb{S}}e = \exp(\eta)e.$$

As before, the operator $\overline{\mathbb{S}}$ is the restriction of $\mathbb{S}$ to payoffs that are only a function of the state variable x. Since S discounts, we expect η to be negative. Additionally, $-\eta$ is the limiting interest rate on a long-term discount bond, provided that $\tilde{e}$ has a finite expectation under the change of measure induced by the positive martingale $\widetilde{S}$.

Alvarez and Jermann (2005) use factorization (6) to argue for the importance of permanent shocks as operating through the martingale component $\widetilde{S}$. Specifically, they interpret the multiplicative factorization analogously to an additive counterpart obtained, say by taking logarithms of S. The additive martingale extraction is familiar from time series analysis and empirical macroeconomics as a device to identify permanent shocks.[4] The martingale component in a multiplicative factorization is positive and has "unusual" sample-path properties. It converges almost surely, and for many example economies with stochastic growth, it converges to zero.[5] Hansen and Scheinkman (2009) and Hansen (2012) instead use the martingale component as a change of measure and show in what sense this change of measure has permanent consequences for pricing. As emphasized by Hansen (2012), if $\log S$ has a nondegenerate martingale component, then so does S, and conversely. This relation gives a different but less direct way to motivate the analysis of permanent shocks in Alvarez and Jermann (2005). While there is a tight connection between the multiplicative martingale component of S and the additive martingale component of $\log S$ for log-normal specifications, in general there is no simple relation. In what follows we discuss further the implied change in probability distribution associated with the martingale component.

As we argued in Section 2, we may use $\widetilde{S}$ to define a distorted conditional expectations operator as featured in Hansen and Scheinkman (2009) and Hansen (2012):

$$(7) \quad \widetilde{E}[g(X_{t+1}, y_{t+1})|X_t = x] \doteq E\left[\left(\frac{\widetilde{S}_{t+1}}{\widetilde{S}_t}\right)g(X_{t+1}, Y_{t+1})|X_t = x\right]$$
$$= \exp(-\eta)\tilde{e}(x)[\mathbb{S}(ge)](x)$$

where as before, $\tilde{e} = \frac{1}{e}$. When markets are (dynamically) complete, there is a unique operator $\mathbb{S}$ compatible with the observed asset prices and the absence of arbitrage. If a researcher has at her disposal the relevant information on asset prices, she can infer the operator $\mathbb{S}$, and the (relevant) associated Perron-Frebenius eigenfunction e and eigenvalue $\exp(\eta)$. Alternatively, she might have a more limited amount of asset market data and instead infer $\mathbb{S}$ by parameterizing an underling economic model. Thus the right-hand side of (7) sometimes can be identified in a formal econometric sense, revealing the distorted expectation operator on the left-hand side. The recovered transition distribution is *not* the actual one-period transition distribution. Instead it is an altered measure that provides a convenient way to characterize value implications for long investment horizons. It can be viewed as the limiting analog of a forward measure used sometimes in mathematical finance.

Example 3 *It is revealing to consider the special case of a finite-state Markov chain for X. For the time being, we abstract from the role of Y and consequently restrict $\mathbb{S} = \overline{\mathbb{S}}$. The conditional expectation for such a process can be represented as a $n \times n$ matrix of transition probabilities, $P = [p_{ij}]$, and functions of the Markov state can be represented as vectors f, where entry i is the value that the function takes in state i. Thus as in Example 1, there is also a matrix depiction $A = [a_{ij}]$ of the operator $\overline{\mathbb{S}}$ with n^2 entries, and applying $\overline{\mathbb{S}}$ to the ith coordinate vector (a vector with all zeros except in entry i) reveals the ith column of the matrix used to represent the operator $\overline{\mathbb{S}}$. In matrix terms, we solve*

$$A\mathbf{e} = \exp(\eta)\mathbf{e}.$$

It is of interest to consider the "inverse" of relation (7):

(8) $$[\overline{\mathbb{S}}f](x) = \exp(\eta)\tilde{E}\left[f(X_{t+1})\tilde{e}(X_{t+1})|X_t = x\right]e(x).$$

Perron-Frobenius theory suggests representing $\overline{\mathbb{S}}$ by the expression on the right-hand side of (8). Using the matrix representation A, (8) becomes

(9) $$a_{ij} = \exp(\eta)\tilde{p}_{ij}\left(\frac{\mathbf{e}_i}{\mathbf{e}_j}\right),$$

where the distorted transition matrix is $\tilde{P} = [\tilde{p}_{ij}]$. Restricting the $\tilde{p}_{ij}$ to be transition probabilities in (9) guarantees that if $\tilde{P}$ and the vector $\mathbf{e}$ solve the n^2 equations (9), then we have

$$(Ae)_i = \sum_j a_{ij}e_j = \exp(\eta) \sum_j \tilde{p}_{ij}e_i = \exp(\eta)e_i,$$

and hence e is indeed an eigenvector of A associated with eigenvalue $\exp(\eta)$. *The transition matrix $\tilde{P}$ has $(n^2 - n)$ free parameters. The n-dimensional eigenvector e with positive entries is only identified up to scale and hence depends on $n-1$ free parameters, and the eigenvalue $\exp(\eta)$ gives one more free parameter. Thus, for this example, we may think of (8) or equivalently (9) as providing n^2 equations with input A to be used in identifying n^2 free parameters of $\tilde{P}$, e, and η. While the Perron-Frobenius approach recovers a transition matrix, it is not the transition matrix for the underlying Markov chain.*

If $\tilde{S}$, the martingale component of S, is constant over time, the distorted and actual probabilities are identical, and one obtains the recovery result of Ross (2013), who also uses Perron-Frobenius theory in his construction. This is a remarkable result, because it allows for the recovery of the transition distribution of the Markov state and thus permits investor beliefs to be subjective. When marginal utility of an investor is a time-invariant function of the Markov state, we may interpret $\delta = -\eta$ as a subjective discount rate and $\tilde{e}$ as the marginal utility of consumption expressed as a function of the Markov state.

To justify the recovery of the actual (as opposed to distorted) transition density, we had to restrict the martingale component to be constant over time. Alvarez and Jermann (2005) argue why it is important empirically to allow for the martingale component in a stochastic discount factorization (6). In an equilibrium model, a specification where the martingale component is constant is unlikely to hold unless consumption is stationary, an assumption that typically is not made in the macro-asset pricing literature.[6] In general, the application of Perron-Frobenius theory to one-period valuation recovers a transition distribution, but one that characterizes long-term valuation. This transition distribution will differ from the actual conditional distribution when there is a martingale component to the stochastic discount factor.

Example 4 *Consider the dynamic normal mixture model from Example 1. In that example, it is assumed that*

$$\log S_{t+1} - \log S_t = \bar{\beta} \cdot X_t + (X_{t+1})'\bar{\alpha}'Y_{t+1}.$$

This dynamics for S can be justified from more primitive assumptions. For instance, if the representative consumer has log utility and a subjective discount rate δ, the dynamics for S follow, provided we postulate that the consumption process C satisfies

(10) $$\log C_{t+1} - \log C_t = \tilde{\beta} \cdot X_t + (X_{t+1})' \tilde{\alpha}' Y_{t+1},$$

where

$$\bar{\beta} = -\tilde{\beta} - \exp(-\delta)\mathbf{1}_n,$$
$$\bar{\alpha} = -\tilde{\alpha},$$

and $\mathbf{1}_n$ is an n-dimensional vector of ones. In (10), the expected change in log C between t and t + 1 is given by $\tilde{\beta} \cdot \mathsf{u}_i$ (the ith component of $\tilde{\beta}$) when state i is realized at date t. The variance of the change in log C is $(\mathsf{u}_j)' \tilde{\alpha}' \tilde{\alpha} \mathsf{u}_j$ (the jth diagonal entry of $\tilde{\alpha}' \tilde{\alpha}$) conditioned on state j being realized at date t + 1. The vector $\bar{\beta}$ and matrix $\bar{\alpha}$ have analogous interpretations for the process log S.

We use this example to better illustrate the link between P and $\widetilde{P}$. We presume that state vector (X, Y) is observable to investors and consider the recovery of the transition matrix for the state vector x. For this example, (2) and (9) show that the recovered transition matrix implied by (7) is $\widetilde{P}$, where

$$\tilde{p}_{ij} = \exp(-\eta)p_{ij}\xi_{ij} \left(\frac{\mathsf{e}_j}{\mathsf{e}_i} \right).$$

Direct verification shows that $\widetilde{P}$ is indeed a transition matrix. This transition matrix agrees with P when

(11) $$\exp(-\eta)\xi_{ij} \left(\frac{\mathsf{e}_j}{\mathsf{e}_i} \right) = 1$$

for all (i, j), but this will not be true in general. Equation (11) implies that

(12) $$\xi_{ij} = \exp(\eta) \left(\frac{\mathsf{e}_i}{\mathsf{e}_j} \right).$$

The ξ_{ij}s depend on 2n parameters, the n means of $\log S_{t+1} - \log S_t$ and the n variances of $\log S_{t+1} - \log S_t$ conditioned on X_t and X_{t+1}. Thus there are

2n parameters that underlie the ξ_{ij} on the left-hand side of this equation, but only n free parameters that we can vary on the right-hand side (where e only matters up to a free scale parameter).[7]

To clarify how restrictive the requirement is in (12), suppose that $n = 2$ and Y is univariate. Then we have

$$\xi_{ij} = \exp\left[\bar{\beta}_i + \frac{1}{2}(\bar{\alpha}_j)^2\right].$$

If $p_{ii} = \tilde{p}_{ii}$, then $\xi_{ii} = \exp(\eta)$, and thus we have $\bar{\beta}_1 + \frac{1}{2}(\bar{\alpha}_1)^2 = \bar{\beta}_2 + \frac{1}{2}(\bar{\alpha}_2)^2$.

Appendix A describes an alternative recovery strategy but also argues why this approach will not work under more general circumstances.[8]

A reader might be concerned that our focus on the finite state case is too special. What follows is an example based on an underlying Markov diffusion specification, except that we allow for more shocks to be priced than the underlying state variable.

Example 5   *Suppose that X is a Markov diffusion:*

$$dX_t = \mu(X_t)dt + \Lambda(X_t)dW_t,$$

and

$$d\log S_t = \beta(X_t)dt + \alpha(X_t) \cdot dW_t.$$

The counterpart to Y_{t+1} in this example is any component of the dW_t increment that is not needed for the evolution of X. To construct the counterpart to $\bar{\mathbb{S}}$ in continuous time, we consider the operator $\mathbb{G}$ that associates to each function f the "expected time derivative" of $\frac{S_t}{S_0}f(X_t)$ at $t = 0$, that is, the drift of $\frac{S_t}{S_0}f(X_t)$ at $t = 0$:[9]

$$[\mathbb{G}f](x) = \left[\beta(x) + \frac{1}{2}|\alpha(x)|^2\right]f(x) + \left[\mu(X_t)' + \alpha(x)'\Lambda(x)\right]\frac{\partial f(x)}{\partial x}$$
$$+ \frac{1}{2}\text{trace}\left[\Lambda(x)\Lambda(x)'\frac{\partial^2 f(x)}{\partial x \partial x'}\right].$$

In this expression, $-\beta(x) - \frac{1}{2}|\alpha(x)|^2$ is the instantaneous interest rate, and $-\alpha$ is the vector of risk prices that capture the expected return reward needed as compensation for exposure to dW_t. To apply Ito's formula to *compute the drift, we may restrict f to be twice continuously differentiable, but we typically have to explore a larger collection of functions in order to solve eigenvalue problem*

(13) $[\mathbb{G}e](x) = \eta e(x)$

for a positive function e. See Hansen and Scheinkman (2009) for a more formal analysis.

The diffusion dynamics implied by the Perron-Frobenius adjustment is

$$dX_t = \left[\mu(X_t)' + \alpha(x)'\Lambda(x)' + \left[\frac{\partial \log e(x)}{\partial x}\right]' \Lambda(x)\Lambda(x)'\right]dt + \Lambda(X_t)d\widetilde{W}_t,$$

where $\widetilde{W}$ is a Brownian motion under the change of measure. See Appendix B. The version of (7) for continuous time allows us to identify the distorted dynamics for X. Thus for this procedure to identify the original dynamics, it is necessary that

$$\alpha(x) = -\Lambda(x)'\left[\frac{\partial \log e(x)}{\partial x}\right].$$

As is shown in Appendix B, when this restriction is satisfied, we can write

$$\frac{S_t}{S_0} = \exp(\eta t)\frac{e(X_0)}{e(X_t)},$$

implying that S has a constant martingale component.

4 Model Misspecification

In this section, we suggest a novel approach to confronting potential model misspecification. We consider transient model misspecifications, whereby the candidate economic model of a stochastic discount factor is restricted to give the correct limiting risk prices and approximately correct processes for long investment payoff horizons. This approach restricts the misspecified model to share the eigenvalue and the martingale component with the true or correctly specified model. We show how to use Perron-Frobenius and cumulative returns to identify the unknown parameters needed to characterize the benchmark misspecified model. We also contrast this approach to models of belief distortions that by design target the martingale components of stochastic discount factors.

As the examples in Section 3 suggest, Perron-Frobenius theory recovers an *interesting* probability distribution but typically one that is distorted. To proceed under stochastic growth, we must bring to bear additional information. Otherwise we would be left with a rather substantial identification problem. Following the literature on rational expectations econometrics, we can appeal to "cross-equation restrictions" if the Markov state vector process X is observable. In what follows we sketch two related approaches for evaluating parametric stochastic discount factor models of valuation. These approaches are distinct but complementary to the nonparameteric approach proposed by Ait-Sahalia and Lo (2000).[10]

4.1 Transient Model Misspecification

Building from Bansal and Lehmann (1997) and subsequent research, in Hansen (2012) we relate factorization (4) to a stochastic discount factor representation,

(14)
$$\frac{S_t}{S_0} = \frac{S_t^*}{S_0^*} \left[\frac{h(X_t)}{h(X_0)} \right],$$

where $\frac{S_t^*}{S_0^*}$ is the stochastic discount factor in a representative consumer power utility model, and h modifies the investor preferences to include possibly internal habit persistence, external habit persistence, or limiting versions of recursive utility. In the case of internal and external habit persistence models, these modifications may entail an endogenous state variable constructed on the basis of current and past consumptions. Introducing this function h modifies the Perron-Frobenius problem by leaving the eigenvalue intact and altering the eigenfunction as follows. If e^* is the eigenfunction associated with S^*, then $e = e^*/h$ is the Perron-Frobenius eigenfunction for S. See Chen and Ludvigson (2009) and Chen et al. (2011) for semiparametric implementations of this factorization for some specific examples.

Let us turn to the specific application of Chen et al. (2014) but adopt a discrete-time counterpart to a formulation in Hansen and Scheinkman (2009). Let R be a cumulative return process and C be a consumption process. Both are modeled with the "multiplicative" structure described in Section 2. We assume it takes the form

$$\frac{M_t}{M_0} = \frac{R_t}{R_0} \left(\frac{C_t}{C_0} \right)^{-\gamma},$$

where γ is the risk aversion parameter for a power utility model of investor preferences. Chen et al. (2011) presume that the actual stochastic discount factor is

$$\frac{S_t}{S_0} = \exp(-\delta t) \left(\frac{C_t}{C_0} \right)^{-\gamma} \left[\frac{h(X_t)}{h(X_0)} \right],$$

where X is the growth rate in consumption and any other variables that might forecast that growth rate. They motivate h as arising from a consumption externality in which lagged consumption is viewed as being socially determined, as in Abel (1990). In contrast to Abel (1990), Chen et al. (2011) aim to be nonparametric, and h becomes a multiplicative adjustment to a marginal utility of consumption that they seek to identify with limited restrictions. Thus they presume that the stochastic dynamics can be inferred and allow for growth in consumption.

A fundamental result in asset pricing is that RS is always a martingale, and as consequence, we have

$$\frac{M_t}{M_0} = \exp(\delta t) \left(\frac{\tilde{M}_t}{\tilde{M}_0} \right) \left[\frac{h(X_0)}{h(X_t)} \right].$$

Thus $\exp(\delta)$ is the associated Perron-Frobenius eigenvalue, and h is the eigenfunction. In contrast to Ross (2013), the actual transition dynamics are presumed to be directly identifiable. Perhaps surprisingly, h and δ can both be inferred from a single return process, provided that we can infer the underlying conditional distributions from historical data.[11] The use of multiple returns allows for the identification of γ along with overidentifying restrictions. The same eigenvalue and eigenfunction should be extracted when we alter the return process.[12]

We suggest an alternative approach based on a similar idea. Let S^* be a benchmark economic model that is possibly misspecified. We no longer limit our specification S^* to be the stochastic discount factor associated with power utility. Instead we allow for a more general starting point.

We restrict the potential misspecification to have transient implications for valuation, with the actual stochastic discount factor representable as (14). The function h is introduced to capture transient sources of misspecification. We call this modification "transient," because the modified stochastic discount factor shares the same eigenvalue η and hence the same long-term interest rate; in addition, it shares the same martingale component, which determines the long-term risk prices as argued in Hansen and Scheinkman (2009), Borovička et al. (2011), Hansen and Scheinkman (2012b), and Hansen (2012). The presumption is that we have little a priori structure to impose on h other than limiting its long-term consequences.

Let

$$M = RS^*,$$

and recall that $RS = \tilde{M}$ is itself a martingale. Thus we write

$$\frac{M_t}{M_0} = \left(\frac{\tilde{M}_t}{\tilde{M}_0} \right) \left[\frac{h(X_0)}{h(X_t)} \right].$$

The Perron-Frobenius eigenvalue $\exp(\eta)$ is now one, and the eigenfunction $\mathsf{e} = h$. This representation using the unit eigenvalue and the eigenfunction h must hold whenever R is a cumulative return process for a feasible self-financing strategy. This link across returns allows for the identification of unknown parameters needed to characterize the benchmark model S^* under misspecification.

This is a rather different approach to misspecification from that suggested by Hansen and Jagannathan (1997). The approach we choose here explicitly restricts the misspecification to have transient consequences for valuation. The true S and the modeled S^* must share the same asymptotic decay rate (long-term interest rate) and the same martingale component. This approach does not restrict the magnitude of h in any particular way. This leaves open the possibility that while h has "transient" consequences for pricing, these consequences might well be very important for shorter time investment horizons. Thus in practice, one would also want to assess impact of this proposed transient adjustment over investment horizons of interest in order to characterize the impact of the economic restrictions and the role of misspecification.

4.2   Distorted Beliefs

In the previous subsection, we used a long-term perspective to introduce a structured way for economic models to fit better over longer investment horizons. One motivation for this could be a misspecification of the utility functions used to represent investor preferences, but there may be other reasons to suspect model misspecification. The stochastic discount factor specification, as we have used it so far, presumes a correct specification of the transition probabilities for (X, Y), because the discount factors are only defined relative to a probability distribution. We now consider the impact of incorrectly specifying the stochastic evolution of the state variables, and we allow this to have permanent consequences on valuation. Investors themselves may have "incorrect" beliefs, or they may act as if they have distorted beliefs. Motivations for this latter perspective include ambiguity aversion or investor ambitions to be robust to model misspecification. See, for instance, Hansen and Sargent (2001) and Chen and Epstein (2002).

To capture belief distortion as a form of model misspecification, construct

$$\frac{S_t}{S_0} = \left(\frac{S_t^*}{S_0^*}\right)\left(\frac{N_t}{N_0}\right),$$

where S^* is the modeled stochastic discount factor process, and N is a martingale. Both processes are assumed to be of the "multiplicative" form introduced in Section 2. The process S is the pertinent one for pricing assets, while the process N is introduced to capture distorted beliefs.

Allowing for arbitrary belief distortions is counterproductive from the perspective of building economic models. While introducing investors with preferences that display ambiguity aversion and concerns about robustness give one way to add some structure to this analysis, this approach still depends on parameters that limit the class of alternative probability models to be considered by an investor. More generally, it is valuable to characterize or to limit the size of this source of misspecification from a statistical perspective. Here we consider Chernoff's (1952) notion of entropy motivated explicitly by the difficulty in statistically discriminating among competing models. Markov counterparts to this approach rely on Perron-Frobenius theory; see Newman and Stuck (1979). The Chernoff-style calculations are "large-deviation calculations," because mistakes occur when there is an unusual realization of a sequence of observations.

To define Chernoff entropy for the statistical discrimination among Markov processes, we focus on the martingale process N. Since N is a martingale, N^θ is a supermartingale for $0 \le \theta \le 1$. Consider

$$\epsilon(\theta) = - \lim_{t \to \infty} \frac{1}{t} \log E \left[\left(\frac{N_t}{N_0} \right)^\theta |X_0 = x \right].$$

Notice that $\epsilon(0) = 0$, and since N is a martingale, $\epsilon(1) = 0$, but more generally, $\epsilon(\theta) \ge 0$, because N^θ is a supermartingale. As the asymptotic rate of growth of $\exp(\theta \log N) = N^\theta$, $\exp[-\epsilon(\theta)]$ can be seen as the Perron-Frobenius eigenvalue associated with this process. Chernoff entropy is the asymptotic decay rate for making mistakes in determining the correct model from historical data. It is given by solving

$$\max_{\theta \in [0,1]} \epsilon(\theta).$$

When the maximized value is close to zero, it is difficult to distinguish between the original model and the distorted model captured by N. Anderson et al. (2003) suggest this as a way to assess when investor concerns about model misspecification might be reasonable. More generally, this can used to assess how large the misspecification is from a statistical standpoint.[13] Such calculations give us a way to see whether statistically small but permanent distortions in probability specifications can have notable consequence for valuation.

5   Recursive Utility Valuation

Recursive utility of the type proposed by Kreps and Porteus (1978) and Epstein and Zin (1989) represents the valuation of prospective future risky consumption processes through the construction of continuation values. This approach avoids the reduction of intertemporal compound lotteries and thus allows for the intertemporal composition of risk to matter. Bansal and Yaron (2004) use this feature of recursive preferences to argue that even statistically subtle components of growth rate risk can have an important impact on valuation. Hansen and Scheinkman (2012a) establish a link between Perron-Frobenius theory and Kreps and Porteus (1978)–style recursive utility. We show that this link provides a new perspective on the valuation impacts of stochastic growth and volatility in consumption as they are compounded over time, and it further clarifies the roles of the parameters used in representing the utility recursion.

We use the homogeneous-of-degree-one aggregator specified in terms of current period consumption C_t and the continuation value V_t:

(15) $$V_t = \left[(\zeta C_t)^{1-\rho} + \exp(-\delta) \left[\mathcal{R}_t(V_{t+1}) \right]^{1-\rho} \right]^{\frac{1}{1-\rho}},$$

where

$$\mathcal{R}_t (V_{t+1}) = \left(E\left[(V_{t+1})^{1-\gamma} | \mathcal{F}_t \right] \right)^{\frac{1}{1-\gamma}}$$

adjusts the continuation value V_{t+1} for risk. With these preferences, $\frac{1}{\rho}$ is the elasticity of intertemporal substitution, and δ is a subjective discount rate. The parameter ζ does not alter preferences but gives some additional flexibility that is valuable when taking limits. Next, we exploit homogeneity-of-degree-one in (15) to obtain

(16) $$\left(\frac{V_t}{C_t} \right)^{1-\rho} = \zeta^{1-\rho} + \exp(-\delta) \left[\mathcal{R}_t \left(\frac{V_{t+1}}{C_{t+1}} \frac{C_{t+1}}{C_t} \right) \right]^{1-\rho}.$$

In finite horizons, using the aggregator requires a terminal condition for the continuation value. In what follows, we consider infinite-horizon limits, leading us to consider fixed-point equations. Thus we explore the construction of the continuation value V_t as a function of $C_t, C_{t+1}, C_{t+2}, \ldots$.

Suppose that the consumption dynamics evolve as

$$\log C_{t+1} - \log C_t = \kappa(X_{t+1}, Y_{t+1}, X_t).$$

Given the Markov dynamics, we seek a solution:

$$\left(\frac{V_t}{C_t} \right)^{1-\rho} = f(X_t), \quad f \geq 0.$$

Writing

$$\alpha = \frac{1-\gamma}{1-\rho},$$

and for $f \geq 0$,

$$[\mathbb{U}f](x) = \zeta^{1-\rho} + \exp(-\delta) \left(E \left[f(X_{t+1})^{\alpha} \right. \right.$$
$$\left. \left. \times \exp[(1-\gamma)\kappa(X_{t+1}, Y_{t+1}, X_t)] | X_t = x \right] \right)^{\frac{1}{\alpha}},$$

we express equation (16) as

(17) $\hat{f}(x) = [\mathbb{U}\hat{f}](x).$

The solution to the fixed-point problem (17) is closely related to a Perron-Frobenius eigenvalue equation.[14] To see this relation, consider the mapping

$$[\mathbb{T}f](x) = E\left[\exp[(1-\gamma)\kappa(X_{t+1}, Y_{t+1}, X_t)]f(X_{t+1})|X_t = x\right].$$

The eigenvalue equation of interest is

(18) $[\mathbb{T}e](x) = \exp(\eta)e(x),$

for $e > 0$. Hansen and Scheinkman (2012a) construct a solution to (17) using the eigenfunction $e(x)$, provided the following parameter restriction

(19) $\delta > \dfrac{1-\rho}{1-\gamma}\eta$

is satisfied, along with some additional moment restrictions.

Why might there be a connection between the eigenvalue equation (18) and the fixed-point equation (17)? Consider (17), but add the following modifications:

  i) Set $\zeta^{1-\rho} = 0$;
  ii) Raise both sides of the equation to the power α;
  iii) Set δ to satisfy inequality (19) with equality.

This modified version of (17) is essentially the same as the eigenvalue equation (18).

What do we make of this observation? The positive number ζ is merely a convenient scale factor. Its specific choice does not alter the preferences implied by the recursive utility model. This gives us some flexibility in taking limits. The limit that we must take entails letting the subjective discount rate δ approximate the bound in (19). In effect, this makes the future as important as possible in the utility recursion. Hansen and Scheinkman (2012a) discuss more formally how this limit effectively reduces the infinite-horizon value function problem to a Perron-Frobenius eigenvalue problem. For many common model parameterizations, the eigenfunction is the exponential of a quadratic, and the eigenvalue equation can be solved in a straightforward manner. This solution then can be used to construct a solution to the infinite-horizon utility recursive under the stated parameter restrictions.

In the notation of the previous sections, the process M_t used in conjunction with the Perron-Frobenius theory is

$$\frac{M_t}{M_0} = \left(\frac{C_t}{C_0}\right)^{1-\gamma}.$$

The martingale component for this process provides a convenient change of measure to use for evaluating the utility recursion as it absorbs the stochastic growth component to consumption pertinent for valuation. This approach thus features the risk-aversion parameter γ in the construction of a martingale component relevant for the analysis of investor preferences.

6 Conclusion

In this paper, we studied three problems using a common approach. This approach assumes a Markov environment and applies Perron-Frobenius theory to characterize the long-run impact of compounding in a stochastic environment. Given a possibly nonlinear stochastic process describing growth or discounting, this approach identifies three multiplicative components: i) a deterministic growth or decay rate rate, ii) a transient component, and iii) a martingale component. The latter two components are typically correlated. We use the martingale component to produce a distorted probability measure that helps reveal the long-term contribution to valuation induced by stochastic growth or discounting.

First, we applied these methods to investigate how compounding interacts with the assignment of risk prices and to examine the possibility of disentangling risk adjustments from investor beliefs using asset market data. We showed that, in the presence of stochastic growth, application of Perron-Frobenius theory does *not* recover the actual probability used by investors but instead recovers the distorted probability measure. This measure is informative about the implications for risk prices over long payoff and investment horizons.

Second, we used the decomposition to examine misspecification of parametric models of valuation. These models, while tractable, are surely misspecified. Departures from economic fundamentals may be of a temporary nature, and econometric identification should reflect this possibility. This can be accomplished in the framework developed in this paper by assuming that the true stochastic discount factor and the parametric model of the discount factor share the same deterministic growth rate and martingale component, differing only in their respective transient components to valuation. We also discussed how to treat the impact of assuming that investors have "wrong" beliefs in environments in which we allow for the misspecification to have permanent consequences for valuation.

Third, we discussed how to use Perron-Frobenius theory to obtain existence results for infinite-horizon Kreps-Porteus utility functions, and highlighted the role of the risk-aversion parameter in the construction of the stochastic growth component of consumption that is pertinent to long-run valuation.

The methods we describe here can also be applied to study the valuation of unusual episodes as they emerge over multiple time periods. While the episodes might be disguised in the short run, they could become more prominent over longer horizons. In our analysis here, we applied a generalized version of Perron-Frobenius theory for Markov processes, an approach that has much in common with large-deviation theory as developed by Donsker and Varadhan (1976). To better appreciate this connection, see Stutzer (2003) and Hansen and Scheinkman (2012a). An alternative approach analyzes such phenomena with a different type of limiting behavior. In future work, we plan to study the pricing of rare events using a large-deviation theory in continuous time, whereby we hold fixed the valuation time interval while progressively reducing the exposure to Brownian motion shocks.

Appendix A: Mixture-of-Normals Example

Consider an alternative approach to recovery for Example 4. The positive random variable

$$\frac{\frac{S_{t+1}}{S_t}}{E\left(\frac{S_{t+1}}{S_t} | X_{t+1}, X_t\right)}$$

alters the distribution of Y_{t+1} conditioned on X_{t+1} and X_t in the same manner as described previously. The adjustment induced by

$$E\left(\frac{S_{t+1}}{S_t} | X_{t+1}, X_t\right)$$

is captured in the A matrix. Consider now a payoff of the form $g_1(Y_{t+1})g_2(X_{t+1}, X_t)$, where g_2 is one when X_t is in state i and X_{t+1} is in state j. We may compute this price by first evaluating the distorted expectation of g_1 conditioned on X_{t+1}, X_t and then multiplying this conditional expectation by a_{ij}. Since the a_{ij}s are can be inferred by asset market data, so can the altered distribution for Y_{t+1} conditioned on X_{t+1}, X_t. Thus $\bar{\alpha}$ is revealed. The terms $\bar{\beta} \cdot \mathsf{u}_i$ and the p_{ij}s can be solved in terms of the a_{ij}s and the $\frac{1}{2}(\mathsf{u}_j)'\bar{\alpha}'\bar{\alpha}\mathsf{u}_j$s. Thus P can be recovered but not by a Perron-Frobenius extraction. In the more general case,

$$\log S_{t+1} - \log S_t = (X_t)'\tilde{\beta}X_{t+1} + (X_{t+1})'\bar{\alpha}'Y_{t+1},$$

where $\tilde{\beta}$ is an $n \times n$ matrix, then it is typically not possible to recover P without additional restrictions.

Appendix B: Markov Diffusion Example

Here we give some supporting arguments for the discussion of Example 5. Suppose that X is a Markov diffusion

$$dX_t = \mu(X_t)dt + \Lambda(X_t)dW_t,$$

and we have

$$d \log S_t = \beta(X_t)dt + \alpha(X_t) \cdot dW_t.$$

To construct a transformed generator, we compute the drift of $\exp(-\eta t)f(x_t)\left(\frac{e(X_t)}{e(X_0)}\right)$. This gives rise to the transformed generator:

$$[\widetilde{\mathbb{G}}f](x) = \frac{1}{e(x)}[\mathbb{G}(ef)](x) - \eta f(x)$$

$$= [\mathbb{G}f](x) + \frac{f(x)}{e(x)}[\mathbb{G}e](x) - \left[\beta(x) + \frac{1}{2}|\alpha(x)|^2\right]f(x)$$

$$+ \left[\frac{\partial \log e(x)}{\partial x}\right]' \Lambda(x)\Lambda(x)' \left[\frac{\partial f(x)}{\partial x}\right] - \eta f(x)$$

$$= [\mathbb{G}f](x) - \left[\beta(x) + \frac{1}{2}|\alpha(x)|^2\right]f(x) + \left[\frac{\partial \log e(x)}{\partial x}\right]'\Lambda(x)\Lambda(x)'\left[\frac{\partial f(x)}{\partial x}\right]$$

$$= \left[\mu(X_t)' + \alpha(x)'\Lambda(x)' + \left[\frac{\partial \log e(x)}{\partial x}\right]' \Lambda(x)\Lambda(x)'\right]\frac{\partial f(x)}{\partial x}$$

$$+ \frac{1}{2}\text{trace}\left[\Lambda(x)\Lambda(x)'\frac{\partial^2 e(x)}{\partial x \partial x'}\right].$$

As expected, the coefficient on the level $f(x)$ is zero, because we want this to be the generator of a stochastically stable Markov process. The matrix of coefficients for the second derivative of f remains the same, as the absolute continuity between the implied probability measures over finite time intervals requires that the diffusion matrix remain the same. The important change is in the vector of coefficients for the first derivative of f. This modification alters the drift of the diffusion in the manner stated in the discussion of Example 5.

This approach recovers the original generator of the Markov process when e solves the eigenfunction equation (13) and

$$\alpha(x) = -\Lambda(x)'\left[\frac{\partial \log e(x)}{\partial x}\right].$$

Given these restrictions, it follows that

$$\eta = \beta(x) - \frac{1}{2}\left[\frac{\partial \log e(x)}{\partial x}\right]'\Lambda(x)\Lambda(x)'\left[\frac{\partial \log e(x)}{\partial x}\right]$$

$$+ \mu(x)'\frac{\partial \log e(x)}{\partial x} + \frac{1}{2e(x)}\text{trace}\left[\Lambda(x)\Lambda(x)'\frac{\partial^2 e(x)}{\partial x \partial x'}\right]$$

$$= \beta(x) + \mu(x)'\frac{\partial \log e(x)}{\partial x} + \frac{1}{2}\text{trace}\left[\Lambda(x)\Lambda(x)'\frac{\partial^2 \log e(x)}{\partial x \partial x'}\right].$$

As a consequence, $\beta(x) = \eta - \text{drift} \log e(x)$, where

$$\text{drift} \log e(x) = \mu(x)' \frac{\partial \log e(x)}{\partial x} + \frac{1}{2} \text{trace} \left[\Lambda(x) \Lambda(x)' \frac{\partial^2 \log e(x)}{\partial x \partial x'} \right]$$

and hence

$$d \log S_t = \eta dt - d \log e(X_t) dt.$$

Integrating between dates zero and t and exponentiating gives

$$\frac{S_t}{S_0} = \exp(\eta t) \left[\frac{e(X_0)}{e(X_t)} \right].$$

Notes

A first version of this chapter was presented at the conference *Après le Déluge: Finance and the Common Good after the Crisis*, held at Columbia University on March 22, 2013. We thank our discussants Jaroslav Borovicka, Xiaohong Chen, Steve Durlauf, Ed Glaeser, Valentin Haddad, Paul Ho, Kyle Jurado, and Narayana Kocherlakota for their comments.

1. See also Alvarez and Jermann (2005) for a discussion of the empirical importance for a martingale component of stochastic discount factors.

2. Thus we consider payoffs that are functions of both X_{t+1} and Y_{t+1}. To infer the prices of multiperiod payoffs, we iterate on the one-period valuation operator. Given a characterization of the pricing of these "primitive" payoffs, we can extend the valuation operator to an even richer collection of asset payoffs with more complicated forms of history dependence.

3. See Backus et al. (1989) for an early use of Perron-Frobenius theory in their study of the term structure implications.

4. The "left over" part in additive decomposition is correlated with the permanent part, making it hard to use directly as a statistical decomposition. This correlation has led many researchers to identify "transitory shocks" as those that are uncorrelated with the martingale increment. Similarly, the Peron-Frobenius eigenfunction is correlated with the martingale component, making it difficult to interpret (6) directly as a decomposition.

5. In contrast, the martingale from an additive extraction obeys a central limit theorem when appropriately scaled.

6. As Alvarez and Jermann (2005) point out, even if consumption is stationary, the more general recursive utility model could imply a martingale component to the stochastic discount factor process.

7. In this example, the ξ_{ij}s depend on $2n$ parameters, but one can construct examples in which there are n^2 free parameters.

8. One might argue that we should expand our search for eigenfunctions to a broader set of functions. For instance, we might add S_t to the state vector along with X_t and Y_t, even though $\log S_{t+1} - \log S_t$ is constructed from X_{t+1}, Y_{t+1}, and X_t. Since S is typically not stationary, this would require relaxing some of our maintained assumptions and would require that we dispense with the selection rule in Hansen and Scheinkman (2009). A potential gain from this approach is that we might view $\frac{1}{S_t}$ as a Perron-Frobenius eigenfunction associated with the unit eigenvalue based on the observation that $\frac{1}{S_t}$ is strictly positive. One could modify the selection rule of Hansen and Scheinkman (2009), requiring only the stochastic stability of X. This, however, would allow potentially for both candidate solutions. Alternatively, we could identify the eigenfunction of interest by "zeroing out" the dependence on X_t and Y_t. If this is our selection criterion, we would choose $\frac{1}{S_t}$, but in this case, the use of Perron-Frobenius theory adds no information concerning the dynamics of X.

9. This operator is called the "generator for the pricing semigroup" in Hansen and Scheinkman (2009).

10. Ait-Sahalia and Lo (2000) show how to recover a stochastic discount factor nonparametrically over a given investment horizon by using option prices to extract a forward measure and forming the ratio of the forward transition density to the actual transition density measured from the observed data.

11. A researcher may actually prefer to place some restrictions on h consistent with an underlying preference interpretation. Even so, the identification result in Chen et al. (2011) remains interesting, as additional restrictions should only make identification easier.

12. In external habit models, such as the one in Campbell and Cochrane (1999), the habit stock is a constructed state variable, one for which there is no direct observable counterpart. An additional challenge for identification is to infer, perhaps with weak restrictions, the law of motion for this endogenous state variable.

13. Anderson et al. (2003) also explore a local counterpart to the Chernoff measure.

14. See Duffie and Lions (1992) for a related application of Perron-Frobenius theory as an input into an existence argument.

References

Abel, A. B. (1990). Asset prices under habit formation and catching up with the Joneses. *American Economic Review* 80 2), 38–42.

Ait-Sahalia, Y., and A. W. Lo (2000). Nonparametric risk management and implied risk aversion. *Journal of Econometrics* 94(1–2), 9–51.

Alvarez, F., and U. J. Jermann (2005). Using asset prices to measure the persistence of the marginal utility of wealth. *Econometrica* 73(6), 1977–2016.

Anderson, E. W., L. P. Hansen, and T. J. Sargent (2003). A quartet of semigroups for model specification, robustness, prices of risk, and model detection. *Journal of the European Economic Association* 1(1), 68–123.

Backus, D. K., A. W. Gregory, and S. E. Zin (1989). Risk premiums in the term structure: Evidence from artificial economies. *Journal of Monetary Economics* 24(3), 371–399.

Bansal, R., and B. N. Lehmann (1997). Growth-optimal portfolio restrictions on asset pricing models. *Macroeconomic Dynamics* 1(2), 333–354.

Bansal, R., and A. Yaron (2004). Risks for the long run: A potential resolution of asset pricing puzzles. *Journal of Finance* 59(4), 1481–1509.

Borovička, J., L. P. Hansen, M. Hendricks, and J. A. Scheinkman (2011). Risk price dynamics. *Journal of Financial Econometrics* 9(1), 3–65.

Campbell, J. Y., and J. H. Cochrane (1999). By force of habit. *Journal of Political Economy* 107(2), 205–251.

Chen, X., and S. Ludvigson (2009). Land of addicts? An empirical investigation of habit-based asset pricing models. *Journal of Applied Econometrics* 24(7), 1057–1093.

Chen, X., V. Chernozhukov, S. Lee, and W. Newey (2014). Local identification of nonparametric and semiparametric models. *Econometrica* 82(2), 785–805.

Chen, Z., and L. Epstein (2002). Ambiguity, risk, and asset returns in continuous time. *Econometrica* 70(4), 1403–1443.

Chernoff, H. (1952). A measure of asymptotic efficiency for tests of a hypothesis based on the sum of observations. *Annals of Mathematical Statistics* 23(4), 493–507.

Donsker, M. E., and S. R. S. Varadhan (1976). On the principal eigenvalue of second-order elliptic differential equations. *Communications in Pure and Applied Mathematics* 29(6), 595–621.

Duffie, D., and P.-L. Lions (1992). PDE solutions of stochastic differential utility. *Journal of Mathematical Economics* 21(6), 577–606.

Epstein, L., and S. Zin (1989). Substitution, risk aversion and the temporal behavior of consumption and asset returns: A theoretical framework. *Econometrica* 57(4), 937–969.

Granger, C. W. J. (1969). Investigating causal relations by econometric models with cross-spectral methods. *Econometrica* 37(3), 424–438.

Hansen, L. P. (2012). Dynamic valuation decomposition within stochastic economies. *Econometrica* 80(3), 911–967. Fisher-Schultz Lecture at the European Meetings of the Econometric Society.

Hansen, L. P., and R. Jagannathan (1997). Assessing specification errors in stochastic discount factor models. *Journal of Finance* 52(2), 557–590.

Hansen, L. P., and S. F. Richard (1987). The role of conditioning information in deducing testable restrictions implied by dynamic asset pricing models. *Econometrica* 55(3), 587–614.

Hansen, L. P., and T. J. Sargent (2001). Robust control and model uncertainty. *American Economic Review* 91(2), 60–66.

Hansen, L. P., and J. Scheinkman (2009). Long-term risk: An operator approach. *Econometrica* 77(1), 117–234.

———— (2012a). Recursive utility in a Markov environment with stochastic growth. *Proceedings of the National Academy of Sciences 109*(30), 11967–11972.

———— (2012b). Pricing growth-rate risk. *Finance and Stochastics 16*(1), 1–15.

Hansen, L. P., J. C. Heaton, and N. Li (2008). Consumption strikes back? Measuring long-run risk. *Journal of Political Economy 116*(2), 260–302.

Kreps, D. M., and E. L. Porteus (1978). Temporal resolution of uncertainty and dynamic choice. *Econometrica 46*(1), 185–200.

Newman, C. M., and B. W. Stuck (1979). Chernoff bounds for discriminating between two Markov processes. *Stochastics 2*(1–4), 139–153.

Ross, S. A. (2015). The recovery theorem. *Journal of Finance 70*(2), 615–648.

Stutzer, M. (2003). Portfolio choice with endogenous utility: A large deviation approach. *Journal of Econometrics 116*(1), 365–386.

van Binsbergen, J., M. Brandt, and R. Koijen (2012). On the timing and pricing of dividends. *American Economic Review 102*(4), 1596–1618.

CHAPTER THREE

The Good Banker

Patrick Bolton

1 Introduction

The scandal over the fixing of the London Interbank Offered Rate (LIBOR) prompted the new management of Barclays to commission an in-depth review of the bank's corporate culture by an independent commission headed by Anthony Salz. Following extensive internal interviews with hundreds of Barclays bankers, a detailed and insightful review of Barclays management failings was published in April 2013. It begins with a tactful British understatement: "The public has been encouraged by politicians, regulators and the media to see the banks as having a significant responsibility for the financial crisis and the ensuing economic ills. This has been a cause of the loss of public confidence" (Salz 2013, 4). To be sure, there has been a constant outpouring of negative commentary on bankers ethical blindness ever since the failure of Bear Stearns, fuelled by a seemingly endless stream of revelations about banks' dubious practices before and during the financial crisis.

We thought we had heard the worst about bank misconduct when shady mortgage origination practices—epitomized by predatory lending methods and the rapid growth of "Ninja"[1] loans—were reported, or when later the widespread misselling of mortgage-backed securities was uncovered.[2] Alas, over the past five years we have learned that virtually every major bank has been involved in some form of malfeasance and that essentially every banking activity has been touched by some scandal, whether it was improperly feeding funds to Bernie Madoff, money laundering, facilitating tax evasion for wealthy private clients, collusion in credit derivatives markets, or the manipulation of LIBOR. What is worse, some banks seemed to continue their bad habits undeterred during the crisis, as the robo-signing of foreclosure notices scandal revealed.

In light of all these revelations, it is no wonder that bankers have acquired a bad name and that they have lost the public's trust. But what are the causes of all this misconduct? The answers to this question are important to determine what banking reforms are needed to establish a sounder and more reputable banking industry.

Many commentators have put the blame on financial deregulation, which has allowed banks to gravitate away from their traditional role as lenders and to increasingly engage in speculative trading activities. I differ with this assessment and argue that the gradual dismantling and eventual repeal of Glass-Steagall separations between commercial and investment banking was a necessary evolution reflecting the changed nature of modern banking. I argue instead that the causes behind the erosion of bankers' ethical standards and reckless behavior are largely to be found with how bankers were compensated and the culture of impunity that banks' compensation practices gave rise to. Thus, regulatory reforms should be directed more toward reigning in bank compensation and governance practices than toward structural remedies imposing artificial boundaries between different banking activities.

After laying out the two main contending hypotheses in Section 2, I develop at greater length the basic economic and regulatory logic behind the repeal of separations between lending and trading activities before the crisis in Sections 3 and 4. I then turn to a more detailed discussion of compensation practices and the economic logic for controlling bankers pay in Section 5. Finally, Section 6 summarizes the main argument and concludes.

2 Transactions over Relationships

Two broad explanations for banker misconduct prior to the crisis have been proposed. The first is that banks have increasingly abandoned their traditional commercial banking activities in favor of fee-based transaction services, trading, and speculation. In the process, to borrow the Supreme Court's famous phrasing in its landmark decision ICI vs. Camp (1971), bankers have been carried away by their "salesman interest ... impair[ing] [their] ability to function as an impartial source of credit."[3] In other words, by moving away from their traditional role of deposit taking and lending to businesses and households, bankers have gradually transformed an activity based on long-term relationships with clients into a short-term trading activity focused on maximizing profits from trading. The *Salz Review* reaches a similar conclusion and observes that Barclays'

> rapid journey, from a primarily domestic retail bank to a global universal bank twenty or so years later, gave rise to cultural and other growth challenges. The result of this growth was that Barclays became complex to manage, tending to develop silos with different values and cultures. Despite some attempts to establish Group-wide values, the culture that emerged tended to favour transactions over relationships, the short term over sustainability, and financial over other business purposes. [Salz 2013, 2.13]

But the *Salz Review* also offers another related explanation, one that centers on bankers' compensation practices and banks' bonus culture:

> The structuring of pay was typically focused on revenues and not on other aspects of performance. Encouraging the maximisation of short-term revenues carried risks of unsatisfactory behaviour, with significant and adverse reputational consequences for the bank.... Based on our interviews, we could not avoid concluding that pay contributed significantly to a sense among a few that they were somehow unaffected by the ordinary rules. A few investment bankers seemed to lose a sense of proportion and humility. [Salz 2013, 2.28 and 2.29]

Two separate points are made here. The first is that Barclays (and other banks) based bankers' compensation on the wrong performance benchmarks; they lavishly rewarded short-term revenue performance without looking too deeply into how the performance was achieved. Was a bankers' sales performance due to misselling, excessive risk taking, or even market manipulation? These questions did not receive much consideration, unwittingly fostering a culture of winning at all costs.

This first point, although systematically ignored even by the most reputable executive pay consultants, is actually in accordance with some of the main contributions of modern agency theory in economics. As the Holmström and Milgrom (1991) multi-task agency theory emphasizes, the obvious risk of offering bankers high-powered incentives to maximize short-term revenue is that they will inevitably respond by neglecting other important tasks that are less well rewarded. And, as Bénabou and Tirole (2016) have recently shown, increased competition for talented bankers can exacerbate this multi-task distortion and give rise to an equilibrium in which a destructive bonus culture can develop inside banks.[4] They consider a multi-task production model, where the output of some tasks is easily measured and rewarded and that of others, which involve some elements of public goods production (such as maintaining the firm's reputation), is not. Agents differ in their productivity, so that firms, which are not able to observe underlying agent productivity types, seek to screen agents based on their observable outputs. Bénabou and Tirole show that under competitive labor markets, individual firms can be led to provide excessive incentives to agents for tasks with easily measured output. Thus, competition for talent can give rise to an equilibrium outcome, where firms foster a potentially destructive bonus culture, as the less well-measured tasks are neglected by agents. They show that in such a model, welfare can be improved by introducing regulations that put a ceiling on the size of bonuses.

The economics literature on short-termism has also emphasized that rewards for short-term performance can be destructive if they induce behavior that boosts short-term performance at the expense of long-term value (see, e.g., Stein 1989). One would think that bank owners and their pay consultants would not be so foolish as to offer such destructive financial incentives to bank managers, traders, and executives. But as Bolton et al. Scheinkman and Xiong (2006) have argued, bank owners themselves, and the financial markets in which they trade their shares, may also have excessively short-run horizons, so much so that they actually are quite happy to encourage bank executives to pursue short-term performance at the expense of long-term value. The key element of their argument is the observation that shareholders often have different opinions and disagree about the fundamental value of a bank's strategy. As a result, bubbles can develop when optimists temporarily drive up stock prices. Shareholders believe they benefit from these bubbles, because they hope to be able to exit before the bubble bursts. As a result, they are happy to encourage bank executives to boost short-term performance even at the cost of excessive risk taking, as higher reported short-term earnings tend to fuel the bubble.

The second point in the analysis of the *Salz Review* on Barclays' pay practices concerns the disproportionate levels of pay of some of the top bankers. The *Salz Review* indicates that top bankers' remuneration had become so extravagantly high that bankers lost any sense of reality. Top Barclays bankers' lavish pay had the unintended effect of isolating them from their clients and ordinary employees. It fostered hubris and gave rise to a sense of entitlement. The lopsided compensation also boosted their egos, making them overconfident, distorting their perceptions of risk, and muffling their sense of caution. Classical agency theory does not allow for any possible psychological side effects of outsize pay. This may be an important gap in the economic theory of incentives that frames compensation practice, especially in view of the abundant anecdotal evidence that people who have the good fortune to rapidly amass wealth can easily become disoriented and squander it, be they successful sportsmen, artists, gamblers, or bankers.

The two broad explanations for the corrosion of bankers' ethical standards and banker misconduct—i) the shift toward a transactions, fee-based, banking model and ii) the growth of a toxic bonus culture—are not mutually exclusive. Indeed, many commentators have conflated the two explanations. A prominent example is Simon Johnson, who asserted that:

> the culture in big Wall Street banks remains just as bad as ever—traders and executives have no respect for their clients and are mostly looking for ways to behave badly (and get away with it). Top people at megabanks make a lot of money under existing arrangements. They get the upside from big bets and, when things go badly, they benefit from downside protection provided by the government. This amounts to a non-transparent, unfair and danger-ous subsidy system. The Volcker Rule will curtail subsidies and cut bankers' pay. You should be careful with your investments and be very skeptical of the advice you receive from big banks. Trust community savings banks and credit unions. Trust the FDIC to protect your deposits. Support politicians who want to reform and rein in the power of the big banks.[5]

It is important, however, to make a clear distinction between these two explanations, for they lead to very different assessments of how banking needs to be reformed. Echoing Robert Shiller (2013), who in his discussion of collateralized mortgage obligations (CMOs), wisely warns that "[we] have to understand human behavior and human ethical standards, to know that the financial system that produced the CMOs and other derivatives was not inherently evil, that it had sound concepts that might sometimes be derailed, that [we] *should not adopt a Manichean view of business that sees the financial community in black and white* [emphasis added]." I shall argue that the transformation of banking away from its traditional role of relationship lender to small and medium-sized firms is a natural and efficient evolution, responding to technological changes and changing needs for financial services in the economy, but that compensation of bankers has gotten out of hand to the point that it has corroded bankers' ethical standards of conduct.

3   What Is a Good Banker?

For many, the idealized image of the good banker is James Stewart playing the role of George Bailey, the selfless manager of a small bank, in Frank Capra's classic, *It's a Wonderful Life* (1946). It is an image that is appealing both for the noble character of the main protagonist and the nostalgic depiction of relationship banking in a small-town savings and loan bank. Recently, Joe Nocera conjured up this very image in singling out Robert G. Wilmers, the CEO of M&T Bank as the personification of a good banker. In Wilmers' own words: "Most bankers are very involved in their communities . . . banks exist for people to keep their liquid income, and also to finance trade and commerce." And Nocera adds

> what particularly galled [Wilmers]—trading derivatives and other securities [that] really had nothing to do with the underlying purpose of banking. He told me that he thought the Glass-Steagall Act—the Depression-era law that separated commercial and investment banks—should never have been abolished and that derivatives need to be brought under government control.[6]

This is a widespread sentiment. Many believe that the origins of the crisis of 2007–2009 can be found in the passage of the Gramm-Leach-Bliley Act of 1999, which essentially repealed Glass-Steagall and allowed for the expansion by commercial banks into investment banking. While the Dodd-Frank Act of 2010 partially reverses some of the Gramm-Leach-Bliley provisions with the Volcker rule prohibiting proprietary trading by banks, this is only seen as a modest step in the right direction, and many continue to call for the return to a complete separation of commercial and investment banking, as vividly illustrated by the "21st Century Glass-Steagall" bill introduced in the Senate on July 11, 2013, by Senators Warren, McCain, Cantwell, and King.

The opposition to the universal banking model, which combines commercial banking, investment banking, and insurance activities, comprises different constituencies invoking different reasons for returning to a Glass-Steagall form of separation. At a general philosophical level, there has long been an ethical condemnation of speculative activities (at least since Aristotle), and several major religions condemn financial speculation (see, e.g., Sen 1993). Interestingly, Robert Shiller (2013, 404) has recently reaffirmed this condemnation by arguing that: "Speculation is selfish in the sense that successful speculators do not share information freely. They buy and sell on behalf of their own account instead of revealing information and generously providing the information to all of society." Shiller's argument in effect is that a good banker is motivated by altruism and to the extent that speculation involves the selfish exploitation of counterparties' ignorance, it cannot be part of the job description of a good banker.

This is a deep insight that goes to the heart of some of the concerns voiced in the *Salz Review* about lost trust in bankers, and to the apprehension expressed by the Supreme Court in ICI vs. Camp about the subtle hazards of mixing lending and securities trading activities in the same bank. In ICI vs. Camp, the Supreme Court had to determine whether First National City Bank's creation and promotion of a collective investment fund (functionally similar to a mutual fund) constituted an infringement of the Glass-Steagall separation between commercial and investment banking. Although the Court recognized that the collective investment fund posed no immediate systemic risk, it nevertheless decided that this was a violation of the law, on the grounds that the extension of commercial banks activities into the fund industry could give rise to *subtle hazards* that the legislators sought to avoid.

In a penetrating analysis of the history of enforcement of the Glass-Steagall Act and the gradual dismantling of the legal barriers separating investment and commercial banking activities in the decades following ICI vs. Camp, Langevoort (1987) shows that while the Supreme Court may have been prescient in pinpointing the subtle hazards of mixing traditional lending with securities trading activities and the risks that "the promotional needs of investment banking might lead commercial banks to lend their reputation for prudence and restraint to the enterprise of selling particular stocks and securities,"[7] the evolution of financial markets, technological change, and the changing financial needs of households and corporations left no choice to the courts but to gradually dismantle the restrictions imposed on commercial banks by the Glass-Steagall Act.

As Langevoort (1987) explains:

> [the] view of banks [underlying Glass-Steagall] as something of public trustees or a public utility, [was] perhaps justified given the regulation-induced monopolistic conditions in the post-1933 banking marketplace, [but] One doubts that many sophisticated people today see the banker as anything but a businessperson under pressure to sell products and generate profits—not a likely source of "disinterested investment advice" unless that service is paid for. Camp's reference to the conservative traditions of commercial banking, in contrast to the promotional emphasis of the securities industry, rings hollow if consumers treat the financial services products offered by the two industries as in fact fungible. The monopoly rents that once could be appropriated by the industry have in many respects disappeared in the face of vigorous competition, and with them the normative basis for expecting any compensating sense of public responsibility.[8]

Indeed, the history of banking of the past 50 years is one of increased competition from the financial services industry, which gradually undermined the traditional, local, undiversified commercial banking model. Whether on the depositor side or on the borrower side, commercial banks increasingly faced competition from close substitutes offered by nonbank entities. When bank depositors moved more and more of their savings into higher-return money market mutual funds, which simultaneously attracted a larger and larger fraction of corporate issuers away from banks, Congress had little choice but to significantly relax the interest rate ceiling restrictions imposed on commercial banks under regulation Q in the early 1980s.

A further relaxation of the commercial banking regulatory straitjacket followed when commercial banks were allowed to offer discount brokerage services and individual retirement accounts (IRAs) to their depositor clients. While the Supreme Court had adhered to a strict interpretation of Glass-Steagall in the early 1970s in ICI vs. Camp, both it and the lower courts gradually retreated from this fundamentalist interpretation in the 1980s and ruled that the provision of these services was not incompatible with Glass-Steagall. Further erosion of the strict separation between securities markets and commercial banking was brought about when securities firms in the mutual funds business were allowed to also offer FDIC-insured checking accounts to their clients, when banks were permitted to privately place commercial paper for their corporate clients, and finally when securities affiliates of bank holding companies were allowed to underwrite stock and bond issues.

In sum, the erosion of the strict separation of lending and trading activities in the 1980s and 1990s took both the form of commercial banks extending their footprint into (among others) the mutual fund business, and investment banks offering traditional commercial banking services (such as checking accounts). From the perspective of their corporate and retail clients, the distinction between commercial and investment banking activities became increasingly blurred: for a corporate borrower, what is the difference between a commercial paper issue held by a money market mutual fund and a short-term loan extended by a commercial bank? Moreover, the separation between the two banking sectors imposed increasingly onerous artificial barriers preventing the offering of complementary services, such as commercial loans together with hedging, trade credit, and cash-management services. Most importantly, the Glass-Steagall separation between commercial and investment banking introduced a form of destabilizing competition between the two sectors, artificially favoring the less tightly regulated sector. The pressure to deregulate largely came from the sector at risk of losing ground and of becoming unviable. Thus, when the competitive distortions from Glass-Steagall became evident, the courts responded by relaxing the most distortionary restrictions in the law in an effort to restore a level playing field.

The passage of the Gramm-Leach-Bliley Act of 1999 is thus mostly a response by Congress to a fait accompli and an affirmation of the new reality of financial markets. Indeed, viewed from a global perspective, commercial banking in the United States was arguably lagging behind leading European, Japanese, and Canadian commercial banking industries, which were much more concentrated and diversified. It is remarkable, for example, that one year prior to the passage of the Gramm-Leach-Bliley Act, Deutsche Bank completed a merger with Bankers Trust, thus allowing the leading German universal bank to expand on a huge scale into the derivatives and swaps business, the fastest growing and most profitable segment of the financial industry.

Of course, the fundamental economic causes for the repeal of Glass-Steagall—technological changes, financial innovation, the global integration of financial markets, the growing competitive pressure from the nonbanking sector—do not magically erase the subtle hazards that the

Supreme Court pointed to in ICI vs. Camp. As is amply evident from the stream of revelations about banks' wrongdoing over the past five years, subtle hazards in universal banks were real and widespread. Arguably, however, the bankers' salesman interest, which the Supreme Court was intent on suppressing, was stoked more by the relentless stock market pressures to meet return-on-equity targets and by the increasingly high-powered financial performance incentives given to bankers.

What is more, a narrative of the crisis that finds its main origin in financial deregulation and the repeal of Glass-Steagall is at best highly incomplete. After all, the first institutions to fail were entirely specialized banks, whether they were savings and loan institutions dedicated to the origination and distribution of residential mortgages, such as New Century Financial (which failed in April 2007), or pure investment banks, such as Bear Stearns (which collapsed in March 2008) and Lehman Brothers (which filed for bankruptcy on September 15, 2008).

Perhaps the main revelation of the financial crisis was the fundamental fragility of the specialized investment banking model inherited from Glass-Steagall. As formidable competitors as sophisticated securities firms could be in a bull market, the crisis has also starkly revealed that standalone investment banks are much more vulnerable to runs, given the very short-term nature of their wholesale funding, the absence of anything analogous to deposit insurance to buttress their funding, and the lack of access to the central bank backstop. Indeed, a remarkable outcome of the financial crisis is that virtually no significant investment bank without a bank holding company license remains; and with Morgan Stanley and Goldman Sachs, only two standalone large investment banks are left standing.

However, in the wake of the crisis, the banking industry is now more integrated and concentrated than ever before. A new category of banks has emerged, the global systemically important financial institutions (SIFIs), with its attendant too-big-to-fail problem. The importance of these banks to the economy inevitably transforms their status, as the *Salz Review* lucidly recognizes: "The implicit and explicit government support of banks and the systemic risks they pose to financial stability make them semi-public institutions" (Salz 2013, 2.5). To be sure, because of their semi-public status, SIFIs should not be allowed to be guided only by bankers' "salesman interest." In effect, their status as SIFIs puts them in the same position as the "public trustees or public utilities" implicitly envisaged by Glass-Steagall for community banks in the 1930s, albeit on a much bigger scale. If SIFIs are allowed to reap the full benefits of scale and scope a bank can ever hope to reach, they must also shoulder greater responsibility for safeguarding the health of the economy and the entire financial system.

The alternative course for SIFIs advocated by many is to break them up or shrink them down to size (see, e.g., Tarullo 2012). An important lesson from the history of bank regulation post-Glass-Steagall, however, is that a regulatory approach that seeks to strictly divide the financial system into separate parts, based on somewhat arbitrary distinctions among different financial activities, may not be sustainable and will introduce an artificial destabilizing competition among the separated parts of the system. If savers see no clear difference between a bank checking account and a money market mutual fund, if they overlook the fact that one contract is insured against investment losses but not the other, then inevitably the regulated, but more costly, commercial banking sector will be vulnerable to unfair competition from the more lightly regulated securities industry. And if corporations can obtain credit in the form of cheaper commercial paper issues or wholesale funding, then the viability of traditional commercial banks could be threatened. Every time two similar services or products are offered that receive different regulatory treatment, the forces of arbitrage will push out the product that is hampered by more burdensome regulations, whether this is a product offered by the securities industry or by banks.

4 The Future of Banking

What is the source of returns to scale and scope of large, systemically important financial institutions? What added economic value do these banks contribute to the economy? How SIFIs should be regulated and whether they should be barred from investment banking activities or proprietary trading depends in large part on the answer to these questions. Unfortunately, there is little existing research in finance and economics on bank returns to scale and scope that we can rely on. First of all, only a tiny fraction of the academic research literature on banking is devoted to universal banks (see Drucker and Puri (2007) for a recent survey). Second, the literature on universal banks mostly focuses on the narrow issue of the costs and benefits of combining underwriting services and lending activities in the same institution. Indeed, most of the theoretical literature on universal banks is cast in terms of the following trade-off: the informational returns to scope from combining both activities (the information acquired through lending makes for better underwriting) are limited by conflicts of interest (for example, as suggested in ICI vs. Camp, the temptation to help a weak issuer raise funds through a bond or equity issue in order to repay an outstanding loan).

As plausible as such a conflict of interest sounds, there appears to be no evidence so far of such abuse of securities investor-clients by universal banks. And this is not for lack of research, as a significant fraction of the empirical studies on universal banking are devoted to this question. The evidence from these studies is that securities issues underwritten by universal banks, who have a lending relationship with the issuer, have lower yields (or less underpricing) and also lower fees, which is difficult to reconcile with a the view that these underwriters are conflicted. Drucker and Puri (2007, 210) summarize the findings of this empirical research as follows: "Overall, the empirical evidence shows that using relationship banks as underwriters improves the pricing of issues and lowers fees, and both prior lending relationships and lending around the time of a security issuance increase the probability that an underwriter will be selected as underwriter." In fact, the combined findings of this research are so strong in their eyes that Drucker and Puri are led to ask the rhetorical question: "Given these facts, is it possible for [standalone] investment banks to remain viable underwriters?"

Even a cursory read of the annual reports of JPMorgan Chase (2012) and Citigroup (2012) immediately reveals how oversimplified existing economic models of universal banks are. It is easy to see from these reports that there is much more to universal banking than deposit taking and lending combined with securities underwriting. In a nutshell, the business model of global universal banks on the corporate and investment banking side is to provide bundled financial services to the world's largest nonfinancial companies and to meet the special financial needs of these corporations. For example, firms that operate in multiple countries rely on JPMorgan Chase, Citigroup, and a handful of other global banks for a number of financial services, which include cash, foreign exchange, and payroll management, payments and settlement, trade credit, and other transaction services. But the role of global banks can go much further and also covers customized hedging and insurance services built around the analysis of large datasets, along with the more traditional lending and funding functions. It is instructive to consider, for example, the list of services mentioned by the Corporate and Investment banking division of JPMorgan Chase in its annual report of 2012 under the heading *Evolution of Product Set Usage among Clients.* These include: "Advisory; Equity Capital Markets; Debt Capital Markets; Lending; Rates, Credit, Foreign Exchange, Securitized Products; Equities, Futures & Options; Commodities; Cash Management; Liquidity; Trade; Depositary Receipts; Custody."

Large banks also reap substantial economies of scale by delivering many of these services through sophisticated electronic platforms: "We have 20,000 programmers, application developers and information technology [IT] employees who tirelessly keep our 31 data centers, 56,000 servers, 22,000 databases, 325,000 physical desktops, virtual desktops and laptops, and global networks up and running. We spend over $8 billion on systems and technology every year" (JPMorgan Chase annual report, 2012, 22). The fixed costs of setting up and running these IT platforms are so high that these technologies are basically out of reach for medium-sized banks and all but a small number of large nonfinancial corporations. This is why global banks like JPMorgan Chase are able to offer significant value added by bundling financial services with lending. The total value of these services is what attracts large firms to global banks, as the evidence in Parthasarathy (2007) confirms. As much as one-stop banking may remain an elusive concept on the retail banking side, it is a model that appears to be working on the corporate banking side (at least for the largest corporations), as the study by Parthasarathy (2007) suggests. Blue chip firms, the study shows, tend to get all their financial services from the same bank, while smaller firms value more highly the local networks and knowledge of regional banks.

A major challenge for SIFIs, however, is to be able to successfully integrate the retail banking side, a critical source of liquidity, with the thriving corporate banking side, which relies on the delivery of cost-effective liquidity and lending services to corporations. The value added from the one-stop universal banking model, however, seems to be harder to deliver on the retail side, where public trust in bankers is of greater importance and has been eroded the most. Retail customers must have confidence that the services and products they are being offered by their bank are not peddled to them because of the high commissions and fees attached to them. This is where banking scandals and banker misbehavior has

damaged the universal banking model the most. This is where reining in
the toxic bonus culture that has led bankers astray matters the most, and
where regaining the public's trust will pay off the most.

5 Bank Governance and the Regulation of Bankers' Pay

How can banks regain the public's trust? To a large extent, the answer lies
in governance and pay reform. As far reaching as the regulatory response
to the crisis of 2007–2009 has been—ranging from more stringent capital
requirements, limits on proprietary trading, the creation of a new systemic risk regulator charged with supervising (bank and nonbank) SIFIs,
tighter regulations and the creation of a special resolution procedure for
SIFIs, new regulations for derivatives and swaps, registration of hedge
funds, and tighter "skin-in-the-game" rules for securitization—it is still
remarkable how little attention has been devoted to governance and pay
reform.

This is unfortunate, given that bankers' high-powered performance-
based pay has in all likelihood overly stimulated their "salesman interest"
in the run-up to the crisis. As Cheng et al. (2015) have shown, it is striking
that most of the worst performers in the crisis were financial institutions
that also offered the most high-powered financial incentives to their executives. The list of companies for which residual CEO compensation (that
is, the component of compensation not driven by firm size and industry)
varied the most with the underlying risk exposure of the financial institution (as measured, for example, by the institution's daily equity beta)
speaks for itself: it includes AIG, Lehman Brothers, Bear Stearns, Merrill Lynch, Morgan Stanley, Bank of America, Citigroup, and Goldman
Sachs (see Cheng et al. 2015, figure 2). A related analysis by Balachandran et al. (2010) looking at how the risk of default varied with the extent
of stock-based compensation of bank executives also finds that the risk of
default was higher at those banks offering higher equity-based pay.

Equally striking are the findings of Ellul and Yerramilli (2013). Their
study directly measures banks' risk controls and seeks to determine how
effective these controls were in limiting risk taking and losses during the
crisis. They construct Risk Management, Indices (RMI), which take into
account dimensions of bank risk management, such as the presence of a
chief risk officer (CRO) and his/her seniority, the ratio of CRO to CEO
pay, whether the CRO reports directly to the board, and the banking

experience of independent directors on the risk committee. Their first finding is that risk management varies considerably across banks. About half the banks had a CRO reporting directly to the board, or a CRO with a senior management position, and only one in five CROs was among the highest-paid executives. Their second finding is that the importance of the CRO position in the bank—what they refer to as "CRO centrality"—is the key component of the RMI. Third, they find that banks with more risk controls (higher RMI) took fewer risks and suffered fewer losses during the crisis. These studies and others (see Becht et al. (2011) for a selective review of this research) provide more systematic evidence consistent with the conclusions of the *Salz Review* (Salz 2013) for Barclays that established a link between senior bankers' lavish compensation and their willingness to take unconsidered risks.

Bankers have not always been so abundantly compensated. According to Philippon and Reshef (2012), who track average compensation across industries over the past 100 years in the United States, pay levels in the financial and nonfinancial sectors for jobs requiring similar educational backgrounds have been roughly in line from the Great Depression to the 1990s. However, in the quarter century preceding the crisis of 2007–2009, pay raises in the financial sector have increasingly outpaced those in other sectors, with bankers earning a 50% premium by 2006 and bank executives earning a 250% premium, after controlling for firm size and job tenure. This rise in relative banker pay may well reflect a remarkable relative growth in bankers' productivity over the past 30 years. But the fact that most of the increase in pay has occurred in the shadow finance sector also suggests an alternative explanation, which has more to do with bankers' greater ability to extract informational rents by skimming the most valuable investments away from the uninformed investor public (see Bolton et al. 2016). Indeed, it is revealing that one of the most bitterly fought regulatory battles in the aftermath of the financial crisis of 2007–2009 has been and still is over the regulation of trading activities of swaps, derivatives, and other instruments in unregulated over-the-counter (OTC) markets, where banks are generating an increasingly large share of their earnings.[9]

If disproportionately high remuneration fosters a culture of entitlement, if high-powered incentives for bankers give rise to pushback by traders against the constraints and risk limits imposed by lower paid and less senior CFOs, and if as a result of these pressures banks end up taking excessive risks or skirting the law, then a natural regulatory response would seem to be to reign in pay and to bolster the authority of risk managers. Indeed, European legislators have recently taken steps to control banker pay. However, the idea that regulators should intervene and control executive pay remains largely a taboo in the United States.

The ambiguities around unrestricted market-based pay for bankers and traders at systemically important financial institutions have been sharply brought to light in the context of the rescue of AIG and the negotiations between the U.S. Treasury and Congress around the Troubled Asset Relief Program (TARP). Banker compensation quickly became an important issue for Congress, and one closely followed in the media and by public opinion. When TARP was proposed to Congress, a key issue that was debated is whether there would be conditions on pay of executives and traders at institutions receiving TARP funding. The brief exchange between Hank Paulson and Barney Frank on this question recounted in Kaiser (2013) superbly summarizes both sides of this issue. To justify the lack of any pay conditionality in the initial TARP proposal by Treasury to Congress, Paulson simply said that: "If you put in a compensation requirement? I cannot say that [TARP] will work." To which, Barney Frank replied: "If there are no compensation requirements, I cannot say that [TARP] will pass" (Kaiser 2013, 11).

Ever since the first negotiations around TARP, the regulation of banker compensation has been a contentious political issue. A particularly controversial decision was to allow AIGFP, the AIG entity responsible for building a systemically risky net credit default swap (CDS) short position of nearly half a trillion dollars, to pay retention bonuses of up to $165 million to its traders as part of the $85 billion bailout deal from the Fed. The main argument against intervention to reign in pay is, of course, that compensation should be left to market forces, and that artificial limits on pay will simply prevent banks from attracting or retaining top talent. It is based on such logic that it was deemed more efficient to pay the market rate to retain AIGFP managers with the necessary skills to unwind AIG's huge CDS position in an orderly way. But this free-market logic was swept aside by the general moral outrage sparked by the revelations of these bonuses.

Was it morally justified to reward those directly responsible for the financial crisis in such a way? Very few thought so.

Economists generally shy away from ethical arguments to justify interventions to regulate pay. It is not their comparative advantage. They prefer to rest their reasoning on efficiency grounds, that is, on welfare efficiency grounds. Thus, intervention to regulate pay is justified for economists if market forces are shown to lead to distortionary pay practices such as those highlighted by Bénabou and Tirole (2016) and Bolton et al. (2006). Similarly, intervention is justified if market forces result in investment or occupational misallocations due to the extraction of informational rents by bankers, as shown by Bolton et al. (2016).

As well grounded as these economic arguments are, it is still worth pointing out that they all abstract from the basic reality that pay of government employees, regulators, and officials is not determined by market forces. It is well known that government officials are generally paid significantly less than their private sector counterparts (for jobs requiring similar educational backgrounds). Differences in job security can explain part of the pay difference, but fundamentally, this pay difference rests on the notion that working for the government is a public service, and unlike for private sector jobs, compensation of public servants cannot be solely driven by "salesman interests." Of course, the lower pay in the public sector does mean that government is not always able to attract and retain top talent. Public service is valued by many very talented people who want to make a difference. A particularly striking, but admittedly extreme, example of pay disparity is that of Ben Bernanke. The Federal Reserve was recently described by Warren Buffett as "the greatest hedge fund in history." Picking up on this comment, the *Wall Street Journal* further observed: "If it were really a hedge fund, Ben Bernanke would be the worst-paid manager in history. A typical 'two-and-20' hedge-fund payday structure on the Fed's $3 trillion in assets and 'profit' paid to the Treasury would equal fees of $78 billion. Mr. Bernanke's actual remuneration: $199,700."[10]

If pay restraint in the public sector is accepted on the notion that public service must be shielded from "salesman interests," then one might argue by extension that, some form of pay restraint is called for at SIFIs, which already are in effect "semi-public institutions," as the *Salz Review* (Salz 2013) describes. Or put slightly differently, if the economic viability of SIFIs rests in part on an implicit or explicit government backstop, then shouldn't the government be entitled to scrutinize and regulate pay practices at SIFIs? After all, it is somewhat paradoxical to limit pay at the Fed acting as a lender of last resort while allowing for unrestrained compensation at the institutions that are the main beneficiaries of cheap public liquidity.

Part of the reticence in pursuing a more forceful policy regulating compensation at SIFIs is that it is not obvious a priori how best to approach the problem. The European Union's move to ban banker bonuses in excess of fixed salary in April 2013 struck many as a rather crude and heavy-handed intervention. Switzerland chose a different approach, giving greater power to shareholders to approve CEO pay packages, and altogether banning golden parachutes. The U.K. business secretary Vince Cable has proposed extending personal liability for bank directors in the event of a large loss or collapse of the bank.[11] Others have advocated putting a limit on the level of pay based on a multiple of the lowest wage paid to a bank's employee (say, 50 or 100). The difficulty of course with this latter intervention is that any multiple that is chosen could be seen as arbitrary. Still, the difficulty in determining a reasonable cap on executive pay at SIFIs is not a sufficient argument for giving up entirely. Perhaps the regulation of pay is approached more straightforwardly by focusing more on the structure than the level of pay. Thus, for example, if stock-based compensation induces excess risk-taking by bankers and puts taxpayers at risk, it makes sense to introduce structural requirements, such as extending performance-based pay to include exposure to the bank's own CDS spread so as to penalize risk shifting, as Bolton et al. (2015) among others have proposed. Such structural pay requirements alone, along with corporate governance rules specifically designed for SIFIs—such as giving more authority to the CFO, as Ellul and Yerramilli (2013) have advocated—are likely to go a long way toward reigning in bankers' "salesman interests" and in fostering good banker behavior.

6 Conclusion

A good banker should not be driven excessively by "salesman interests." A good banker is a responsible steward, seeking to enhance the long-run sustainability of the bank and internalizing the systemic risks the bank might inflict on the financial system. A good banker is not necessarily someone who favors deposit-taking and lending activities over trading and the provision of other fee-based financial services. I have argued that a modern bank can bring greater value added by integrating lending with other complementary financial services. This is especially the case for the global systemically important banks that are able to generate significant returns to scale and scope by offering one-stop access to a whole range of banking services to large corporations with multiple financial needs. But given that many of these services are fee based, they can sharpen bankers' "salesman interests," particularly if these activities are strongly incentivized. In addition the value added that systemically important banks are able to generate rests in a crucial way on a government backstop. In this respect, systemically important banks are more like semi-public institutions than full-fledged private entities. For all these reasons, bankers' compensation at systemically important banks needs to be kept in check. In sum, a good banker is a steward that is not overly incentivized or overpaid.

Notes

I am grateful to Edward Glaeser, Jeffrey Gordon, Ailsa Rell, Charles Sabel, Tano Santos, and Glen Weyl for helpful conversations and comments.

1. See, for example, Agarwal et al. (2014); Ninja stands for "no income, no job, and no assets."

2. See, for example, Piskorski et al. (2015).

3. Investment Company Institute vs. Camp, 401 U.S.C. 617 (1971).

4. See also Marinovic and Povel (2014) and Bijlsma et al. (2012) for related analyses.

5. Simon Johnson, "Making banks play fair," March 19, 2012, on BillMoyers .com.

6. Joe Nocera, "The Good Banker," *New York Times,* May 30, 2011.

7. 401 U.S.C. at 632.

8. Langevoort 1987, 700, 703–704.

9. See Kara Scannell, "Big companies go to Washington to fight regulations on fancy derivatives," *Wall Street Journal,* July 10, 2009; and Gillian Tett, "Calls for radical rethink of derivatives body," *Financial Times,* August 26, 2010.

10. *Wall Street Journal,* September 23, 2013, *Overheard* column.

11. David Oakley and Helen Warrel, "UK to crack down on negligent directors," *Financial Times,* July 14, 2013.

References

Agarwal, S., I. Ben-David, G. Amromin, S. Chomsisengphet, and D. Evanoff (2014). Predatory lending and the subprime crisis. *Journal of Financial Economics 113*(1), 2952.

Balachandran, S., B. Kogut, and H. Harnal (2010). The probability of default, excessive risk, and executive compensation: A study of financial services firms from 1995 to 2008. New York: Columbia Business School.

Becht, M., P. Bolton, and A. Röell (2011). Why bank governance is different. *Oxford Review of Economic Policy 27*(3), 437–463.

Bénabou, R., and J. Tirole (2016). Bonus culture: Competitive pay, screening, and multitasking. *Journal of Political Economy 124*(2), 305–379.

Bijlsma, M., J. Boone, and G. Zwart (2012). Competition for traders and risk. Working paper, Tilburg University.

Bolton, P., J. Scheinkman, and W. Xiong (2006). Executive compensation and short-termist behavior in speculative markets. *Review of Economic Studies* 73(3), 577–611.

Bolton, P., H. Mehran, and J. D. Shapiro (2015). Executive compensation and risk taking. *Review of Finance* 19(1), 1–43.

Bolton, P., T. Santos, and J. A. Scheinkman (2016). Cream skimming in financial markets. *Journal of Finance* 71(2), 709–736.

Cheng, I.-H., H. G. Hong, and J. A. Scheinkman (2015). Yesterday's heroes: Compensation and creative risk-taking. *Journal of Finance* 70(2), 839–879.

Drucker, S., and M. Puri (2007). Banks in capital markets. In E. Eckbo (Ed.), *Empirical Corporate Finance. Handbooks in Finance.* Amsterdam: North-Holland.

Ellul, A., and V. Yerramilli (2013). Stronger risk controls, lower risk: Evidence from U.S., bank holding companies. *Journal of Finance* 68(5), 1757–1803.

Holmström B., and P. Milgrom (1991). Multi-task principal-agent analyzes: Incentive contracts, asset ownership, and job design. *Journal of Law, Economics and Organization* 7, 24–52. Special issue from the conference on the New Science of Organizations.

Kaiser, G. R. (2013). *Act of Congress: How America's Essential's Institution Works, and How It Doesn't.* New York: Alfred A. Knopf.

Langevoort, D. (1987). Statutory obsolescence and the judicial process: The revisionist role of the court in federal banking regulation. *Michigan Law Review* 85, 672.

Marinovic, I., and P. Povel (2014). Competition for talent under performance manipulation: CEOs on steroids. Rock Center for Corporate Governance, Working Paper 160, Stanford University.

Parthasarathy, H. (2007). Universal banking deregulation and firms' choices of lender and equity underwriter. Washington, DC: World Bank.

Philippan, T. and A. Reshet (2012). Wages and human capital in the US finance industry: 1909–2006. *Quarterly Journal of Economics* 127(4), 1551–1609.

Piskorski, T., A. Seru, and J. Witkin (2015). Asset quality misrepresentation by financial intermediaries: Evidence from RMBS market. *Journal of Finance* 70(6), 2635–2678.

Salz, A. (2013). *Salz Review: An Independent Review of Barclays Business Practices.* London: Barclays.

Sen, A. K. (1993). Money and value: On the ethics and economics of finance. *Economics and Philosophy* 9(2), 203–227.

Shiller, R. J. (2013). Reflections on finance and the Good Society. *American Economic Review* 103(3), 402–405.

Stein, J. (1989). Efficient capital markets, inefficient firms: A model of myopic corporate behavior. *Quarterly Journal of Economics 104*(4), 655–669.

Tarullo, D. K. (2012). Industry structure and systemic risk regulation. Presented at the Brookings Institution Conference on Structuring the Financial Industry to Enhance Economic Growth and Stability, Washington, DC.

Whitehead, C. K. (2011). The Volcker rule and evolving financial markets. *Harvard Business Law Review 1*(1), 39–73.

CHAPTER FOUR

How to Implement Contingent Capital

Albert S. Kyle

1 Introduction

How can an economically efficient set of policies be designed to prevent financial institutions from receiving costly bailouts in the future? The scenario that ends in bailouts is familiar: As a result of looming loan losses, the financial condition of banks weakens. Banks delay raising capital and continue to pay dividends; the financial condition of the banking system weakens further. Government regulators do little to force banks to raise capital. Eventually, banks refuse to lend to one another, and uninsured creditors run by refusing to roll over their debt securities. To prevent imminent defaults, the government bails out bank creditors by providing collapsing banks with collateralized loans, loan guarantees, and equity injections. The bailout may even give value to otherwise worthless bank equity securities.

To prevent such a bailout scenario, two different sets of policies are typically proposed: i) more regulation and ii) more capital.

Proponents of more regulation believe that increased restrictions on banking activities, stronger reporting requirements, and more intrusive inspections will enable government regulators to avert bailouts by detecting undercapitalized banks and requiring them to raise more capital before they become too undercapitalized to do so. Proponents of more capital, such as Admati and Hellwig (2013), argue that dramatically higher capital buffers will prevent banks from becoming so weak that they cannot raise new equity in stressed situations.

This paper shows how contingent capital securities, included in a bank's capital structure as a substitute for additional common stock, can amplify the effectiveness of both increased government regulation and higher capital requirements. Contingent capital is a hybrid security that has the risk characteristics of debt when a bank is healthy but converts to riskier common stock when a bank becomes undercapitalized. Conversion replaces a lengthy, messy bankruptcy process with a fast, clean conversion of the contingent capital securities into common stock. Since "bailing in" the contingent capital securities makes the bank dramatically better capitalized without threatening the value of more senior debtholders, contingent capital conversions reduce political pressure for government bailouts.

Contingent capital securities follow a template mandated by the banks' regulator. The market determines terms like maturity and coupon rate. The template defines trigger events, which set in motion a process that might lead to conversion of contingent capital securities into common stock. The most important trigger event is a choice by contingent capital holders not to roll over their securities when they mature; when owners of contingent capital securities try to run, they instead set in a motion a process that leads to conversion of their securities into equity. In addition, there may be regulatory triggers, such as failure to meet a target capital ratio, or market triggers, such as the market price of the bank's common stock falling below a given target fraction of its book value. Regulatory triggers and market triggers interact in a positive manner, making regulation supplemented by contingent capital more effective than increased regulation alone. When regulators are practicing forbearance by allowing banks to delay raising needed capital, market triggers can force conversion, thus keeping the regulators honest. When contingent capital holders and equity holders "collude" by pretending that a bank is healthier than they know it to be, regulatory triggers can call the market's bluff, thus keeping the market honest. This paper explains why both regulatory and market triggers are necessary to make contingent capital work effectively.

There are two distinct advantages of replacing some common stock with contingent capital in the capital structure of a bank. First, if the owners of the contingent capital do not collude with the owners of common stock, the arm's-length relationship between the contingent capital owners and the equity owners incents the former to exert pressure on the bank to remain well capitalized. The potential benefits of market discipline resulting from monitoring by contingent capital holders is a central issue discussed in this proposal. Incentive problems associated with both debt overhang and managerial agency issues are mitigated if contingent capital securities are structured so that the owners of the contingent capital securities can force the bank to maintain healthy levels of capital while allowing reasonable levels of leverage. Furthermore, well-capitalized banks have less incentive to lobby regulators to practice forbearance with respect to requiring new equity issuance.

Second, the debt-like nature of contingent capital makes it less information sensitive than common stock, without "clogging up" the bank's capital structure. Other securities with low information sensitivity, such as very junior debt or preferred stock, contain protective features that increase the costs of future issuance of more senior securities and dilute the common stockholders' incentives to issue more common stock. As a result, issuance of such securities increases the fragility of the bank's balance sheet; the path to recapitalization becomes so painful that banks avoid recapitalizing at all. Contingent capital does not clog up the capital structure in this way. In circumstances where additional issuance of information-insensitive securities is reasonable, contingent capital makes room in the capital structure by converting into equity first.

The effectiveness with which contingent capital securities can prevent bailouts depends on the details of how the securities are structured. These details include precise definitions of trigger events as well as provisions designed to force weak banks to conserve cash. The proposed structure for contingent capital securities describes examples of the types of triggers and other terms made necessary by the logic of contingent capital securities. The proposed structure converts contingent capital into 80% equity ownership. The other terms include limitations on dividend payments and requirements to pay high interest rates on contingent capital securities "in kind," using shares of newly issued common stock, rather than in cash. The proposed structure avoids cash-settlement features, which use market prices to calculate the amount of dilution when conversion occurs.

This paper does not attempt to optimize the security structure by claiming that illustrative numerical values for various quantities are optimal. Instead, the specific numbers are designed to illustrate, using reasonable parameter choices, the trade-offs that optimized securities must deal with.

2   The Economic Policy Problem

2.1   Too Big to Fail: A No-Bailout Policy Is Not Credible

Government promises not to bail out failing banks have little credibility. Even when governments state a policy objective of no bailouts, markets do not believe the stated policy will be carried out, and markets are usually proven correct when the governments provide financial support to failing banks at taxpayer expense. Although this commitment problem is implicit in the cliche "too big to fail," governments also have difficulty committing not to bail out small failing banks, especially in circumstances where failure of one or more small banks can lead to runs on many banks, large and small alike.

In the United States, the Federal Reserve bailed out bondholders of Bear Stearns by acquiring some of its risky assets at prices higher than the market was willing to pay. As the financial crisis unfolded with the collapse of Lehman Brothers in the fall of 2008, the U.S. government guaranteed the debts of AIG and guaranteed both existing and new debt issued by banks. Implicit guarantees to Fannie Mae and Freddie Mac became explicit as insolvency became clear. Although the FDIC did not insure the assets of money market mutual funds prior to the collapse of Lehman Brothers, these assets became insured shortly thereafter, when losses incurred by the Reserve Fund triggered an industry-wide run. The U.S. Treasury even bailed out equity owners of Citigroup and Bank of America. They did this by allowing shareholders to maintain ownership of a majority of outstanding shares, which were intrinsically worthless without government support. It then gave these shares value by providing financial support to both banks with ring-fenced loan losses, guaranteed debt issuance, and capital provided on generous terms relative to what was available in the market at the same time.

In the Eurozone, German taxpayers bailed out governments and banks of other countries, including Greece, Portugal, and Cyprus, contradicting the policies on which the euro was based. In the United Kingdom, the central bank stated a policy of not supporting Northern Rock as it failed; a few weeks later, it bailed out Northern Rock. In Ireland, the government tried to implement a policy of not bailing out its overextended banks at high cost to taxpayers; it subsequently imposed on Irish taxpayers substantial bailout costs.

Governments fail to keep their promises not to bail out failing banks for understandable reasons. If failing banks' creditors are not bailed out, governments fear the possibility of bank runs, severe credit squeezes, recession, and social unrest.

2.2   Adverse Selection, Moral Hazard, Good Governance, and Forbearance

The lack of credibility of a no-bailout policy leads to a toxic interaction involving adverse selection, moral hazard, good governance, and regulatory forbearance.

Bankers believe that issuing new equity in stressed conditions is prohibitively expensive. High equity issuance costs result from an adverse selection problem. Since the true financial condition of banks depends on private information, which is difficult to share in a credible manner, a bank that attempts to issue new equity sends a bad signal to the market. When a large amount of equity is issued over a short period of time, the signal becomes worse, and "fire sale" prices may result. A rational undercapitalized bank with vigilant short-term depositors would be willing to incur high equity issuance costs in the short run if the alternative were even higher issuance costs in the long run. If the bank and its creditors instead expect that the bank will benefit from a taxpayer-funded bailout in disaster scenarios, then the bank has an incentive to delay issuing new equity when its financial condition first begins to weaken.

As banks become more undercapitalized by failing to raise capital, the moral hazard problem associated with risk shifting is magnified. When undercapitalized banks fail, the equity owners do not bear all the risks associated with failure. Some of the risks are shifted to debtholders or, if a bailout occurs, to taxpayers. The resulting option to default is valuable to equity owners. Equity owners have incentives to practice moral hazard by taking actions that increase the value of this option. In addition to avoiding issuing new equity, which dilutes the value of the option to default, such actions include paying higher dividends and increasing the riskiness of the bank's portfolio. These actions increase the probability of bailouts.

"Good governance," associated with the idea that banks operate in the interests of their shareholders, makes this moral hazard problem worse, not better. The expectation of valuable future bailouts increases the value of the bank's equity. Therefore, a well-governed bank not only has an incentive to avoid expensive dilutive equity issuance when bailouts might otherwise be obtained, but also has an incentive to practice as much moral hazard, at the expense of taxpayers, as it can get away with.

To prevent moral hazard from making things worse, bank regulators should require undercapitalized banks to recapitalize promptly. In practice, "prompt corrective action" does not occur promptly enough. Instead, bank regulators practice forbearance. Responding to political pressure from banks that have a lot to lose, regulators allow undercapitalized banks to delay raising new capital. These delays often look reasonable ex post, because undercapitalized banks often become better capitalized by becoming profitable in the future. It is a fundamental fact about options that out-of-the money options tend to expire worthless; in other words, there is a substantial probability that the option to default will not be exercised, because the bank will become healthy again and not need a bailout.

How can government policy deal with this toxic interaction involving adverse selection, moral hazard, good governance, and regulatory forbearance?

Consider the problem of adverse selection. Although regulators might collect otherwise private information about the financial condition of banks and make such information public, it is unlikely that such policies will make the problem of adverse selection go away completely. The standard solution to intractable adverse selections, often applied to health care, is to subsidize the bad risks at the expense of the good risks. Applied to banks, this would have the dubious effect of using government policy to encourage capital to move to banks with track records of earning low returns in the past. It is doubtful that government policy can make the problem of adverse selection go away.

Now consider the problem of moral hazard. Moral hazard is not a traditional "market failure" based on public goods, externalities, or market power. Instead, it is a technological problem associated with the inability to observe or control actions associated with "bad behavior," like draining capital from a bank or excessive risk taking. Compared with the private sector, the government has a particularly poor ability to deal with moral hazard problems.

Thus, to deal with the toxic mix, the public policy problem boils down to a trade-off between undermining good governance to make bad incentives weaker or to improve regulation by lessening the incentive for the private sector to pressure the regulators to practice forbearance.

Consider first the possibility of undermining good governance, weakening the manner in which incentives operate in the private sector. The private sector aligns the incentives of top executives with shareholders by using bonuses, stock options, and stock ownership. Government policy could sharply curtail the use of incentive pay in executive compensation, instead requiring that top executives be paid fixed salaries. Since fixed salaries represent claims similar to debt, the incentives of top executives would become more aligned with those of the banks' debtholders than those of equity holders. This would reduce the moral hazard associated with risk shifting but lead to another moral hazard problem. Top executives on fixed salaries would have less incentive to work hard and less incentive to implement efficient decisions. They would be more likely to carry out the wishes of government regulators by making loans to non-credit-worthy borrowers which government regulators favor. The government could go further in this direction by appointing the top managers itself or by nationalizing the banking system. Ultimately, this approach is likely to lead to inefficient banks that either need bailing out anyway or pay inefficiently low interest rates on deposits, because their incentives to make profitable loans are undermined.

Consider next the possibility of reducing incentives for government regulators to practice forbearance. To the extent that forbearance results from political pressure by regulated banks who have significant value at stake, this approach should involve weakening the value banks believe they have at stake when regulators attempt to enforce capital requirements. If banks are financially healthy and there is freedom of entry, implicit promises to bail out failing banks are of limited value, because more capital will flow into banking, lower the returns to banking, and thus erode the value of the promised subsidies. Rent seeking generates private value to bankers only when they are already in trouble. Therefore, the regulatory problem is to design a regulatory mechanism that prevents banks from becoming unhealthy in the first place, even when the regulator itself has a tendency to practice forbearance at least some of the time.

This trade-off between good governance and forbearance resembles the trade-off between populism and corruption proposed by Glaeser (2012). In this context, "populism" is associated with a policy of undermining good governance. Populism implies giving the government a greater role in bank governance by subsidizing credit to politically favored customers of banks, such as subprime borrowers, even if this policy makes bank profits low. In this context, "corruption" means allowing private sector incentives to drive bank policies, including policies that pressure regulators to practice forbearance.

2.3   How Contingent Capital Addresses the Policy Problem

Contingent capital lessens the pressure on regulators to practice forbearance by providing private sector incentives for banks not to become undercapitalized in the first place. At times when government regulators would be practicing forbearance by allowing modestly undercapitalized banks to delay raising capital properly designed contingent capital securities will be inducing banks to become better capitalized. Either the owners of the contingent capital securities will be threatening not to roll over their securities, or the terms of the securities themselves will make banks improve their financial healthy by, for example, reducing dividends.

It may be tempting to think of the policy problem as a mechanism design problem, where the regulator designs a game in which bank equity holders and contingent capital holders are the players and the regulator sets the rules of the games. Carefully crafted rules might lead to a game that, if played optimally by both equity holders and contingent capital holders, leads to an equilibrium in which banks remain well capitalized. This is not the best way to think about the problem. Even if optimal strategies could be calculated, equity holders might not play optimal strategies. Instead, they might "cheat" by avoiding capital raising in the short run, hoping instead to pressure regulators to change the rules of the game in the long run.

A better approach is to think of the policy problem as designing a game that keeps banks well capitalized even if the banks' equity holders attempt to cheat by playing the game sub-optimally in the short run. A good contingent capital mechanism is a robust security design that keeps banks well capitalized even if the equity holders do not play optimally, thus providing weak incentives for the equity holders to pressure regulators to change the rules of the game by allowing forbearance. The approach taken in this chapter is not to solve for optimal strategies by equity holders but rather to show that even if equity holders follow suboptimal strategies by avoiding raising capital, banks do not become undercapitalized, and therefore incentives to change the rules of the game remain weak.

As discussed in the introduction to this chapter, contingent capital has two main advantages: i) contingent capital owners have an incentive to monitor a bank's capital level and force capital raising even when the bank's regulator is practicing forbearance; and ii) contingent capital is a security with low information sensitivity, which does not clog up the bank's capital structure. Contingent capital securities incentivize capital raising while also making it less painful.

Contingent capital is not a panacea for the problem of low bank capitalization. A well-designed contingent capital security should deal with numerous additional incentive problems, including the following:

- Contingent capital owners and common stockholders may "collude" to shift risks to taxpayers, bondholders, or depositors.
- Market prices of common stock and contingent capital may not generate accurate signals of the value of a bank due to illiquidity, actual or perceived price manipulation, or the belief by common stockholders and contingent capital holders that government bailouts will occur.
- Bankers may delay taking write-offs of bad debts, making book values of assets a poor measure of the health of an undercapitalized bank.
- A bank nearing failure tends to hemorrhage cash as result of depositor withdrawals, excessive dividend payments, and excessive executive compensation.
- A bank with a very high level of capital and imperfect corporate governance may suffer from an agency problem associated with excessive executive compensation, perhaps enabled by hidden carry trades.

3 The Proposed Contingent Capital Structure

3.1 Summary of Features

The main features that differentiate this proposed structure from the literature are the following:

- The threat by contingent capital holders not to roll over maturing securities is likely to be the binding constraint that induces banks to maintain healthy capital levels.
- A combination of regulatory triggers (based on measures of capital adequacy) and market triggers (based on common stock prices or credit default swap (CDS) spreads), forcing conversion when either trigger is pulled and not necessarily both, enhances the ability of a contingent capital regime to ensure that banks can raise new capital when they become undercapitalized.

- While the threat by regulators to force conversion due to missed regulatory targets is not likely to be binding most of the time, the possibility that it might be binding will lessen incentives for contingent capital holders and common stockholders to collude by delaying new common stock issuance to increase the ex ante value of potential bailouts.
- The proposed structure does not rely on cash settlement or "death spiral" features that are implicitly based on the assumption that market prices will be accurate at times when markets are most stressed.
- The proposed structure contains specific features—limits on cash interest to contingent capital holders and increased capital requirements when dividends or high cash executive compensation is paid—that encourage banks to retain cash equity when they become stressed.
- To deal with the incentives banks have to avoid writing down bad assets to pass regulatory tests, the proposed structure encourages mandatory write-downs when a bank's common stock trades below book value for an extended time. In addition, the requirement that banks issue new common stock equal to the book value of interest paid to contingent capital holders in shares actually encourages banks to reduce book value by writing down bad assets.
- It is quite possible that contingent capital securities will have short maturities, structured like auction rate securities. If the securities do not roll over, suspension of convertibility may occur for a few months, during which the bank pays a penalty rate while it attempts to recapitalize or find other investors. If the securities are not redeemed at par after this period of suspended convertibility, a conversion event occurs. The penalty rate and the period of suspended convertibility are subject to negotiation between the bank and contingent capital investors. Note that short-term debt contracts, including auction rate securities, tend to make markets fragile by triggering messy bankruptcy processes when the debt cannot be rolled over. Since contingent capital securities are expressly structured to convert gracefully into common stock when they do not roll over, failure to roll over contingent capital securities makes market less fragile, because the capitalization of a bank is improved after conversion and there is no messy bankruptcy process.

The remainder of this paper discusses how the proposed contingent capital structure is designed to achieve its goal of preventing banks from failing as a result of not having appropriate incentives to recapitalize in times of stress.

3.2 Literature

The contingent capital structure proposed here incorporates various features that can be found in a growing literature on the subject.

A 20% capital level is consistent with other proposals favoring higher capital levels. For brevity, let "20 + 0" denote a 20% capital structure that is all common stock, while "15 + 5" denotes a capital structure consisting of 15% common stock and 5% contingent capital. Admati and Hellwig (2013) and Admati et al. (2013) propose dramatically higher capital levels, consistent with the a 20+0 capital structure. Calomiris and Herring (2012) also propose dramatically higher levels, including examples based on a 10 + 10 capital structure.

Kashyap et al. (2008) argue that too much equity in a bank's capital structure exacerbates agency problems within a bank, because it insulates bank managers too much from the market discipline provided by bondholders. Consider, for example, a 20 + 0 bank in which the executives have captured control of the board, pay themselves lavish salaries at the expense of common stockholders, and pay common stockholders meager dividends. In this situation, market discipline does not work effectively through the market for corporate control. Debtholders, however, do exert market discipline. They can impose restrictive covenants or, even better, keep maturity of debt contracts short, refusing to roll over debt unless their demands are met. Since contingent capital holders are like debtholders, with interests diametrically opposed to bank's management and common stockholders, more effective market discipline is provided by a 10 + 10 capital structure than a 20 + 0 structure.

Coffee (2011) and Calomiris and Herring (2012) emphasize this monitoring role of contingent capital holders or subordinated debtholders, who can discipline common stockholders (see also Calomiris 1999).

In contrast to the proposal here, Kashyap et al. (2008) propose that contingent capital not be funded with cash. Consistent with Bolton and Samama (2012) and Hart and Zingales (2011), the contingent capital structure proposed here is fully funded. It is likely to be purchased by long-term investors seeking to enhance yield in good times by risking losses in bad times.

Kashyap et al. (2008) also propose that contingent capital incorporate aggregate insurance not connected to specific bank losses. This aggregate insurance feature undermines the incentives for monitoring, which they identify as the major problem making bank capital expensive. Aggregate insurance is not included in the structure proposed here.

Consistent with Sundaresan and Wang (2010), the contingent capital proposed here may sell at par.

Like Glasserman and Nouri (2012), regulatory capital ratios play an important role in the proposed contingent capital structure, and issuance of new equity may be a gradual process. In the proposal here, gradual issuance of common stock is incented by the threat of forced conversion and by paying dividends to contingent capital holders in shares.

The proposed contingent capital security avoids "death spiral" features, which result from trying to increase the number of shares into which contingent capital converts to achieve a market value target. In this respect, it is consistent with the spirit of Pennacchi et al. (2014) and differs from Flannery (2016).

Although regulatory triggers may refer to market prices, the proposed structure for contingent capital places minimal faith in the assumption that market prices are accurate indicators of the value of the bank. It is therefore robust to the possibility that asset prices may be overvalued due to short sale constraints and agreement to disagree, as in Scheinkman and Xiong (2003). In this respect, my proposed structure is different from Squam Lake Working Group (2010), Flannery (2016), Hart and Zingales (2011), and others.

The proposed contingent capital structure has multiple triggers. McDonald (2013) and Squam Lake Working Group (2010) propose dual microprudential and macroprudential triggers such that contingent capital converts when *both* bank-specific market triggers (low common stock price) and macroeconomic triggers (low index price for bank stocks) are simultaneously pulled. The proposed contingent capital has multiple microprudential triggers that fire when either one of multiple regulatory targets are missed *or* when the contingent capital holders force a conversion event. The purpose of these multiple triggers is to provide regulatory discipline when market discipline fails due to collusion between contingent capital holders and common stockholders or due to expectations of bailouts, which undermine market discipline. Although the proposed structure has no specific macroprudential triggers, such triggers could easily be incorporated into the proposed regulatory triggers.

Calomiris and Herring (2012) propose that contingent capital securities be required for large institutions with deep and liquid markets for common stock. In contrast, the proposal here is also compatible with contingent capital being mandatory for smaller banks, even those that are not publicly traded.

3.3   Higher Capital Levels

Measuring capital for regulatory purposes is a potentially difficult exercise that involves translating conceptual financial risks into operational accounting rules. Such an exercise is not attempted here. To keep matters simple, let us think of capital levels as a percentage of "risk-weighted assets," using informal intuition consistent with the spirit of the Basel I or Basel II frameworks. The Basel framework distinguishes between tier 1 and tier 2 capital. In what follows, common stock is tier 1 capital, and contingent capital is tier 2 capital.

Risk weights are based on rules designed to makes risks comparable across assets of different riskiness. The numeraire capital level appropriate for a bank asset of "typical" risk is 8%. We think of this typical debt instrument as being on the boundary between investment grade and junk, perhaps with a risk equivalent to a bond rating of BBB−.[1]

If a bank's capital level is substantially above 8% of risk-weighted assets in the Basel framework, then the bank's capital level is considered healthy; if it is far below 8%, the bank is considered to be undercapitalized and should be required to take steps to improve its capitalization. Although Basel I can be interpreted as usually calculating risk-weighted assets based on book values, the regulator can mandate calculations based on book values, market values, or a combination of both. In the simplified discussion below, the terms "risk-weighted assets" and "book value" are used interchangeably. The discussion below does not depend on whether the regulator uses market values or book values. It does not depend on whether the regulator uses Basel I, Basel II, Basel III, or a different regulatory mechanism.[2]

Neither the Basel I process nor the Basel II process prevented massive bank failures during the financial crisis. This suggests that target capital levels should be far higher than the 8% numeraire level. The obvious regulatory policy to reduce costs associated with bailing out failing banks is higher capital requirements.

For the sake of discussion, assume that the regulator structures capital requirements so that a bank is incentivized to have a target capital level of 20% of risk-weighted assets, 2.5 times the 8% numeraire level of Basel I. A 20% capital level can be implemented either with all common stock or with a mixture of common stock and contingent capital. The following discussion focuses on a "10 + 10" capital structure (half common stock and half contingent capital).

The 10 + 10 capital level is to be interpreted as an equilibrium target, not a minimum. As the discussion below makes clear, contingent capital may not be forced to convert into common stock until a lower minimum level is hit, here assumed to be 7 + 7.

Multiple tiers of contingent capital might be useful. For example, a 10 + 10 + 10 capital structure would consist of 10% common stock, 10% contingent capital, and 10% backup contingent capital. When contingent capital converts into common stock, backup contingent capital converts into contingent capital. To recapitalize after conversion, a bank needs to issue backup contingent capital, not contingent capital. Backup contingent capital may be a useful feature of a contingent capital proposal, because backup contingent capital is even less information sensitive than contingent capital. To keep the discussion in this paper simple, backup contingent capital is not part of the proposed contingent capital structure.

3.4   Proposed Structure in Detail

The structure for contingent capital securities proposed here has several features, including multiple "either-or" conversion triggers and forced common stock issuance, all designed to deal with the incentive problems. The proposed security features, to be mandated by the bank's regulator, has the following characteristics:

- The only types of equity securities allowed in a bank's capital structure are common stock and contingent capital.
- Contingent capital is structured as reverse convertible preferred stock. The term "reverse convertible" means that, when a conversion event occurs, the bank—not the contingent capital investors—has the option to determine whether the contingent capital is paid off at par or converted into common stock with severe dilution to existing shareholders; either way, there is no potentially disorderly bankruptcy process.
- When a conversion event occurs, the bank has a fixed window of time, assumed for simplicity to be 60 days, during which it can redeem at par some or all of the contingent capital, either with the cash proceeds of new common stock issuance (e.g., with a rights offering after the conversion event, presumably priced above

the conversion rate) or with some fraction of cash proceeds of new common stock issuance in the recent past. For the sake of discussion, the fraction of cash proceeds from recent new common stock issuance that can be used to redeem contingent capital is assumed to be reduced by 5% for each month that has passed since the common stock was sold, falling to zero after 20 months. For example, if a bank issued new equity for cash three months before the conversion event, then 85% of the cash proceeds of this equity issuance can be used to redeem contingent capital at par after a conversion event. Unredeemed contingent capital converts to common stock at the end of the fixed window of time; the conversion process cannot be reversed at the end of the window, even if the bank's financial situation has improved dramatically. During the 60-day conversion window, corporate governance should be subjected to some oversight by the regulator or contingent capital investors; for example, dividends and bonuses should not be allowed.

- Conversion is based on a highly dilutive fixed ownership percentage of the outstanding common stock, assumed for the sake of discussion to be 80% ownership of the common stock. Regardless of the book value or market value of the contingent capital and common stock, this $80 - 20$ conversion rule implies that if none of the contingent capital is redeemed, then all contingent capital converts into common stock representing 80% ownership of the bank, with all issues of contingent capital converting proportionally based on their par value. For example, if 25% of the contingent capital is redeemed at par after the conversion event, the remaining 75% of the contingent capital converts into 60% ownership of the common stock.

- Contingent capital shares have equal seniority. If one share is affected by a conversion event, then all shares are affected.

- If a bank fails to replace maturing contingent capital with new contingent capital or defaults on an interest payment to contingent capital holders, then a conversion event occurs. The bank does not undergo a potentially destabilizing liquidation, bankruptcy, or other resolution process.

- The regulator may declare a conversion event when a bank is deemed undercapitalized for any of a variety of reasons, such as i) low book capital, ii) failing grades on a stress test, iii) persistently low common stock prices, iv) persistently high CDS spreads, v) ratings downgrades, vi) accounting irregularities, or vii) persistently high levels of borrowing from the central bank. These are "either-or" tests, implying that failing only one test triggers a conversion event. These tests may interact with other regulatory tools, such as mandatory common stock issuance, limits on dividends and executive compensation (discussed further below), immediate forced conversion of contingent capital (without a 60-day window), replacing management, or placing a bank directly in a resolution process. For example, it would be reasonable for the regulator to replace management and liquidate a bank after discovering massive fraud that makes it unlikely the bank will have value, even after conversion of all contingent capital. To ensure that market prices are not affected by private information about regulator's behavior, the automatic triggers should be based on rules and not on regulatory discretion.

- After a conversion event, the bank must promptly replace the converted contingent capital with new contingent capital. If it does not do so after a reasonable period of time—say, 90 days after the end of the 60-day conversion period—the central bank or other bank resolution authority either forces the bank into a resolution process or automatically purchases new contingent capital securities, holds the proceeds of the securities as cash, puts restrictions on the bank's activities, and charges a very high interest rate in shares (assumed for the sake of discussion to be 3% per month) until either nationalization automatically occurs or the bank has replaced all of the government-provided contingent capital with new market-contingent capital.

- Cash interest on contingent capital is capped at a rate assumed for the sake of discussion to be 200 basis points over Treasury rates.

- Contingent capital is also allowed to be paid interest in shares of common stock, but such shares must result from recent new issuance of common shares that raise cash equity equal to a multiple of the book value of the shares issued to contingent capital holders in lieu of cash interest. For the sake of discussion, the multiple is set at 2. For example, assume contingent capital holders holding $400 par value of contingent capital receive one share of common stock as annual interest paid in kind; assume the market value of a share is $10, implying a 250-basis-point yield to contingent capital investors; assume the book value of a share is $25; then the bank must issue new equity with cash proceeds of $50 by issuing some number of new shares of common stock; presumably, the number of shares issued to give contingent capital investors one share worth $10 is, in this example, more than two shares worth $20 (due to the multiple of 2) and perhaps about five shares worth $50 (since the book value of the stock is 2.5 times its market value).

- Maturities of contingent capital securities should be limited. For example, such securities might have a maximum five-year maturity; alternatively, contingent capital securities should be both put-able and callable at par (with modest penalties), given a reasonable notice period (say, two years). Contingent capital securities are not allowed to have incentive payments or delayed interest payments, such as cumulative preferred stock. The par value of the securities must be equal to the capital raised.

In addition to these provisions, the proposed structure also includes other features of bank regulation that are not, strictly speaking, intrinsic to the contingent capital securities themselves:

- The bank regulator may require a bank to write down the book value of assets when the market value of its equity is low. For example, if the market value of common stock during a quarter is less than 10% of the value of risk-weighted assets during the quarter, the regulator may require the bank to write down the book value by some percentage of the difference between market value and book value, say, 10% each quarter.
- When a bank pays cash dividends to common stockholders (or buys back common stock for cash) or pays high cash executive compensation, its forward-looking capital requirement is raised by a multiple of the amount paid for a given period of time. For the sake of discussion, we assume a multiple of 3 (half common stock and half contingent capital), a forward-looking period of four years, and an unrestricted executive compensation limit of $1 million for any employee. For example, if a bank has two employees with cash compensation in excess of $1 million, one with cash compensation of $1.5 million and one with cash compensation of $3 million, the high cash executive compensation amount is $2.5 million, calculated as $(1.5 - 1.0) + (3.0 - 1.0) = 2.5$. Compensation in shares is not restricted.

To illustrate how the forward-looking capital requirement works, suppose that $10 + 10$ is the target capital structure, but the regulator does not declare a conversion event until the level falls below $7 + 7$ for a bank that has paid no dividends and no high cash executive compensation for the past four years. Now consider a bank in a steady state where risk-weighted assets are constant, common stock is 10% of risk-weighted assets, and contingent capital is 10% of risk-weighted assets. Suppose that the bank has been paying cash dividends and high cash executive compensation equal to 5% of the book value of its common stock per year (0.5% of risk-weighted assets); then its steady state capital requirement is raised by 6% of risk-weighted assets, calculated as $5\% \times 0.10 \times 3 \times 4 = 6\%$. Since half of the 6% is required to be common stock and half contingent capital, the bank's required capital level is raised from $7 + 7$ to $10 + 10$. This is the sense in which $10 + 10$ is the steady state for this bank; it is a function of the steady state dividend yield and steady state level of high cash executive compensation. Note that this regulatory principle creates a procyclical capital level, which allows the $10 + 10$ steady state capital structure to fall to $7 + 7$ gradually over four years if the bank pays no dividends and no high cash executive compensation; it rises above $10 + 10$ if the bank pays higher dividends or higher cash executive compensation.

- Institutions that own bank common stock or contingent capital securities cannot count the value of such securities as bank capital for regulatory purposes. This provision effectively prevents circular cross-holdings of contingent capital securities.
- Cash interest on contingent capital securities should be tax deductible as long as interest is not also being paid in common stock. If interest is also being paid in common stock, both the cash interest and the interest paid as common stock are taxed like payments to equity.

This structure for contingent capital is designed to balance incentives in such a manner that the bank has a reasonable level of high-quality common stock in its capital structure; the regulator can credibly threaten forced contingent capital conversion to induce the bank to recapitalize without a disorderly resolution process; the regulatory threat and the contingent capital holders' threat to force conversion interact in a positive manner; the bank has an incentive to conserve cash and issue common stock when it becomes undercapitalized; and the low information sensitivity of contingent capital lessens the cost of recapitalizing a bank with new issuance of contingent capital after a forced conversion. All these features are designed to avoid situations in which governments bail out failing banks to avoid disorderly bank failures.

4   Contingent Capital as Reverse Convertible Preferred Stock

At its simplest, the purpose of contingent capital is to ensure that a bank that needs to raise additional capital can, with very high probability, do so by converting its outstanding contingent capital into common stock and then replacing the contingent capital by issuing more of it. Since the conversion does not involve a potentially disorderly bankruptcy process, it is painful only for the bank's common stockholders, not for the bank's debtholders or for the rest of the economy. To avoid the severe dilution of forced conversion, the common stockholders have an incentive to keep the bank well capitalized in the first place. In principle, contingent capital can be structured in many ways: as put options with a striking price well below market, as deeply subordinated debt that can be washed out or "bailed in," or as preferred stock with a reverse conversion feature.

4.1 Permanent Capital

Regardless of whether it is structured like a put option, like subordinated debt, or like preferred stock, contingent capital should be thought of as permanent capital. This implies that the maturing contingent capital securities must be converted into common stock if new securities are not immediately issued to replace maturing securities. If the contingent capital is structured as put options, the bank must be required to exercise the put options at expiration if new put options have not been issued to replace the expiring ones. Similarly, if the securities are structured as preferred stock or subordinated debt, these securities must be converted into common stock if new preferred stock or subordinated debt is not issued to replace maturing securities.

After a conversion of contingent capital securities into common stock, the bank should be required promptly to issue new contingent capital securities. Since the old contingent capital securities have just been converted into common stock, the bank presumably should have a solid cushion of common stock in its capital structure, making issuance of new contingent capital easier. Clearly, issuance of new contingent capital should be easier than issuance of more new common stock, because the contingent capital securities are senior to common stock and therefore less information sensitive.

4.2 Disadvantage of Put Options

Structuring contingent capital as a put option has one obvious disadvantage. The seller of the put option can only be assured of honoring its obligation to buy the shares issued as a result of put option exercise if the seller itself is solvent. The put options are likely to be exercised at times when a banking crisis is in progress and there is a credit crunch. Ensuring the solvency of the option sellers in such circumstances is a more difficult a regulatory problem than the problem of inducing banks to be adequately capitalized in the first place. Structuring contingent capital as put options therefore does not solve the problem of ensuring that banks can issue more common stock if needed. It merely passes the problem along to different institutions: those which issue put options. It therefore obviously makes sense to structure contingent capital as a security that is fully funded in advance, either as subordinated debt or as preferred stock.

4.3   Advantages of Preferred Stock

Given a choice between subordinated debt and preferred stock, there are multiple reasons to structure contingent capital as preferred stock and not as subordinated debt.

First, it is more difficult politically to force losses on debtholders than on equity holders. Calling the securities equity rather than debt therefore makes it easier to force losses on the contingent capital holders.

Second, default on contingent capital securities that are structured as subordinated debt might trigger a messy bankruptcy process. One of the purposes of contingent capital is to avoid the threat of such a process. Bank resolution tends to be more disorderly and complicated when a bank holding company is involved. Discussing whether contingent capital securities are issued by a bank holding company or its subsidiaries is a topic beyond the scope of this proposal.

Third, contingent capital can play a useful monitoring role if the contingent capital holders have interests different from common stockholders. To enforce their interests, the contingent capital holders may ask for some rights that usually belong to equity holders, especially for small banks that are privately held. Such rights might include the ability to attend board meetings or to examine the bank's books on a regular basis. To the extent that contingent capital holders demand rights usually not associated with debtholders, these securities look more like equity than like debt.

4.4   Taxation of Contingent Capital Interest

One disadvantage of structuring the securities as equity is that coupon payments may be taxed like dividends and not like interest. The proposed structure recommends restructuring tax laws so that cash interest paid on contingent capital is tax deductible like debt, as long as no interest is being paid in shares. Since the proposed maximum cash interest rate allowed is 200 basis points over Treasuries, the contingent capital securities must be very safe, debt-like securities to qualify for tax deductibility. If the interest rate is higher than 200 basis points over Treasuries, the additional interest is required to be paid in shares financed with new common stock issuance and all the interest—whether paid in cash or paid in common stock—is taxed like payments to equity, not debt. This required structure gives the common stockholders and contingent capital holders an incentive to keep the bank well enough capitalized so that the contingent capital securities are perceived as being safe. It thus mitigates the perverse incentives that otherwise occur with debt overhang. This feature emphasizes the hybrid nature of contingent capital securities, which are like debt when safe and like equity when risky.

4.5 Comparison with Convertible Preferred Stock Used in Venture Capital Transactions

If thought of as an equity security, contingent capital is a form of reverse-convertible preferred stock. As such, it shares similarities and differences with "straight" preferred stock and regular convertible preferred stock like that typical of venture capital transactions. It is similar to straight preferred stock in that the cash flow rights resemble bond payments. If the bank does well, neither contingent capital nor straight preferred stock participate in the bank's upside, except to the extent that they receive promised coupon and principle payments. The convertible preferred stock used in venture capital transactions, in contrast, converts into common stock when the firm does well. It has a potentially huge upside.

In effect, the convertible preferred stock used in venture capital transactions has an embedded call option that is exercised by the convertible preferred shareholder, while the reverse-convertible contingent capital securities have an embedded put option exercised by the common stockholders. The embedded call option gives the convertible preferred stock used in venture capital transactions a convex payoff structure when the firm does well, as a result of which the convertible preferred shareholders are more tolerant of risk taking by the firm. The embedded put option in contingent capital gives the security a concave payoff structure, as a result of which the contingent capital shareholders want the bank to limit risk taking.

Although contingent capital does not participate in upside gains like the convertible preferred stock used in venture capital transactions, what happens when the venture-capital-backed firm or contingent-capital-backed bank does poorly can be remarkably similar, given the differences between startup firms and banks.

The convertible preferred stock used in venture capital transactions typically has coupon payments that accumulate if they are not paid in a timely manner. If, after some number of years, the venture-capital-backed startup firm has not done well, either by being acquired at a premium valuation or by having a successful initial public offering, the owners of the convertible preferred shares have the right to redeem their shares for cash. If the firm is not able to satisfy the redemption request on the redemption date, the convertible preferred shares often are entitled to receive a very high interest rate, paid in shares, which over a period of a few years transfers control of the firm to the convertible shareholders. In effect these payments are like a reverse conversion in which the common stockholders allow their equity stake to be diluted to meet the conditions defined by the structure of the convertible preferred stock. Thus, when either the startup firm or bank does poorly, both the convertible preferred stock used in venture capital transactions and the contingent capital structure proposed in this paper have "reverse conversion" features that give the securities a concave structure and thus give the preferred stockholders an incentive to lower risk in bad states.

Although both the convertible preferred stock used in venture capital transactions and the reverse-convertible contingent capital securities have similar concave claims on cash flows in bad states, the securities themselves serve quite different purposes. In a typical venture capital situation, the startup firm has little or no debt; if it is efficient to liquidate the firm, reverse conversion allows a venture-capital-backed startup firm to be liquidated in an orderly manner, in a situation where there are typically few assets to liquidate. If it is not efficient to liquidate the firm, it gives the convertible preferred shareholders a strong bargaining position: they can threaten to liquidate the firm and fire its employees. The employees also have a strong bargaining position, to the extent that most of the value of the firm is their human capital and thus the threat to fire them has little credibility. The powerful control rights given to convertible preferred shareholders in bad states compensate them for the fact they otherwise would have little bargaining power with a firm whose assets are mostly in the heads of its employees.

4.6 Why Banks Are Different

If the firm is a bank, the situation is entirely different from that of a startup firm. The bank holds numerous assets and liabilities, is highly leveraged, and typically many of its assets are opaque and therefore difficult to liquidate. The purpose of the contingent capital securities is to allow the bank to continue operating in a well-capitalized manner, not to be liquidated quickly. Since contingent capital owners control 80% of the bank's shares after conversion, they can threaten to replace the bank's management, a market discipline feature emphasized by Calomiris and Herring (2012).

While the contingent capital holders have an incentive to avoid a lengthy period during which debt overhang distorts the incentives of the common stockholders, both contingent capital holders and common stockholders have a common incentive to avoid a conversion that requires new contingent capital to be issued if they believe risks can be shifted to depositors, bondholders, or taxpayers. In contrast, the bank's regulator has strong incentives, both microprudential and macroprudential, to ensure a prompt recapitalization of a weak bank. In addition to the microprudential motive of preventing exactly such risk shifting, the regulator also has an incentive to ensure that banks throughout the economy have enough capital to support new lending and do not have incentives to strengthen their own capital position by squeezing their customers too hard.

For microprudential reasons, the regulator wants cash injected into a failing bank sooner rather than later. Forcing fast conversion of large amounts of contingent capital into common stock makes it easier for banks otherwise in distress to raise new contingent capital securities, by doing it sooner rather than later. The alternative of allowing a weak bank to delay raising new contingent capital encourages a distressed bank to buy time by selling off its good assets, by failing to make good loans to good customers, by exaggerating its financial position, and by allowing too much cash to leave the bank in the form of dividends, executive compensation, and new loans to borrowers headed toward default. These short-term strategies destroy the bank's value while allowing the distressed institution to bet on good luck or a bailout in the future. They also make bailouts more costly.

For macroprudential reasons, the regulator wants a well-capitalized banking system able to support lending to worthy customers. In recessions or financial crises, financial distress tends to be correlated across banks. Recessions are prolonged and exacerbated if many banks are allowed to persist in undercapitalized states year after year. Forcing banks to have high levels of capital makes it easier for banks to raise new capital in times of stress, since high levels of capital reduce the information asymmetries that make raising new capital expensive for the issuer.

While conversion of contingent capital into common stock results in immediate recapitalization, contingent capital holders and common stockholders may actually bargain for a slower-than-optimal recapitalization involving gradually paying interest to contingent capital holders in the form of common stock. Such delayed recapitalization may be motivated by a desire to benefit from potential bailouts if the bank's position deteriorates sharply in the future. The proposed contingent capital structure addresses this incentive problem by taking tax deductibility of cash interest payments away from the contingent capital holders when they are receiving interest in common stock and, more importantly, by requiring the bank to issue new common stock with a book value equal to a multiple of 2 of the interest paid in shares. Contingent capital holders are likely to demand interest payments in stock based on the market value of the common stock. To the extent that the market value of the common stock is below its book value, many shares of common stock will have to be issued, and this will speed up the bank's recapitalization process. For example, if the bank's shares are trading at 25% of book value, each dollar's worth of interest payments to contingent capital holders in shares must be accompanied by $8 of new common stock issuance.

The bank can reduce the amount of common stock it must issue by writing down the value of bad assets. For example, if the bank writes the book value of its assets down by 5%, then the common stock will trade at 50% of book value, and only $4 of new common stock needs be issued to pay $1 in-kind interest. This incentive to write down bad assets is beneficial, since a bank otherwise has an incentive to overstate its capitalization to appear healthy to its regulator.

5   Market Discipline from the 80-20 Conversion Rule

The proposed structure converts contingent capital into 80% ownership of the common stock of the bank, regardless of the book value or market value of the bank's contingent capital and common stock.

The market discipline that results from the highly dilutive 80-20 conversion rule depends strongly on whether contingent capital holders collude or do not collude with bankers representing common stock owners. Contingent capital tends to provide effective market discipline only when the contingent capital owners do not collude or cooperate with common stockholders. When they do collude, the result is the same as a $20+0$

capital structure with no contingent capital. The banks is protected from failure by higher capital requirements (20% instead of, say, 10%) but not by the market discipline exerted by contingent capital owners.

5.1 No Collusion between Contingent Capital Owners and Common Stockholders

To illustrate the mechanics of conversion of contingent capital into common stock, consider the following simple example based on three assumptions:

- The contingent capital owners do not collude with common stockholders. Instead, they aggressively threaten to force conversion, so that the value of their holdings does not fall below a par value of 10% of the book value of assets.
- The bank reports book capital of 10% of assets, and the outstanding par value of contingent capital represents another 10% of assets.
- The combined value of the common stock and contingent capital does not change as a result of conversion of the contingent capital into common stock (i.e., the value of expected bailouts is zero).

As contingent capital owners contemplate whether to roll over their maturing contingent capital, they will be keeping an eye on the market value of the bank's common stock. If the market does not trust the bank's book value numbers, the bank's common stock will trade at a steep discount to its book value.

Assume an 80-20 conversion ratio and assume outstanding contingent capital is 10% of risk-weighted assets and trades at par. This implies that common stockholders are indifferent between allowing contingent capital to convert and allowing it to roll over when the common stock is trading at a value equal to 2.5% of risk-weighted assets. To see this, note that the combined market value of the common stock and contingent capital is 12.5% of assets. If the value of the bank does not change post-conversion, then the post-conversion new common stock will be worth 12.5% of assets. The holdings of the former contingent capital owners will represent 80% of this value, or 10% of the book value of assets, and the holdings of the legacy common stock holders will represent 20% of this value, or 2.5% of assets.

Now assume also that the book value of common stock is 10% of risk-weighted assets. This indifference point now corresponds to the common stock trading at 25% of book value. After conversion, the common stock trades at 62.5% of the new combined book value of 20% of assets represented by common stock and converted contingent capital.

The contingent capital owners have an incentive not to lose money on conversion. They are therefore likely to threaten a conversion event by not rolling over the securities when the market value of the common stock is substantially greater than 25% of its book value. The common stockholders have little incentive to resist the threat of conversion when the combined market value of the contingent capital and common stock is less than 62.5% of its book value. By offering very high interest rates to encourage rolling over when the value of the common stock and contingent capital is less than 62.5% of its book value, the common stockholders might induce rollover, but the present value of their common stock would be less than what they would obtain with conversion, even after dilution. If contingent capital holders threaten conversion when the common stock is trading at, say, 30% of its book value, common stockholders are likely to attempt a rights offering to raise enough new common stock to induce the contingent capital to roll over. The rights offering is likely to be priced somewhat above 25% of the book value of common stock, because the common stockholders have nothing to gain over an 80-20 forced conversion from a successful rights offering priced at 25% of book value.

When choosing a conversion ratio, such as 80 to 20, the regulator will want to align incentives of the common stockholders and the contingent capital holders, so that neither common stockholders nor contingent capital holders have an incentive to resist conversion at the point when the regulator believe it is microprudentially reasonable for the bank to recapitalize. The above analysis is therefore consistent with the interpretation that the regulator will want a bank to increase its common stock dramatically when the market value of its common stock and contingent capital fall to 12.5% of the bank's risk-weighted assets. A ratio with more dilution, such as 90 to 10, will induce the common stockholders to delay conversion. There will be a potentially greater incentive problem between contingent capital holders and common stockholders due to debt overhang (with contingent capital playing the role of debt). A ratio with less dilution, such as 70 to 30, will induce contingent capital holders to force conversion earlier, at a point when bad incentives related to debt overhang are less of a problem.

The 80-20 conversion rate proposed is for the purposes of discussion. It is chosen to illustrate the effects of a substantial degree of dilution.

5.2   Conversion Incentives of Common Stockholders

As the market value of common stock falls toward 2.5% of the book value of assets, the common stockholders can attempt to forestall conversion of contingent capital using three mechanisms: i) increase the interest rate paid on the contingent capital; ii) issue new common stock, perhaps through a rights offering; or iii) "deleverage" by selling off risky assets, refusing to make new loans, and refusing to roll over maturing loans.

It is likely that the bank will first increase the interest rate paid on contingent capital to its maximum rate of 200 basis points over Treasuries.

A question of practical importance is whether common stockholders will voluntarily attempt to forestall conversion of the contingent capital by issuing new common stock before conversion is forced by contingent capital holders refusing to roll over their securities. When a conversion event occurs, the proposed contingent capital structure allows the bank to use a portion of the cash received from recent common stock issuance to redeem contingent capital at par. Without this feature, conversion would dilute the common stock to a 20% ownership stake regardless of the amount of new common stock recently issued; this would strongly discourage new common stock issuance by a weak bank anticipating contingent capital conversion in the not-too-distant future. With this feature, the proposed capital structure essentially gives the common stockholders a valuable option either to use the cash proceeds of the common stock issuance to redeem contingent capital or to allow it to migrate gradually into the bank's permanent capital structure.

The proposed migration rate of 5% per month represents a trade-off. A low rate encourages the bank to issue common stock sooner, since more of the proceeds can be used to redeem contingent capital at future conversion events. A high rate improves the bank's permanent capital structure more quickly. If the regulator exercises prompt diligence in forcing banks to issue capital when needed, a low rate would be appropriate. Since, however, regulators around the world have a proven track record of not mandating common stock issuance in a timely manner, the rate needs to be high enough to migrate the new common stock into the permanent capital structure reasonably quickly.

If the pressure to issue new common stock comes from contingent capital holders (not colluding with common stockholders) or from the bank's regulator (when collusion is occurring), the ability to use a portion of cash raised from common stock issuance to redeem converting contingent capital should make the bank less resistant to the demands of the contingent capital holders or regulator. It thus helps align incentives.

After conversion of contingent capital to common stock, a bank that has more than 10% common stock may consider itself overcapitalized and may therefore want to increase dividends or engage in stock buybacks. Temporarily higher capital requirements for higher cash dividend yields should induce a bank to pay dividends gradually rather than as a lump sum.

5.3   Monitoring by Arm's-Length Contingent Capital Holders

One way in which unaccountable bank managers justify lavish salaries is by engaging in hidden carry trades, paying out the profits from such trades in good times as generous performance-based bonuses. Loosely speaking, we can think of a carry trade as financing a long position in a risky debt instrument at safe low interest rates. Such speculative positions conceptually incorporate short positions in out-of-the-money embedded put options. By choosing to invest in risky debt in a typical carry trade, the bank sells an out-of-the-money option to default, which gives the risky borrower the option to put assets (collateral) to the bank by defaulting. The positions are profitable when the embedded put options expire out of the money. Of course, carry trades have a tendency to blow up occasionally (i.e., they give rise to a "peso problem" associated with large losses when the embedded put options expire in the money).

When carry trades blow up in a highly leveraged bank, there is a risk that stockholders will be wiped out and bondholders will suffer losses too. Even if corporate governance does not allow common stockholders to deal with this agency problem effectively, bondholders can deal with the problem by insisting on fully collateralized loans with short maturities. In the limit, this becomes overnight repo financing with haircuts commensurate with the risk of the assets being financed. To the extent that shareholders realize that they cannot effectively limit the risk taking in hidden carry trades, they can motivate bondholders to limit risks for them by deliberately increasing the amount of debt in the bank's capital structure. Using this logic, Kashyap et al. (2008) point out that low capital levels can address a fundamental agency problem arising in banks.

Contingent capital is a useful device for generating both the benefits of reduced risk taking coming from monitoring by debtholders and reduced bankruptcy costs from having contingent capital conversions replace bank failures. Contingent capital holders may not be able to limit risk taking as efficiently as repo lenders, because they are not fully collateralized on a daily basis, but they can limit risk taking more effectively than common stockholders can by keeping maturities short and threatening a conversion event when the bank appears to be engaging in excessive risk taking associated with extensive carry trades. To make sure that carry trades are not hidden, contingent capital investors might demand more transparency than do common stockholders. Alternatively, if the bank finances risky positions in the repo market, the contingent capital investors might demand that the bank keep some assets in unleveraged trust accounts that the contingent capital investors can observe; this will allow contingent capital investors to limit the amount of capital tied up in repo haircuts.

To the extent that high leverage addresses the agency problem associated with carry trades, contingent capital owners and a bank have an incentive to negotiate terms in which contingent capital is paid a very high interest rate in exchange for tolerating very low levels of capital in the bank. In other words, the solution to the agency problem may make the bank vulnerable to a costly failure, which in the absence of a bailout threatens to impose on the rest of the financial system costs not internalized by the contingent capital holders and the bank in their negotiations. To deal with these external costs, the proposed contingent capital structure requires a banks that pays interest rates higher than 200 basis points over Treasuries also to issue common stock at the same time. This feature frustrates the bank's and contingent capital investors' joint incentive to seek higher leverage.

It might be argued that an alternative way to limit bank risk taking is to prohibit it directly. For example, the Dodd-Frank Act includes the Volcker rule, which limits speculative proprietary trading by large banks. Effective implementation of the Volcker rule is likely to push more speculative trading out of banks and into hedge funds. The hedge fund model is a good example of high leverage being used to control agency costs, consistent with Kashyap et al. (2008). The investors in hedge funds are often unable to monitor the hedge fund's risk taking on a daily basis. They often cannot directly observe the hedge fund's positions and therefore cannot determine whether a hedge fund's profits are influenced by hidden carry trades. The investors in hedge funds deal with this problem by allowing the hedge fund to use leverage and by delegating to the hedge fund's prime brokers the task of limiting the hedge fund's leverage and risk taking. Of course, the prime brokers are the same banks that formerly would have engaged in proprietary trading on their own account. Ironically, prime brokerage itself has elements of a risky carry trade. A prime broker that gives its hedge fund customers more favorable terms (e.g., lower haircuts and higher leverage) may be able to charge higher fees. The high fees are like premiums on out-of-the-money put options. When these hidden options expire in the money, the catastrophic result may resemble the collapse of the highly leveraged hedge fund Long-Term Capital Management in 1998. It remains to be seen to what extent implementation of the Volcker rule will result in banks hiding risks in opaque prime brokerage arrangements with hedge fund customers.

5.4   Collusion between Contingent Capital Holders and Common Stockholders

The logic implying that contingent capital holders will enforce market discipline by threatening conversion when a bank becomes undercapitalized is based on the assumption that contingent capital holders represent a different group of investors from common stockholders. The proposed structure therefore works best if contingent capital owners do not collude with common stockholders and instead enforce market discipline. As a practical matter, this might not be true. For example, the holders of contingent capital might be pension funds with long holding horizons. If such pension funds also invest in common stock issued by banks, the pension funds have an incentive to maximize the combined value of the common stock and contingent capital, not the value of the contingent capital alone.

A more difficult problem also occurs when the bank is closely held and the contingent capital holdings are also highly concentrated. This is likely to be an important issue for small banks. Even large publicly traded banks with liquid market sometimes have large sophisticated investors— like Warren Buffett's Berkshire Hathaway or sovereign wealth funds—in the more senior part of their complex equity structure. Even if contingent capital securities are only issued by large banks with deep liquid markets for their common stock, it is possible that their contingent capital securities will be held by concentrated investors like insurance companies (both life and casualty), large public and private pension funds, and sovereign wealth funds. It will be easy for such sophisticated investors to communicate with bank management; indeed, they already have a long history of doing so. Concentrated holdings make it easier for the common stockholders to collude by making side deals unobserved by the regulator.

5.5   Expectations of Bailouts

The logic implying that common stockholders of a bank with a 10 + 10 capital structure have little incentive to resist conversion when the market value of the common stock falls to 25% of book value is based on the assumption that the combined value of the bank to common stockholders and contingent capital holders is not affected by the conversion itself. This assumption is likely to be violated if the market expects government bailouts of common stockholders, contingent capital holders, bond holders, or depositors. If bailouts are expected, they give the bank more value than implied by the value of the bank's assets alone. This extra value will be impounded in the prices of the bank's common stock, contingent capital, and debt. Since the value of expected bailouts is higher the more poorly the bank is capitalized, common stockholders and contingent capital holders have an incentive to collude to delay conversion of contingent capital even when the bank is unhealthy. Such collusion implies that the monitoring function of contingent capital is lost.

The lack of monitoring is quite severe when market participants expect bailouts. Conceptually, there are two debt overhang problems. First, there is the debt overhang problem between common stockholders and contingent capital holders, where we think of contingent capital as debt. This problems is addressed by the contingent capital holders' threat of forcing a conversion event, which can be made frequent if maturities are kept short enough. It is also addressed if contingent capital holders collude with common stockholders, because they then have an incentive to make efficient common investment decisions.

Second, there is the debt overhang problem between common stockholders plus contingent capital holders (viewed together as "equity") and bondholders, depositors, plus resolution authorities (viewed together as "debt"). When contingent capital holders aggressively protect their interests relative to common stockholders, the bondholders, depositors, and resolution authorities receive an external benefit as a result of their more senior position in the capital structure. When common stockholders collude with contingent capital holders, these benefits are lost, and this second debt overhang becomes a moral hazard or risk-shifting problem. Furthermore, the usual debt overhang problem is exacerbated to the extent that colluding common stockholders and contingent capital holders believe they may benefit from bailouts.

To remedy the perverse incentives resulting from collusion when bailouts are expected, it is important that contingent capital has automatic conversion triggers in addition to the conversion that occurs when contingent capital owners threaten not to roll over. For contingent capital to work properly when common stockholders and contingent capital holders collude, these triggers must be implemented in a credible enough manner to ensure that banks remain well capitalized. This point is discussed in more detail next.

6   Need for Both Regulatory and Market Triggers

What kinds of additional triggers should be built into the required structure of contingent capital securities? When common stock owners collude with contingent capital owners, the bank effectively has a 20 + 0 capital structure (i.e., the incentive structure is the same as if the bank's equity consisted only of common stock). To the extent that discipline is not provided by the market (contingent capital), it must be provided by its regulator.

The regulator's main objective is to ensure that banks do not rely on government-financed bailouts to prevent them from failing. This regulatory objective is achieved when banks can raise significant new equity capital, even after bad news has lowered the value of their assets.

For contingent capital to work effectively when common stockholders collude with contingent capital owners, there must be at least two kinds of triggers, which can be called regulatory triggers and market triggers. To see why, let us examine what happens when only one type of trigger exists.

6.1   Why Market Triggers Alone Do Not Work

To illustrate why a regulatory trigger is needed, suppose there is only a market trigger. For example, McDonald (2013) proposes conversion if the bank's common stock trades in the market below a trigger price while an index of financial stocks also trades below a trigger level. Calomiris and Herring (2012) propose conversion if the 90-day moving average value of the bank's common stock is less than 8% of assets. Hart and Zingales (2011) propose conversion when CDS spreads on the bank's debt or contingent capital stay above a trigger level for some period of time. For example, a conversion event might be triggered if CDS spreads average more than 200 basis points over Treasuries for six months.

There are two problems with relying on these kinds of market-based triggers alone. First, the market may believe creditors or equity owners of failing banks will be bailed out. Since the common stock and contingent capital prices impound the present value of the anticipated bailouts, the stock price can remain high, or the CDS spread can remain low, even as a bank's inherent strength deteriorates. When it becomes apparent that a bank is undercapitalized and the conversion triggers are being hit, the bank may already be effectively insolvent and unable to raise new capital, even after conversion of contingent capital to common stock. This situation makes a bailout more likely to occur.

Second, if the common stockholders and the contingent capital holders collude, they may manipulate common stock prices or CDS spreads to give a misleading indication of the financial health of the bank. This is a more severe problem when the common stock and contingent capital are closely held, in which case there can effectively be a squeeze in the supply of common stock and contingent capital. As a result of a squeeze, both the common stock and the contingent capital can trade in the market at artificially high prices. If prices are artificially high due to a squeeze, the common stock or contingent capital securities may be hard to borrow. Furthermore, CDS spreads may be squeezed as well, under the assumption that an auction to establish a value for contingent capital securities after a conversion event effectively or actually requires delivery of squeezed securities. The regulators may have little incentive to see through the artificial prices until it is too late.

As a practical matter, these two problems interact in a confusing, complicated, and ambiguous manner. For example, suppose that market participants do not believe that the debt of banks will be bailed out, and market participants do not know that the prices of the banks' assets are being squeezed to artificially high prices. Then the high prices for bank common stock and the low CDS spreads send a misleading signal of financial health, which the market can easily misinterpret. When it becomes apparent that the banks are not financially healthy, it is too late to avoid a bailout.

If the market expects bank bailouts but the regulator surprises the market by requiring that banks raise substantial new capital, the market will immediately subtract the reduced present value of previously expected bailouts from debt and equity prices, resulting in a collapse in the price of both. The banks may be unable to raise new equity, they will fail to have adequate capital to support economic growth, and the government may wind up owning them.

To avoid these problems, the regulator must implement triggers for conversion events not based solely on market signals. As a practical matter, some regulatory measure of capital adequacy will be required.

Short sale restrictions have been proposed as a device to make market prices more accurate, thus perhaps making capital adequacy measures less important. In fact, short sale restrictions are likely to undermine the effectiveness of market triggers. As Scheinkman and Xiong (2003) discuss, short sale restrictions lead to an upward bias in prices if investors agree to disagree about the value of a firm. Such disagreement is particularly likely when ambiguity about the probability of bailouts exists. The upward bias can induce confusion and lead market participants to believe that financially unhealthy banks are healthy.

Calomiris and Herring (2012) worry about conversions that occur as a result of artificially low market prices. They therefore propose disallowing short sales of common stock by contingent capital holders. Disallowing short sales by contingent capital holders makes collusion between contingent capital holders and common stockholders somewhat easier. If, for example, some contingent capital holders collude with common stockholders and some do not, those who do not collude will not be able to punctuate their lack of collusion with short sales. Sundaresan and Wang (2010) argue that expectations of a severely dilutive forced conversion based on a market trigger can lead to a multiple equilibrium problem in which a healthy bank suffers forced dilutive conversions. Calomiris and Herring (2012) correctly point out that if the market trigger is based on the ratio of the market value of the common stock to the risk-weighted value of assets (not the book value of the common stock), such dilutive forced conversions can be avoided if the bank increases its market capitalization by issuing more common stock, even if the common stock is issued at a discount. For example, a rights offering at a deeply discounted price will prevent the multiple equilibrium suggested by Sundaresan and Wang (2010).

A better way to look at this short sale issue is from the perspective of the contingent capital holders seeking to force conversion, not from the perspective of the common stockholders seeking to prevent it. If contingent capital holders want to force additional capital raising by the bank, they do not need to go through the costly and risky process of shorting the bank's common stock in an effort to force a market trigger. Instead, they can follow the simpler strategy of keeping the maturity of the contingent capital short, then threatening not to roll it over when it matures. To deal with this threat, the bank must either find new contingent capital holders or issue more common stock.

Contingent capital holders may also want to hedge their exposure by shorting the bank's common stock, similar to the manner in which convertible arbitrage strategies might short a company's stock. Such short hedge positions tend to keep contingent capital owners at arm's length from the bank whose common stock they are shorting. In this way, allowing contingent capital owners to short the stock of the banks they invest in tend has the beneficial effect of limiting collusion.

6.2   Why Triggers Based on Regulatory Capital Alone Do Not Work

To illustrate why a market trigger is needed, suppose there is only a regulatory trigger, such as a capital adequacy ratio.

Even if market signals are known to ignore important information or to incorporate information into prices in a biased manner and the regulator's calculations are known to incorporate information into valuations accurately, it is nevertheless a mistake for the regulator to rely exclusively on its own calculations and ignore market signals.

Consider the following hypothetical example. Suppose that BBB tranches of assets backed by subprime mortgages trade in the marketplace at 60% of par, but the bank's regulator has accurately calculated that a valuation of 90% of par reflects expected defaults and also incorporates an adequate risk premium. In other words, the regulator is 100% certain that market prices are incorrect based on available information and is 100% certain its own valuations are correct. Suppose further that the regulator is also correct in its assessments. Should a regulator force a bank that owns such subprime assets to write them down to 60 cents on the dollar or allow the bank to value the assets at 90 cents on the dollar?

Suppose that a 60-cent valuation will require the bank to raise new equity capital now, while a 90-cent valuation will not. If the regulator does not require the bank to raise new capital now, it is setting the stage for a costly future disaster. It is possible that information changes in such a way that the regulator's valuations, although accurate at the time they were made, subsequently deteriorate due the arrival of new bad information. It is possible that this could make the regulator's accurate valuation fall to 60, while the market's more irrational and more pessimistic valuation falls to, say, 20. If the regulator at this point were to ask the bank to raise more capital, the market price of 20 for a significant portion of the bank's assets might be so low that the bank could not raise new equity from the market at any price. As a result, the bank becomes insolvent and invites government ownership.

Since it is the regulator's plan for the market ultimately to buy the bank's equity to keep it well capitalized, the regulator must respect market valuations, even if the regulator believes them to be irrational.

Therefore, at best, the idea that a regulator's accurate hold-to-maturity valuation should trump a market valuation should apply only to assets known by the regulator to be extremely safe if held to maturity, even when the market appears to be building substantial default premiums and risk premiums into valuations. To justify ignoring market prices, the regulator must not only know that its valuations are accurate based on the information at the time the valuations are made, but the regulator must also know that its valuations are not going to change much if new adverse information arrives in the future.

If a bank holds assets known by the regulator to be safe with probability one (or perhaps close to one), then there is a strong case to be made that the central bank should be willing to buy such assets at a discount to their known-to-be-safe hold-to-maturity value. Similarly, the central should be willing to finance portfolios of risky assets with a repo haircut large enough to cover hold-to-maturity losses under very pessimistic scenarios. Such purchases will force the market prices of such assets to reasonable levels and therefore help defeat a credit squeeze.

Contingent capital does not directly address the problem of bank liquidity. It does address the issue indirectly by making more capital available in the bank's capital structure; this capital can be used for haircuts associated with collateralized lending. Thus, stronger capital levels will enable a central bank lending facility to safely make larger amounts of low-default-risk collateralized loans to banks facing liquidity problems.

6.3   Multiple Triggers

These arguments imply that effective implementation of contingent capital should, at a minimum, incorporate both market signals and calculations conducted by the bank's regulator. Furthermore, these triggers should operate in an either-or manner, not a both-and manner. For example, it is reasonable for the regulator to value a bank's assets in a conservative manner, based on the lowest of several different methodologies: i) book value, ii) the regulator's conservative estimate of correct values,

iii) the market prices for the assets, and iv) a value backed out of the market price of the bank's common stock and contingent capital securities.

These triggers might also include information from outside experts, such as accountants or ratings agencies. For example, the regulator might require a bank's senior debt to be rated A or better, or require that contingent capital securities be rated BBB or better. A satisfactory audit or a satisfactory bond rating should not be a sufficient condition for a bank to avoid raising new capital, but a sufficiently unsatisfactory audit result or a sufficiently unsatisfactory bond rating might well be sufficient to trigger a conversion event or other forced capital raising. For multiple triggers to prevent a bank from getting into a position where it cannot issue new equity, the multiple triggers should consider the probability that the bank becomes undercapitalized in the future.

Using an analogy with option pricing, the triggers should keep the option to default (by not being able to raise capital) far enough out of the money that the bank does not face significant risk of failing. This requires addressing both the "money-ness" of the option and the bank's volatility. Market triggers address both money-ness and volatility by using triggers based on both common stock prices (money-ness) and CDS spreads, contingent capital yields, or bond yields (volatility). Regulatory triggers address both money-ness and volatility by measuring capital adequacy using risk-weighted assets (money-ness) and stress tests (volatility). When regulatory capital is high and common stock prices are high, both the market and the regulator agree that the bank is currently well capitalized. When a bank's CDS spreads are low and the bank passes a regulatory stress test, both the market and the regulator agree that the bank is expected to remain well capitalized in the future with high probability.

7 Additional Considerations

7.1 Incentives to Conserve Cash

As a weak bank heads toward failure, it tends to lose cash in two ways. First, a weak bank tends to lose cash that can be used as capital by paying out high cash interest rates on debt or contingent capital securities (as a result of market perceptions that it is weak), by paying excessive dividends or executive compensation (as a result of moral hazard), and by forgoing opportunities to issue new equity (as a result of expecting bailouts or shifting risks to bondholders).

Second, a weak bank tends to become illiquid as a result of losing short-term financing, as maturing unsecured debt is not rolled over, secured (repo) borrowing is not rolled over, and depositors flee to other institutions. Higher haircuts on repo borrowing also make a weak bank less liquid.

The proposed contingent capital structure addresses the first problem directly and addresses the second problem indirectly by addressing the first problem. It addresses the first of these problems in three ways:

- By requiring the bank to issue new common stock as a multiple of 2 of book value when shares are used to pay interest on contingent capital, the proposed structure prevents capital from leaving the bank when the market prices the contingent capital in a risky manner. Indeed, it requires the bank to raise new capital.
- By raising capital requirements by a multiple of 3, of cash dividend payments and cash executive compensation payments over $1 million for a period of four years, the proposed structure limits excessive dividends and executive compensation when the bank's capital is in adequate.
- By allowing the bank to repurchase contingent capital in the event of a conversion event, with a portion of cash raised from recent common stock issuance, the proposed structure incentivizes the bank to issue new common stock even when there is a substantial possibility of a highly dilutive forced conversion of contingent capital into common stock.

All three of these features interact in a positive manner. Suppose that a weak bank delays writing down bad assets so that it can report to its regulator high enough capital levels to allow large bonuses and high dividends. If the market believes that bank is weak, contingent capital owners will demand high interest rates on contingent capital. To the extent that these rates exceed 200 basis points over Treasuries, the bank will be forced to issue new common stock to pay the extra interest. Since the amount of new common stock to be issued is proportional to the book value and not to the market value of the common stock, the bank will be severely punished for not writing down the value of its common stock. Since a portion of newly issued common stock can be used to redeem contingent capital in the event of conversion, this reduces the cost of issuing new common stock. Since the portion that can be used to redeem contingent capital declines over time, this incents a weak bank that is issuing common stock to allow conversion sooner rather than later.

To discuss how these features might work in practice, suppose that a bank is required to maintain levels of 7% common stock and 7% contingent capital if the bank has paid no dividends and no executive compensation in excess of $1 million for at least four years. Suppose further that the bank's book value has been constant for more than four years, and the bank has been paying out dividends and cash executive compensation in excess of $1 million at a rate equal to 5% of book value for more than four years. Taking into account the bank's dividend and executive compensation history, the banks's capital requirement will be common stock equal to 10% of the book value of assets and contingent capital equal to 10% of the book value of equity, for a total of 20%, calculated as $7\% \times 2 + 5\% \times 0.10 \times 3 \times 4 = 20\%$.

Now suppose that the quality of the bank's assets deteriorates, and the bank begins to write down the value of some of its assets. By canceling cash dividends and reducing cash executive compensation, the bank can reduce its capital requirement from $10 + 10$ to $7 + 7$ over a period of four years. This gives the bank substantial flexibility to take write-downs without having to issue new common stock. It also gives the bank flexibility to allow some contingent capital to mature without being rolled over.

Let us suppose that after four years of no dividends and low executive compensation, the capital structure is $7 + 7$. Suppose that this occurs as a result of writing down bad assets and by allowing contingent capital to mature without being rolled over. Now suppose that the contingent capital holders threaten to force conversion into common stock by not rolling over their securities. The bank may respond to this threat either by issuing new common stock or by raising the interest rate it offers on new contingent capital.

Suppose that the bank follows the path of paying a higher interest rate on the contingent capital, with contingent capital owners receiving the Treasury rate plus 200 basis points in cash interest (the maximum allowed) plus common stock worth an additional 250 basis points per year. Suppose that the common stock is trading at 50% of book value (i.e., at 3.5% of risk-weighted assets). In terms of book value of shares and par value of contingent capital, the cost of the extra interest paid in shares is 500 basis points, not 250 basis points. Applying the multiplier of 2 based on book value, the bank must issue enough common stock to raise the book value of its outstanding common stock, before the extra 250 basis points of interest paid in shares, by 0.70% of risk-weighted assets per year, calculated as $7\% \times 0.0500 \times 2 = 0.70\%$. After the interest is paid to the contingent capital holders in shares, 3/4 of this amount, 0.525% of risk-weighted assets per year, is left over to improve capital adequacy. The remaining 1/4 of this amount is paid to contingent capital holders, who receive the interest of 250 basis points on shares representing 7% of risk-weighted assets. This costs the bank 0.175% of risk-weighted assets per year, calculated as 7% × 0.0250 = 0.175%.

Thus, as a result of the combination of paying high interest rates to contingent capital holders and issuing required new common stock, the book value of common stock rises from 7.00% of assets to 7.525% of assets after one year, and the market value of common stock rises from 3.75% of assets to slightly less than 4.275% of assets (assuming $1 of common stock issuance raises common stock prices by slightly less than $1). This will have the effect of substantially recapitalizing the bank and eventually driving down the interest rate on contingent capital.

If the bank had not written down the values of bad assets, so that its book value of common stock remained at, say, 10%, then it would have to issue even more common stock to pay high interest rates to contingent capital holders. This would make the bank recapitalize even faster. This example is consistent with the interpretation that 7 + 7 is the rock-bottom minimum capital structure tolerated by the regulator, and the bank has already minimized the short-run amount of new common stock it is required to issue by writing down assets as much as possible and by allowing contingent capital to mature and roll over.

7.2   The Bank's Cost of Capital

Bankers are likely to argue that significant contingent capital requirements raise their cost of capital and therefore increase the equilibrium interest rate on loans to customers. Many such arguments are bogus. Typical bogus arguments contradict the Modigliani-Miller principle that relates high expected returns on common stock to high leverage. Other arguments confuse accounting with economics. It is not the purpose here to review all of these arguments in detail.

The relationship between taxpayer-financed bailouts and a bank's cost of capital is particularly confusing. If the market anticipates that the bank's debt will be bailed out by taxpayers with some probability, it is likely that the present value of the anticipated bailouts will be passed along to the bank's common stockholders. Debt that is in fact risky will pay an interest rate appropriate for safer debt, and this interest cost savings will show up as cash flow to common stockholders. The extra cash flows will increase the value of the bank's common stock and in this sense will lower the bank's cost of equity capital. If contingent capital requirements shift the costs of bailouts from taxpayers to contingent capital investors, then the bank's common stockholders will lose the value of the bailouts, because they will either have to pay an interest rate to the contingent capital holders high enough to cover losses given default, or they will have to issue more common stock to make the debt safer. Since the newly issued common stock does not benefit from the subsidies implicit in bailouts, the cost of this equity capital is higher than it would be if bailouts were anticipated. Contingent capital requirements may indeed raise banks' cost of capital, by removing the present value of subsidies expected to be received at taxpayer expense.

Since the value of the subsidies depends on how well capitalized the bank is, if the regulator forces the bank to convert contingent capital unexpectedly, the unexpected decline in the value of the subsidies will disappear from the bank's value. The value of its shares may well plummet. Thus, a plummeting share value on imposition of a contingent capital regime or on unexpected forced conversion of contingent capital may not be a sign that the bank's intrinsic cost of capital has increased but rather a sign that the bank was expecting its cost of capital to be subsidized by bailouts.

It has also been argued that high equity requirements increase the adverse selection costs of issuing equity. For example, Calomiris and Herring (2012) suggest that the higher capital requirements proposed by Admati et al. (2013) incorporate significant incremental adverse selection costs. In fact, contrary to Calomiris and Herring (2012), higher equity requirements probably reduce adverse selection costs, because the Modigliani-Miller principle applies to adverse selection in a manner similar to the way it applies to risk premia.

If the Modigliani-Miller principle is respected and bailouts do not occur because they are unnecessary, then the total value of the securities a bank issues will be a function of the risk structure of the bank's assets. How this value is divided among the various security owners will depend on the rules governing the structure of the various securities.

Suppose that contingent capital holders are occasionally expected to be able to "steal" the bank from the common stock holders at a time of market crisis by forcing an artificial, highly dilutive conversion not justified by the underlying forces of supply and demand. If so, then the occasional windfall expected by contingent capital holders should be priced into the contingent capital securities and show up as a below-market interest rate in normal times. The interest rate will be particularly low to the extent that dollars in crisis states are more valuable than dollars in good states of the economy. Conversion events that benefit existing contingent capital holders at the expense of existing common stockholders do not affect the cost of capital for a bank; they merely redistribute these costs between equity and contingent capital in a manner that the market prices into the various securities, without having any effect on the bank's overall cost of capital.

7.3   No Cash Settlement

Although the proposed structure does use market signals to trigger conversion events, the proposed conversion rule for contingent capital does not have a variable conversion price or variable number of common shares into which contingent capital converts. In this sense, the proposed conversion rule lacks cash settlement features (i.e., features that rely on market prices to determine the cash flows on the securities themselves).

If contingent capital converts into a fixed dollar value of shares based on the market price of the stock at the time of conversion, contingent capital owners may hedge this equity exposure by selling the shares they receive on exercise. This potentially places very large price pressure on the price of the common stock, exactly at a time when information asymmetries are great. To the extent that markets become confused about how much trading is due to hedging as opposed to information asymmetries, this may make the stock price highly sensitive to information asymmetries. If, furthermore, the contingent capital holders dynamically hedge their exposure, they will sell more shares as the value of the shares falls. The result is a potentially unstable stock price whose value is not easily defined. The proposal by Flannery (2016) has such destabilizing cash settlement features.

7.4   Who Would Own Contingent Capital?

Contingent capital securities are likely to be demanded by longer-term bond investors with a tolerance for bearing some degree of risk. This includes life insurance companies; pension funds; endowments; or, more generally, any investors with long horizons and low leverage who are seeking to increase returns by reaching for yield. They would fit well into mutual funds that balance holdings between stocks and bonds. They would be highly appropriate for life-cycle index funds attempting to hold the market portfolio with varying degrees of leverage. Assuming the interest payments are taxable, the securities are, like bonds in general, appropriate for tax-free investors like retirement accounts and foundations.

The ownership structure of contingent capital securities is likely to create tension between two types of investors: i) sophisticated, concentrated investors with the ability to monitor the capitalization and riskiness of the banks they invest in and ii) less sophisticated investors reaching for yield in diversified portfolios that balance risk and expected returns. Some life insurance companies may have the ability to monitor directly the banks that issue the contingent capital securities they invest in. Pension funds and endowments are likely to invest through skilled asset managers with specialized monitoring capabilities.

If contingent capital securities become widely mandated, it is possible that specialized institutional asset managers will structure funds to invest specifically in such securities on behalf of sophisticated institutional clients like pension funds and endowments. If the asset managers are compensated on the basis of the performance of the funds, this will tend to create a separation between the owners of the common stock of banks and the managers of the funds specializing in contingent capital securities. Such structures will tend to prevent collusion between banks and contingent capital owners. Note that the asset manager structure will tend to prevent collusion, even if the institutional investor clients themselves hold a diversified portfolio of contingent capital securities managed by asset manger's specializing in contingent capital securities and bank common stocks managed by a different arms'-length asset manager. Institutional investors, by owning bank common stock through one asset manager and contingent capital through another, can hedge themselves against random redistributions of bank value that occur as a result of unpredictability in the frequency and outcome of conversion events.

Contingent capital securities are not likely to be safe enough to be a reasonable investment for money market funds. Regulators should probably prohibit such securities from being owned by money market funds at all. Indeed, the recent financial crisis was probably exacerbated by the fact that money market funds inappropriately chased yield by buying securities too junior in the capital structure of the banks whose paper they purchased. As a general regulatory principle, money market funds are like highly leverage banks; thus, contingent capital investments by such institutions should have a risk weight of 1,250%; this would prevent money market funds from investing in contingent capital securities.

7.5   What Contingent Capital Might Look Like

The proposed structure does not dictate terms like maturity and interest rate. It is tempting to think of contingent capital as a substitute for "permanent" capital, which therefore should have a long maturity. This thinking is erroneous, because contingent capital securities cannot be paid off unless new contingent capital is issued. In other words, the contingent capital structure proposed here automatically provides "permanent" capital, even if the securities themselves have a maturity of one day. A bank permanently retires its contingent capital by reducing the size of the bank, winding down its operations, and returning capital to investors.

Given that the threat not to roll over contingent capital is likely to be the binding threat that disciplines a bank, it is likely that implementation of the proposed structure would result in contingent capital that has a relatively short maturity, with perhaps many issues outstanding with multiple staggered maturity dates. When outstanding securities are reaching maturity on a frequent basis, relatively frequent monitoring by contingent capital holders takes place and the market can observe the outcomes. Note that this benefits all contingent capital security investors, because all securities have equal seniority when a conversion event takes place.

One likely possibility is that contingent capital could be structured like commercial paper or auction rate securities, with short maturities and floating interest rates. Short-term financing backed by thin capital requires a well-defined mechanism for suspending convertibility and converting debt into common stock. Suspension of convertibility is different from a conversion event. In the event the holders do not want to roll over maturing securities, suspension of convertibility may take place if the securities contain provisions allowing the bank to delay paying of the securities at par by instead paying a high, escalating interest rate for a prespecified time. This prespecified time is the outcome of negotiations between the bank and its contingent capital investors when the securities are issued; for the sake of discussion, it might be three to six months. During this period, there is no conversion event; instead, the interest rate may escalate based on negotiated contractual provisions. For example, the rate may be 200 basis points over Treasuries before the suspension of convertibility and then may rise by 100 basis points per month during the period of suspended convertibility. Since high interest rates greater than 200 basis points over Treasuries are required to be paid in newly issued securities that issue new common stock, this mechanism will automatically result in gradual common stock issuance, which recapitalizes the bank, thus making its contingent capital securities attractive at low interest rates again. Alternatively, if the penalty interest rate for securities that do not want to roll over is very high, the bank may issue large amounts of new common stock quickly in order to induce the contingent capital securities to roll over at lower interest rates. If, at the end of the three-to-six-month period of suspension of convertibility, the bank does not pay off the contingent capital securities, a conversion event takes place. This gives the bank an additional window of time, during which it can issue common stock to redeem the securities.

It is also reasonable to expect staggered maturities. For example, Calomiris and Herring (2012) suggest a rolling window of five-year maturities, with 1/5 of the contingent capital maturing each year. As a practical matter, banks will probably issue somewhat more contingent capital than the bare minimum its regulator requires, in order to have a cushion that buys time for rolling over the securities in an orderly manner. For example, a bank might issue contingent capital equal to 12% of assets instead of 10%. To make calculations simple, suppose these securities have six-year maturities, with 1/72 of the securities maturing each month. If contingent capital holders demand high rates to roll over securities, the bank can pay off maturing securities each month for one year, allowing the stock of outstanding securities to decline from 12% of assets to 10% of assets. At the end of one year, the maturing securities may have a suspension-of-convertibility feature, allowing the bank to buy three to six months of more time. If a conversion event occurs at the end of this period, the bank still has 60 days in which to issue new common stock.

These considerations suggest that conversions of contingent capital into common stock that result from direct negotiation between contingent capital investors and banks—and not from automatic regulatory or market triggers—are likely to be a relatively slow and orderly processes, generating numerous market signals that the regulator observes as a bank's attempt to recapitalize. These market signals include declining levels of "excess" contingent capital, penalty interest rates during periods of suspension of convertibility, and issuance of bank common stock at depressed prices.

The regulator will want to watch carefully for signs that the bank is colluding with contingent capital owners. Such signs would include, for example, equity kickers associated with new contingent capital offerings. Since an equity kicker is like a payment of interest greater than the maximum rate of 200 basis points over Treasuries, such kickers should either be prohibited or alternatively require a multiple of 2 of additional common stock issuance based on the book value of the bank's assets. Hidden equity kickers should be prohibited. Indeed, a clean approach to deterring collusion is to require all equity issuance to result from rights offerings to common stockholders.

8   Macroeconomic Considerations

Although the proposed contingent capital structure is microprudential in nature, it has numerous features that can promote macroeconomic stability:

- When bank equity values collapse as a result of panic, massive conversions of contingent capital and massive issuance of new contingent capital to replace converted contingent capital will have a tendency to strengthen quickly the capital structure of banks throughout the economy, thus bringing an end to the panic.
- The requirement to increase capital for four years after payments of cash dividends or large cash compensation creates procyclical capital and also encourages banks to conserve cash during periods of financial stress.
- The required conversion of all contingent capital rather than just part of it tends to create a large capital buffer during periods of financial stress.
- To the extent that the value of a bank's equity securities fall dramatically as a result of conversion of contingent capital, the bank's regulator receives a useful signal concerning the extent to which the market was pricing private benefits of expected bailouts into the value of the bank's securities.
- A speedy conversion process should shorten the time during which banks try to deleverage their portfolios. This should have some stabilizing effect due to less contraction in credit supply.

Although the proposed structure does not include explicit macroprudential triggers—such as market-wide indices of CDS spreads or market-wide indices of bank stock prices—macroprudential triggers could easily be incorporated.

It might be a useful policy for the regulator to force conversion of healthy banks from time to time. Suppose that the regulator implements a policy of declaring a contingent capital conversion event for at least one bank in the top 100 per year. For example, the chosen bank might be the one with the lowest score on a stress test, even if all 100 banks achieve an otherwise acceptable score. If the chosen bank is actually quite healthy, it should be able to execute a successful rights offering at a price much higher than the dilutive 80-20 conversion rate, then use the proceeds of the rights offering to replace the converted contingent capital. To the extent that bankers perceive such forced conversions as costly, the bankers have an incentive to keep healthy enough capital levels so that they are not the bank chosen for conversion.

9 Conclusion

The purpose of contingent capital is to incentivize banks to maintain healthy balance sheets, which reduces the expected value of taxpayer bailouts and therefore reduces the inefficiencies that expected bailouts lead to.

To achieve this objective, contingent capital should be structured as a robust security, designed to make banks less fragile. It should work both when contingent capital holders collude with common stockholders and when they do not. It should work when markets agree with regulators and when markets do not agree with regulators. The structure for contingent capital securities proposed in this paper is robust in all these ways.

Notes

This chapter was inspired by comments Robert H. Smith made at a lunch with Smith School faculty in the fall of 2009, where he exhorted the faculty to conduct research that would help prevent another financial crisis. The author thanks Anna Obizhaeva for helpful comments.

1. Assets safer or riskier than typical assets have risk weights that convert them to the numeraire scale based on 8%. A safer asset might have a 50% risk weight, which converts an actual capital level of 4% to the numeraire level of 8%; a riskier asset might have a risk weight of 250%, which converts an actual capital level of 20% into the numeraire level of 8% as well. A typical asset has a risk weight of 100%. The most risky assets, such as defaulted debt with

little prospect for recovery, have the maximum risk weight of 1,250%; since they have a required capital level of 100%, writing such assets off does not affect a bank's capital adequacy. For example, a bank that holds $10 billion in assets with a risk weight of 100%, $5 billion in assets with a risk weight of 50%, $2 billion in assets with a risk weight of 250%, and $1 billion face value in defaulted debt with a risk weight of 1,250% has risk-weighted assets of $30 billion, calculated as $10 \times 1.00 + 5 \times 0.50 + 2 \times 2.50 + 1 \times 12.50 = 30$. If the bank has $2.4 billion in capital, its capital level is equal to 8% of risk-weighted assets. If the bank writes off the defaulted debt, its risk-weighted assets fall to $17.5 billion, and its capital falls to $1.4 billion; its capital level remains 8% of risk-weighted assets.

2. The Basel II framework is designed to allow a sophisticated bank to use its own internal risk management process to measure the riskiness of its assets. Although Basel II can potentially deal with new or complex assets not dealt with adequately in Basel I, it also gives a bank incentives to have internal risk management processes that understate risks. The Basel III framework is intended to address the flaws of Basel I and Basel II.

References

Admati, A., P. DeMarzo, M. Hellwig, and P. Pfleiderer (2013). Fallacies, irrelevant facts, and myths in the discussion of capital regulation: Why bank equity is not socially expensive. Max Planck Institute for Research on Collective Goods, preprint 2013/23, Bonn, Germany.

Admati, A. R., and M. Hellwig (2013). *The Bankers' New Clothes: What's Wrong with Banking and What to Do about It*. Princeton, NJ: Princeton University Press.

Bolton, P., and F. Samama (2012). Capital access bonds: Contingent capital with an option to convert. *Economic Policy 27*(70), 275–317.

Calomiris, C. W. (1999). Building an incentive-compatible safety net. *Journal of Banking and Finance, 23*(10), 1499–1519.

Calomiris, C. W., and R. J. Herring (2012). Why and how to design a contingent convertible debt requirement. Chapter 5 in *Rocky times: Perspectives on financial stability*, Yasumuki Fuhita, Richard J. Herring, and Robert E. Litan (eds.). Washington: Brookings/NICMR Press.

Coffee, Jr., J. C. (2011). Systemic risk after Dodd-Frank: Contingent capital and the need for regulatory strategies beyond oversight. *Columbia Law Review 111*, 795–1878.

Flannery, M. (2016). Stabilizing large financial institutions with contingent capital certificates. *Quarterly Journal of Finance 6*(2), 1650006.

Glaeser, E. L. (2012). The political risks of fighting market failures: Subversion, populism and the government sponsored enterprises. *Journal of Legal Analysis 4*(1), 41–82.

Glasserman, P., and B. Nouri (2012). Contingent capital with a capital-ratio trigger. *Management Science* 58(10), 1816–1833.

Hart, O., and L. Zingales (2011). A new capital regulation for large financial institutions. *American Law and Economics Review* 13(2), 453–490.

Kashyap, A., R. Rajan, and J. Stein (2008). Rethinking capital regulation. In *Maintaining Stability in a Changing Financial System*, Symposium at Jackson Hole, WY. Kansas City: Federal Reserve Bank of Kansas City.

McDonald, R. L. (2013). Contingent capital with a dual price trigger. *Journal of Financial Stability* 9(2), 230–241.

Pennacchi, G., T. Vermaelen, and C. C. Wolff (2014). Contingent capital: The case of COERCS. *Journal of Financial and Quantitative Analysis* 49(3), 541–574.

Scheinkman, J., and W. Xiong (2003). Overconfidence and speculative bubbles. *Journal of Political Economy* 111(6), 1183–1220.

Squam Lake Working Group (2010). An expedited resolution mechanism for distressed financial firms: Regulatory hybrid securities. *The Squam Lake Report: Fixing the Financial System.* Chapter 7. Princeton, NJ: Princeton University Press.

Sundaresan, S., and Z. Wang (2010). Design of contingent capital with a stock price trigger for mandatory conversion. Staff report, Federal Reserve Bank of New York.

CHAPTER FIVE

Bankruptcy Laws and Collateral Regulation: Reflections after the Crisis

Aloisio Araujo, Rafael Ferreira, and Bruno Funchal

1 Introduction

Financial crises highlight the importance of understanding default. The 2008 financial crisis, triggered by problems in the American subprime mortgage market, drew attention to the consequences of widespread default and strengthened arguments for additional restrictions on the borrower-lender relationship.

Indeed, in increasingly sophisticated financial markets, with promises considerably exceeding physical assets, the undesirable general equilibrium effects of default can be exacerbated. Creditors that do not receive their payments in time might find themselves unable to fullfil their own promises of repayment, triggering a succession of nonpayments that leads to a crisis. In Section 3 of this paper, we briefly discuss the role of bankruptcy laws in mitigating this effect.

Nonetheless, the current debate on regulation of some of the markets at the center of the crisis provides a good opportunity to remember another, more desirable property of an incomplete market economy with default: increased welfare.[1] Economists have known for some time that default improves efficiency under incomplete markets.

In the canonical general equilibrium with incomplete markets (GEI) model, there is no default, so the only promises that agents can make are those that they can keep in all states of nature. They are restricted to the incomplete set of available assets.

But if agents are allowed to default on their promises, they endogenously change the set of tradable assets. Agents can choose whether to keep their promises in each state of nature, effectively changing the securities' payoffs to better suit the agents' preferences. Permitting default gives rise to a larger asset span, which can increase risk sharing and social welfare.

But when borrowers with limited commitment to repay their debts can default, it is usually optimal for them to do so. Anticipating that they might not be repaid, lenders are less likely to lend. Defaulting debtors impose an externality on other borrowers restricted to less favorable debt contracts. Leniency toward debtors may increase risk sharing, but it also provides incentives for debtors to misbehave, making strategic default more likely and ultimately limiting risk sharing ex ante.

Thus, the possibility of nonpayment creates the need for effective enforcement mechanisms that provide incentives for debtors to keep their promises in some states of nature. However, if the enforcement mechanisms are too effective, few parties will default on their promises, but there will be little borrowing because of the draconian consequences of default.

This reasoning suggests the existence of an optimal level of enforcement that is intermediate, as a result of the fundamental trade-off between mitigating strategic default and increasing risk sharing. Throughout this chapter, we revisit such trade-offs as this, in the context of two important enforcement mechanisms: punitive provisions of bankruptcy laws and debt collateral.

At least three classes of models have been developed around these mechanisms: GEI with bankruptcy, GEI with penalties, and GEI with collateral. In the pages that follow, we borrow insights from all three of them.

We start with personal bankruptcy. Bankruptcy is an institutional arrangement to deal with situations in which an agent's garnishable assets and income do not cover her debt. In these cases, legal provisions must determine how the debtor's resources are to be distributed among the creditors.[2] Section 2 presents a standard model of bankruptcy that sheds some light on the impact of bankruptcy exemptions on risk sharing and strategic defaults. The section follows the approach taken in Dubey et al. (2005). They include punishment to defaulting debtors—an important characteristic of bankruptcy laws—in a GEI framework and show that the degree of debtor punishment influences the amount of risk sharing. When markets are complete, the optimal level of punishment is very high, but under incomplete markets, an intermediate level of punishment—one that encourages some amount of bankruptcy—induces more risk sharing and increases welfare in the economy.[3]

Section 3 outlines some well-known results on corporate bankruptcy law design and discusses cases when it pays to be lenient toward debtors. In summary, when capital markets fail to promote ex post efficiency, deviations from a pro-creditor distribution rule may increase welfare. We present in greater detail the results of Araujo and Funchal (2013), who investigate how the relative costs of bankruptcy procedures and the production technology affect welfare and the optimal design of a bankruptcy law in a GEI framework.

Also in Section 3, we succinctly discuss how bankruptcy laws can play a role in mitigating and alleviating a crisis. The section concludes by presenting some results of Araujo et al. (2012a). They describe the 2005 reform of the Brazilian bankruptcy law and present it as an example of institutional reform that improved an environment with poor enforcement mechanisms.

Finally, we move to margin requirements, a much debated topic in the aftermath of the 2008 financial crisis. An important issue in the literature on GEI with collateral is the availability of the durable good used as collateral and how it relates to welfare. Geanakoplos and Zame (2014) derive necessary and sufficient conditions for Pareto optimality of competitive equilibria. A necessary condition is that collateral is plentiful. If it is scarce, there is inefficiency. An interesting question that follows is whether welfare can be improved through collateral regulation. Araujo et al. (2012b) examine precisely this issue and find that restricting the set of assets available for trade does not lead to Pareto improvement.[4] In particular, they show that it is never optimal to restrict the market of subprime loans. In Section 4, we reexamine these results in further detail.

2   Efficient Personal Bankruptcy Law

The 2008 financial crisis led to a debate in the media[5] on the consequences of bankruptcy due to job losses and on the difficulties for consumers to erase their debts and get a fresh start. Before that, however, during the discussion that motivated the 2005 Bankruptcy Reform Act, the main concern was about moral hazard.

The change of focus was mostly due to the personal bankruptcy law reform being cited as having contributed to the increase in subprime mortgage foreclosures. Morgan et al. (2009) argue that the 2005 Bankruptcy Reform Act contributed to the surge of subprime foreclosures by shifting risk from unsecured credit lenders to mortgage lenders. Before the bankruptcy reform, any household could file for Chapter 7 bankruptcy and have credit cards and other unsecured credit discharged. The bankruptcy reform blocked this possibility by adding a means test to force those households in better condition to file for bankruptcy using Chapter 13, under which they must continue to pay unsecured lenders using their future income. Depending on the means test, cash-constrained householders who might have saved their home by filing for Chapter 7 are more likely to face foreclosure. As a result, Morgan et al. (2009) found a substantial impact of the bankruptcy reform on subprime foreclosure (the foreclosure rate during the seven quarters after the reform was 12.6% higher than it had been).

In contrast, Dobbie and Song (2015) presented evidences of some beneficial effects of filling for bankruptcy under Chapter 13. The authors show empirically that Chapter 13 increases earnings and the employment for the next five years after the filing.

2.1   A Simple Model

Consider a consumer who lives for two periods and maximizes utility over her consumption c. The consumer is born with some amount D of durable goods (a house, a car, etc.) that she consumes in both periods. The durable goods depreciate at rate δ. Period 1 income w_1 is known, but second period income is uncertain and varies according to the realization of the state of nature $w_{2s} \in \{w_{21}, \ldots, w_{2S}\}$. Each state occurs with probability p_s. The wage is observed by the borrower, but the lender can only verify its value at a monitoring cost, denoted by γB.[6]

A large number of agents are divided into two different groups: borrowers and lenders. Borrowers can be thought of as consumers; lenders, as the financial institutions that offer standard debt contracts.[7] Lenders are endowed with enough resources to supply credit to consumers. These lenders' endowments may be used either to lend to a borrower at rate r or to purchase a risk-free asset paying an exogenously given rate of return r_f.

If the borrowers report bankruptcy, a part of the debt will be discharged, and some of the individuals' assets, including personal goods (D) and their current income will be exempted up to an amount E (like the bankruptcy exemption). The bankruptcy law determines the level of E exogenously, so we call E the bankruptcy exemption level in this paper. Debt contracts are subject to this bankruptcy law. Notice that part of borrowers' goods serves as an informal collateral imposed by the law to unsecured credit.

Definition 1 *Strategic bankruptcy*[8] occurs when the borrower has enough resources to pay her debts but she chooses not to do so.

Definition 2 *Bankruptcy by bad fortune* occurs when the realization of states of nature is bad in such a way that borrowers are unable to fulfill their repayment promises.

Consumption in the first period defines the level of debt B at the beginning of period 2:
$$B = (c_1 - D - w_1),$$
which means that the agent consumes more than the sum of her wage and durable goods.

A loan contract between the borrower and the lender consists of a pair (r, B), where B is the loan size and $(1 + r)$ is the loan rate, subject to the legal imposition on the exemption level E. It applies to the situation in which the borrower does not repay the debt $(1 + r)B$.

If at least some debt will be held, so that $B > 0$, we can divide the borrowers' actions in three distinct choices:

C1 do not file for bankruptcy if:

$$w_{2s} + \delta D \geq (1 + r)B \quad \text{and} \quad (1 + r)B \leq \max(w_{2s} + \delta D - E, 0);$$

C2 file for strategic bankruptcy if:

$$w_{2s} + \delta D \geq (1 + r)B \quad \text{and} \quad (1 + r)B > \max(w_{2s} + \delta D - E, 0);$$

C3 file for bad fortune bankruptcy if:

$$w_{2s} + \delta D < (1 + r)B \quad \text{and therefore} \quad (1 + r)B > \max(w_{2s} + \delta D - E, 0).$$

It is optimal for consumers to file for bankruptcy if and only if their gains in bankruptcy are bigger than their gains when they choose not to file for bankruptcy (i.e., if and only if $(1+r)B > \max(w_{2s} + \delta D - E, 0)$). That is, the consumer will default whenever her debt in the second period exceeds the level of assets that can be seized and whenever her debt cannot be fully enforced. So, the consumer delivers $\min[(1+r)B, \max(w_{2s} + \delta D - E, 0)]$. We can write the probability of no bankruptcy as $(1 - p_{\text{bankruptcy}}) = p(C1) = \sum_{s} p_s \iota_s (1 - \iota_d)$, and the probability of bankruptcy as $p_{\text{bankruptcy}} = p(C2) + p(C3) = \sum_{s} p_s [\iota_s \iota_d + (1 - \iota_s)]$, where $\iota_s = 1$ if $w_{2s} + \delta D \geq (1+r)B$ and $\iota_d = 1$ if $(1+r)B > \max(w_{2s} + \delta D - E, 0)$.

The borrowers' wealth in each situation is given as follows:

$$W_2 = \begin{cases} w_2 + \delta D - (1+r)B & \text{if no bankruptcy,} \\ w_2 + \delta D - \max(w_{2s} + \delta D - E, 0) & \text{if bankruptcy.} \end{cases}$$

Thus, in case of bankruptcy the lender can receive a payment between $w_{2s} + \delta D$ (if the bankruptcy exemption is zero) and zero (if the bankruptcy exemption exceeds the debtors' wealth in the second period).

The expected return on lending must be no less than the risk-free return. Therefore, the lender's participation constraint is given by

(1) $\quad (1+r_f)B \leq \sum_{s} p_s \iota_s (1 - \iota_d)(1+r)B$

$$+ \sum_{s} p_s [\iota_s \iota_d + (1 - \iota_s)] [\max(w_{2s} + \delta D - E, 0) - \gamma B].$$

The extra interest rate paid, $r - r_f$, is exactly the one needed to off-set the loss incurred by the financial institution when the consumer goes bankrupt. It is the same as a risk premium.

Given a menu of contracts, the consumer chooses a pair (r, B) that maximizes her expected utility function u:

$$\max_{(r,B)} \quad u(c_1) + Eu(c) = u(c_1) + \sum_{s=1}^{S} p_s u(c_{2s}),$$

$$c_1 = w_1 + D + B,$$

$$c_{2s} = w_{2s} + \delta D - \min[(1+r)B, \max(w_{2s} + \delta D - E, 0)] \quad \forall s.$$

Constraint (1) is always valid with equality, since a smaller rate of return r makes the borrower strictly better and still satisfies the lender's participation constraint. Also, since the lender pays the monitoring cost to verify the wage value (w), the contract specified above is such that in bankruptcy, borrowers have no incentives to falsely report the state of nature.

Notice that the lenders' expected return, described by their participation constraint, determines the supply of credit in the economy. The supply of credit depends directly on the punishment level imposed by the legislation through the bankruptcy exemption.

Proposition 1 *Any value of exemptions above the critical value E* makes the supply of credit to individuals zero.*

Proof: See Araujo and Funchal (2005b).

Proposition 2 *As the bankruptcy exemption falls, the interest rate charged to individuals decreases.*

Proof: See Araujo and Funchal (2005b).

In contrast to the supply side, if the bankruptcy exemption increases (reducing the debtors' punishment), the consumer has more incentive to demand credit. This happens because the cost of building another asset that is more aligned with debtors' interests decreases, since they can keep a larger amount of their personal goods if bankruptcy occurs. Such an asset—one that allows debtors to file for bankruptcy at a cost lower than the bankruptcy exemption—acts as a substitute for the original debt contract. In the extreme case of unlimited exemption, the cost of bankruptcy goes to zero, making the demand for credit even more attractive. However, if the bankruptcy exemption goes to zero, individuals can lose everything they have in case of a bad realization of the state of nature, inhibiting their demand for credit.

Proposition 3 *As the bankruptcy exemption falls, the individuals' demand for credit decreases.*

Proof: See Araujo and Funchal (2005b).

Therefore, two distinct forces act in the proposed problem. A decrease in the bankruptcy exemption E expands the supply of credit, thus reducing the interest rate charged to borrowers, since the chances of creditors being repaid are bigger, and they receive more in bankruptcy states. But the demand is repressed, since debtors fear losing their goods. With an increase in E, there is an incentive for consumers to demand credit, since they can build assets aligned with their needs. However, such levels of exemption inhibit the lenders' supply of credit, since both the amount and the chances of repayment fall.

The equilibrium level of credit provided by extreme levels of bankruptcy exemption (0 or unlimited) tends to be very low or even zero. An optimal level of bankruptcy exemption E^{**} may exist, where the resulting equilibrium provides a higher level of credit and welfare in the economy.

2.2   *Empirical Findings*

Araujo and Funchal (2005b, 2015) empirically analyzed the relationship between the degree of debtors' punishment and the development of the personal credit market. The authors used the U.S. personal bankruptcy exemptions—which vary across U.S. states—to construct a proxy of debtors' punishment in case of default. By looking at the changes in the degree of debtors' punishment (across time and states), they show whether and how these changes are linked to credit market development. Using a two-way fixed-effects panel regression to estimate the

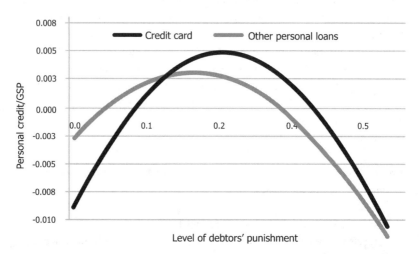

FIGURE 5.1. Non-monotonic shape of the relation between debtors' punishment (measured by the inverse of the normalized exemption) and the credit market development (measured by the ratio of personal credit and Gross State Product [GSP]).

relationship between debtors' punishment and a measure of credit market development, they found that this relationship is not always increasing, and there is actually an intermediate level of punishment that is optimal for credit market development.

Figure 5.1 displays how the amount of personal credit in the economy changes in response to the level of debtor punishment. States with extreme levels of punishment (high or low) tend to have a lower volume of credit relative to states with intermediate levels of protection. These authors' main results suggest that punishment applied by bankruptcy legislation should neither be so harsh that it inhibits credit demand nor so lenient that it reduces credit supply.

3 Optimal Corporate Bankruptcy Law

Writing corporate debt contracts is a complex task. As time passes, firms acquire new debt and more assets. The number of lenders may increase. Prices and firm output change. It becomes increasingly hard to specify how the firm's assets should be allocated under each possible circumstance. Under asymmetry of information, this incompleteness becomes even more pronounced, since creditors cannot write into the contract all the covenants available under perfect information. Bankruptcy laws help mitigate this contract incompleteness by stipulating how the asset division process should take place when firms are bankrupt.

In this section, we review some of the main reasons having good corporate bankrupcy law is important. First, we review some important efficiency-related issues concerning bankruptcy. Then we focus on the case of Brazil, a country that recently conducted a reform in its bankruptcy law. Finally, we look at crises and briefly discuss how a well-designed bankruptcy law can help mitigate their effects and shorten their lengths.

3.1 Efficiency

Corporate bankruptcy laws determine what happens to firms when they can no longer honor their liabilities. Among the main purposes of these laws is reallocating capital from failed firms to more productive activities, leading to higher welfare. However, these laws can also work as an enforcement mechanism of the type discussed in the introduction to this chapter. As such, bankruptcy laws often contain several punitive provisions to provide debtors with the right incentives and increase the payoff of creditors.

The main argument for the inclusion of these provisions is that if bankruptcy is considered sufficiently threatening, managers are less inclined to take excessive risk, expropriate cash flow from the firm, or falsely report the firm's returns. Also, since pro-creditor laws usually increase the recovery rate of credit claims in cases of default, lenders can afford to offer lower rates, increasing the attractiveness of safer projects and limiting risk taking.[9] In doing so, pro-creditor laws reduce the externality that defaulting firms impose on the rest of the borrowing firms.

A feature that is often cited as an important characteristic of pro-creditor laws is the strict observance of the absolute priority rule (APR), a principle stating that debtholders should be paid before equity holders, in descending order of seniority. Legal systems that are prone to liquidating firms in financial distress and follow the APR are often considered to be the pro-creditor benchmark. When capital markets work well, this pro-creditor approach to bankruptcy is known to produce ex-post efficient outcomes.[10]

However, in some cases (specially when capital markets do not work well), ex ante and ex post efficiency do not go hand in hand. These cases provide arguments for legal systems that allow for deviations from the APR and favor firm reorganization rather than liquidation. If managers have specific knowledge about the business and are the only ones capable of restructuring the firm, liquidation is suboptimal. The same is true if creditors' coordination problems lead to inefficient liquidations or if the firm is going through temporary financial distress and is having difficulties obtaining financing due to some sort of credit market friction.

Bebchuk (1988) argues that a bankruptcy code that permits reorganization can increase the value of a distressed firm, particularly if the company is worth more as a going concern or if there are no potential buyers with both accurate information about the company and sufficient resources to acquire it.

Additionally, some authors suggest that APR deviations encourage desirable ex ante investments; that they facilitate the flow of information to creditors, improving the timing of the decision to file for bankruptcy; and that they discourage excessive risk-taking by financially distressed firms (see Eberhart and senbet 1993; Berkovitch et al. 1997; Berkovitch and Israel 1999; Povel 1999).

In summary, when capital markets do not function properly, an efficiency-oriented lawmaker faces a known trade-off between providing the right incentives and preserving firm value.

Araujo and Funchal (2013) also investigate the optimal choice between reorganization and liquidation, but in a different context. They simulate a general equilibrium model with incomplete markets and bankruptcy, in which the optimal bankruptcy law for the economy will depend not only on the costs of each procedure but also on the structure of the productive sector—that is, on how important physical capital is for the economy, relative to variable inputs. Their model has three types of agents: managers; secured creditors, responsible for financing the fixed inputs; and unsecured creditors, who sell the variable input. They compare two types of bankruptcy laws: a pro-reorganization law, in which managers have the right to choose between a reorganization and a liquidation procedure; and a pro-liquidation law, in which firms in financial distress are promptly liquidated.

Figure 5.2 displays the optimal bankruptcy laws, as prescribed by the simulation results from Araujo and Funchal (2013). For physical capital intensive sectors, the best law is pro-liquidation (e.g., Chapter 7 bankruptcy), since it permits secured creditors to recover their claims immediately, making the cost of capital lower. For sectors intensive in variable inputs, the best law is pro-reorganization (e.g., Chapter 11 bankruptcy), since it gives trade creditors another chance to recover their credit, making the cost lower. For extremely high levels of liquidation costs, the best law is pro-reorganization, regardless of the proportion of physical capital.

Araujo and Funchal (2013) also conduct an empirical exercise by using the estimated value of the bankruptcy cost for the United States[11] to assess reorganization and liquidation costs, and the U.S. share of materials and physical capital spent per sector[12] to calibrate the proportion of physical capital and variable input. They use data from the U.S. industrial sector (considered to be industry representative) and identify the technical component—common to the industry in every country—of industry physical capital intensity.

The authors use these data to analyze the optimal bankruptcy law for each country. First they calculating the value-added share of each industry sector for each country (to infer the size of each sector); then they sum the share of each sector that should have a pro-liquidation (or pro-reorganization) procedure. Finally, if the share of the pro-liquidation

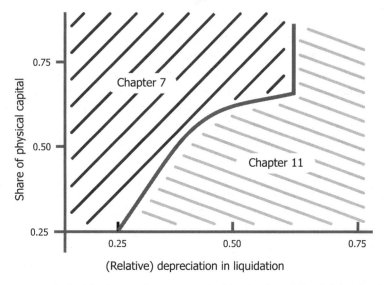

FIGURE 5.2. Optimal bankruptcy law, as prescribed by Araujo and Funchal (2013). For low shares of physical capital and relatively high liquidation costs, the best law is pro-reorganization; when the opposite is true, the best law is pro-liquidation.

sectors is greater than 50%, they consider a pro-liquidation bankruptcy law to be the best for the country. Otherwise, a pro-reorganization bankruptcy law is considered to be the best.

They find that 27 (out of a sample of 44) countries apply procedures aligned with their suggestions. To maximize welfare, approximately 80% of the countries (35 out of 44) should apply a pro-reorganization bankruptcy law. They also find that managers keep a higher proportion of their capital in place when reorganization is available.

These results assume that all countries have bankruptcy costs like those in the United States. If bankruptcy costs are allowed to vary from country to country, Araujo and Funchal (2013) find that countries with higher costs of liquidation (such as Brazil) should move toward a pro-reorganization procedure, while countries with low liquidation costs (like Sweden) should have a more pro-liquidation bankruptcy law.

3.2 The Case of Brazil

Here we present a case of institutional reform that empowered creditors, starting from an environment with very poor creditor protection.

The bankruptcy law reform in Brazil can be seen in light of the trade-off between providing the right incentives to debtors and avoiding inefficient liquidations.

Since the 1990s, several Latin American countries have gone through legislative reforms that have changed the legal framework governing corporate bankruptcy. Brazil was one of these countries. In 1993, the Brazilian Congress initiated an effort to reform the Brazilian corporate insolvency legislation. In December 2004, a new law was finally approved.

The former Brazilian bankruptcy law was part of a very fragmented legal framework governing corporate insolvency, most of which was enacted in the 1940s.

The insolvency process provided both liquidation and reorganization procedures but did not effectively preserve asset values, protect creditor rights during liquidation—leading to an increased cost of capital—or enable viable distressed firms to reorganize. Liquidation was characterized by severe inefficiencies; and reorganization—called *concordata* (composition with creditors)—was extremely rigid and usually unable to provide meaningful options for the firm to recover. There was no formal renegotiation among parties, and the procedure also incentivized informal use of the system to promote consensual renegotiations, notwithstanding an insufficient legislative framework capable of fostering workouts.

Resolving insolvencies used to take, on average, 10 years to complete, making Brazil the country with the slowest insolvency procedures in the world. Figure 5.3 displays the average length of insolvency procedures in Brazil and in seven groups of countries.[13] Notice that the average time to close a business in Brazil was more than twice the average for Latin America. This situation eroded the value of assets and thus lowered the amount received by creditors.

The process of liquidating the firm's assets was usually characterized by procedural inefficiency, lack of transparency, and the so-called succession problem, whereby tax, labor, and other liabilities were transferred to the buyer of the liquidated asset. This liability transfer had the undesirable effect of depressing the market value of the insolvent company's assets.

Another important shortcoming was the bankruptcy priority rule, which was very punitive to creditors. It stipulated that labor and tax claims had priority over all other types of creditors—including secured creditors.

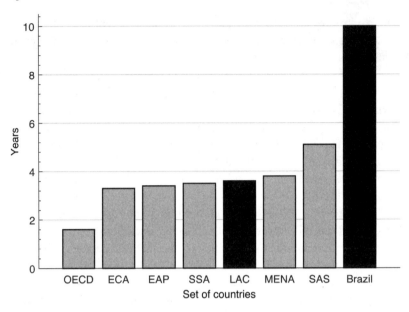

FIGURE 5.3. Average length of insolvency procedures in Brazil compared to seven groups of countries: the Organization for Economic Cooperation and Development (OECD), Latin America and the Caribbean (LAC), the Middle East and North Africa (MENA), Europe and Central Asia (ECA), East Asia and the Pacific (EAP), South Asia (SAS) and sub-Saharan Africa (SSA).

As a consequence of the weak protection given to creditors of insolvent firms, financial markets were characterized by a relatively low credit volume and high interest rates. Distorted incentives and the lack of effective mechanisms to support corporate restructuring resulted in disproportionately high default rates of potentially viable companies. Exit costs were increased for nonviable companies; productivity and employment were reduced.

Creditor recovery rates before the reform illustrate the ultimate effect of an inefficient procedure with poor creditor protection. Until 2005, the recovery rate in cases of bankruptcy in Brazil was a mere 0.2 cents to the dollar, while the averages for Latin American and OECD countries were 26 and 72 cents, respectively. The main reason for such low recovery was the aforementioned priority order, since creditors ranked behind labor and tax claims. After workers and the government were paid, the remaining amount was usually insignificant or even nil.

The ex ante effect of creditors receiving close to nothing from insolvent firms was an increase in the interest rates charged to solvent firms. Before the new law, Brazil had an extremely high interest rate spread (49%), which was more than four times larger than the average spread for Latin American countries (11%) and more than twelve times larger than the average for OECD countries (3.87%). All values refer to the 1997–2002 period.[14]

On June 2005, six months after being signed into law, the new bankruptcy legislation (Law 11,101/05) came into effect.[15] The new law integrated the insolvency system into the country's broader legal and commercial systems, which was an improvement. The new law also provided in- and out-of-court options for reorganization.

The new reorganization procedure—called "judicial reorganiza-tion"[16]—was mostly inspired by Chapter 11 of the U.S. Bankruptcy Code. The new law's aim was to strike a reasonable balance between liquidation and reorganization. It also significantly improved the flexibility of the insolvency legal system by permitting the conversion of reorganization proceedings into liquidation.

Concerning the liquidation and the reorganization procedures, some of the key changes caused by the new Brazilian bankruptcy law are:

1. A change in the priority order in liquidation. Labor credits are now given priority up to an amount equal to 150 times the minimum monthly wage to each worker; residual amounts go to the near-end of the line, together with unsecured creditors; increased priority is given to secured creditors, giving secured claimants priority over tax credits; unsecured creditors have higher priority.
2. Facilitation of the disposal of the firm's assets. The distressed firm may be sold (preferably as a whole) before the creditors' list is formed.
3. Removal of the "succession problem." Labor, tax, and other liabilities are no longer transferred to the buyer of an asset sold in liquidation.
4. Restrictions in the use of bankruptcy for creditors holding low-value claims. Only creditors holding claims higher than 40 times the minimum monthly wages can initiate a bankruptcy procedure.
5. Incentives for lenders of firms under reorganization. Any new credit extended during the reorganization process is given first priority in the event of liquidation.
6. An automatic stay period. Firms under reorganization are granted an automatic injunction, protecting them from secured creditors that seek to seize the debt collateral.

Both the upper bound for labor claims and the increased priority of creditors had a direct impact on expected recovery rates. The second and third changes, in turn, increased the value of the firm in bankruptcy by speeding up the process of valuing the firm in the event of bankruptcy and dissociating the firm's assets from its liabilities.

Another relevant change concerns the new reorganization procedure. Whereas under the previous law, no renegotiation among the interested parties was allowed and only a few parties were entitled to claim assets, now management makes a sweeping proposal for recuperation that must either be accepted by the workers, secured creditors, and unsecured creditors (including trade creditors) or the distressed firm will be liquidated. Therefore, creditors were empowered and play a more significant role in the current procedure than previously, including negotiating and voting on the reorganization plan. These changes motivate creditors to participate more actively in the bankruptcy process.

As stated by Araujo and Funchal (2009), this new design of Brazilian bankruptcy procedures brings new incentives to the interested parties. The incentive for debtors to default strategically is reduced, mainly for two reasons: first, the conditions under which debtors can file for bankruptcy are now limited to those prescribed by law; and second, a reorganization procedure can be converted to liquidation at the creditors' discretion, a feature that nearly eliminates the use of reorganizations as a bargaining mechanism. Figure 5.4 shows the number of liquidation requests and the number of reorganization requests before and after the Brazilian bankruptcy reform. Note that in both cases, the number of requests dropped abruptly after the reform, which is in line with expectations as a consequence of reducing incentives to strategic defaults.

Creditors now have new incentives to actively participate in the bankruptcy procedures, due to three key changes. First, creditors now play a more significant role in the procedures than they did previously, including negotiating the reorganization plan and then voting on its approval. Second, they can file for judicial ratification of out-of-court workouts (facilitating enforcement of the guarantees under the private debt renegotiation contracts). Third, their credit priority in cases of liquidation is higher now than it was under the previous legislation. Figure 5.4C shows an increase in the number of reorganizations in periods of crisis—like the mortgage crises period—when the liquidity default problems were more pronounced. In this case, the number of liquidation

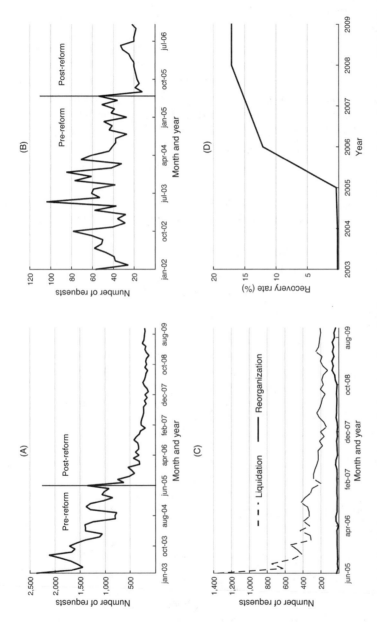

FIGURE 5.4. (A) Liquidation requests before and after the reform; (B) Reorganization requests before and after the reform; (C) Liquidation and reorganization requests after the reform; (D) Creditors' recovery rate.

requests, which was previously more than ten times greater than reorganization requests, dropped to practically the same as the number of reorganization requests. This illustrates the more active behavior of creditors.

Araujo et al. (2012a) study the effect of the Brazilian bankruptcy law reform by employing variations of a difference-in-differences set-up to analyze the behavior of a few debt-related variables. Looking at firm accounting data for 698 publicly traded firms, ranging from 1999 to 2009, they find a reduction in the cost of debt, an increase in total debt, and an even larger increase in long-term debt, following the reform in Brazil. Since secured creditors have benefited more from the new law than the unsecured ones have, the effect is more pronounced on long-term debt, which is known to be more correlated with secured debt. They find no statistically significant effect on short-term debt or loan ownership structures. Araujo et al. (2012a) also look at aggregate data, contrasting the

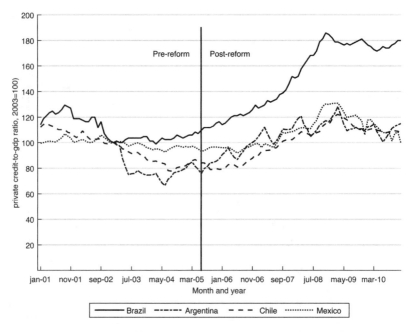

FIGURE 5.5. Ratio between corporate private credit and GDP, in selected countries. The ratio for January 2003, the first period in which information for all countries is available, is normalized to 100. Notice that around mid-2005 all series are close to each other, and as time progresses Brazil detaches itself from the other countries.

time series of the private credit-to-GDP ratio in Brazil with those of
Argentina, Chile, and Mexico. Figure 5.5 provides information on this
variable for these four countries, with January 2003 normalized to 100,
since this is the period when information is available for all countries.
It shows that around mid-2005, all series are close to one another, and
as time progresses, Brazil detaches from the other countries, suggesting
some correlation between the reform and the expansion of private credit.

3.3   Mitigating Crises

In times of economic crisis, the number of bankruptcies usually increases,
so bankruptcy laws can play an important role in alleviating crises and
accelerating turnarounds. Figure 5.6 shows the number of bankruptcies in
selected countries during the 2008 financial crisis, compared to the same
number a few years before.[17]

It is often the case that during crises, some creditors find themselves holding too many claims of bankrupt debtors. If the bankruptcy
law in place produces low recovery rates and slow insolvency resolution, defaults from borrowers can lead to defaults of lenders. The 2008

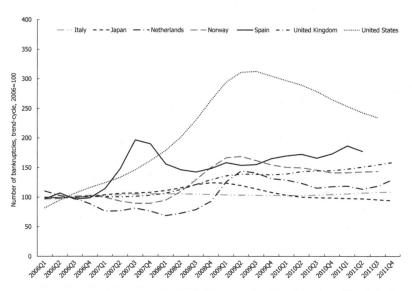

FIGURE 5.6. Number of bankruptcies in selected countries, normalized to 100 for reference
year 2006. Source: OECD (2012).

financial crisis produced numerous examples of creditors facing liquidity problems—and ultimately having to file for bankruptcy themselves—for not being able to recover debt owed to them by defaulting individuals and firms. Similarly, Johnson et al. (2000) report that many bank collapses following the 1998 Russian devaluation were associated with creditors recovering very little of what was owed to them by defaulting debtors. Similar cases were reported throughout Asia during the late 1990s crisis. Ultimately, even lenders not pushed into bankruptcy might find themselves with liquidity problems and be forced to reduce or deny credit to borrowers in sound financial situations.

But if increased recovery rates during a crisis come at the expense of a higher number of liquidations, they may lead to fire sales. If liquidating firms have their assets sold in times when many potential buyers are facing difficulties themselves, the selling price tends to be negatively affected.

Miller and Stiglitz (2010) draw attention to the externalities that arise when bankruptcy laws designed mostly to deal with issues at the firm level are widely used in times of crisis. Following the realization of aggregate shocks with the potential to produce widespread defaults, bankruptcy courts concerned only with idiosyncratic events might fail to consider the potential of large-scale asset disposal to produce fire sales. Miller and Stiglitz (2010) make the case for a "Super Chapter 11" that internalizes these externalities.

Bergoeing et al. (2002) provide an example of how important bankruptcy codes are in facilitating speedy recoveries. They compared the recoveries from the Mexican and Chilean economic crises in the early 1980s. Chile reformed its bankruptcy code in 1982, clearly defining the rights of each creditor and improving the efficiency of bankruptcy procedures. In contrast, Mexico had an obsolete and unwieldy bankruptcy law that dated back to 1943 and stayed in place until 2000. The authors concluded that despite many similarities in initial conditions, the reform of bankruptcy procedures in Chile affected capital accumulation and accelerated the recovery of Chilean economy.

4   Collateral

Debt collateral is one of the most common enforcement mechanisms used in an economy.[18] A substantial portion of debt contracts grants lenders the ability to seize tangible assets belonging to the debtor in case of default. Home mortgages are one example of collateralized debt, and so are many corporate bonds that are backed by equipment and plant.

In the aftermath of the 2008 financial crisis, regulators insisted that collateral requirements be increased, and investors started asking for safer assets, mostly by pressing for more collateral to secure their funds.

Increasing collateral requirements have well-known welfare implications. Since some agents demand the collateral for reasons other than consumption, collateral may not be held by those agents who most wish to consume it. In addition, since the value of the durable good set as collateral limits repayments, reliance on collateral discourages lending.[19]

Moreover, a greater demand for high-quality collateral draws attention to scenarios in which the goods with the potential for collateral are scarce. Araujo et al. (2012b) investigate the implications of several types of collateral regulation in a general equilibrium set-up with incomplete markets and scarce collateral. In their environment, individuals have to put up durable goods as collateral when they want to take short positions in financial markets.[20] Agents are allowed to default on their promises without any punishment other than seizure of the collateral, which is then distributed among creditors. Default will occur whenever the market value of the collateral is lower than the face value of the associated promise.[21]

More precisely, Araujo et al. (2012b) consider a pure exchange economy over two periods, $t \in \{0, 1\}$. In period 1, there is uncertainty regarding the realization of the state of nature $s \in \{1, \ldots, S\}$. The economy is populated by H agents, and there are $L = 2$ goods. Good 1 is perishable, and good 2 is durable without depreciation. Initial endownments are denoted by $e^h \in \mathbb{R}_+^{S^*L}$, where $S^* = S + 1$, and for all goods, there are complete spot markets, with spot prices across states denoted by $p \in \mathbb{R}^{S^*L}$. The utility functions $u^h : \mathbb{R}_+^{S^*L} \longrightarrow \mathbb{R}_+$ represent individual preferences over consumption $x^h \in \mathbb{R}_+^{S^*L}$, and there are J real assets, with prices denoted by $q \in \mathbb{R}_+^J$. Assets are indexed by $j \in \mathcal{J} = \{1, \ldots, J\}$, and their promises are made in units of the perishable good. These promises are denoted by $A_j \in \mathbb{R}^{SL}$.

Also, for each asset there is an associated collateral requirement $C_j \geq 0$, denoted in units of the durable good and always held by the borrower. A key aspect of the model in Araujo et al. (2012b) is its assumption that all assets promise a safe payoff. Thus, assets differentiate themselves only with regard to collateral requirements.

Default happens whenever the face value of the promises made by the agents is higher than the market value of the durable good held by them. So, the payoff of asset j in state s is given by $\min\{1, p_s(s)C_j\}$.

Agent h's portfolio is given by (θ^h, φ^h), where $\theta^h = (\theta_1^h, \ldots, \theta_J^h) \in \mathbb{R}_+^J$ gives the number of units of each asset bought by the agent, and $\varphi^h = (\varphi_1^h, \ldots, \varphi_J^h) \in \mathbb{R}_+^J$ denotes the short positions in the assets.

Agents in this economy choose consumption and portfolios $(x^h, \theta^h, \varphi^h)$, by solving:

$$\max_{x \geq 0, \varphi \geq 0, \theta \geq 0} \quad u^h(x^h)$$
$$\text{s.t.} \quad p(0) \cdot (x^h(0) - e^h(0)) + q \cdot (\theta - \varphi) \leq 0,$$
$$p(s) \cdot (x^h(s) - e^h(s)) - p_2(s)x_2^h(0)$$
$$- \sum_{j \in J}(\theta_j^h - \varphi_j^h)\min\{1, p_s(s)C_j\} \leq 0,$$
$$x_2^h(0) - \sum_{j \in J}\varphi_j^h C_j \geq 0.$$

As usual, a competitive equilibrium is defined by market clearing and agents' optimality conditions.

Definition 3   *A GEI with collateral (GEIC) equilibrium for this economy is a vector $[(\bar{x}^h, \bar{\theta}^h, \bar{\varphi}^h)_{h \in H}; \bar{p}, \bar{q}]$ such that:*

(2) $(\bar{x}^h, \bar{\theta}^h, \bar{\varphi}^h)_{h \in H}$ *solves agents' problem.*

(3) $\sum_{h \in H}(\bar{x}^h(0) - e^h(0)) = 0.$

(4) $\sum_{h \in H}(\bar{x}^h(s) - e^h(s) - \bar{x}_2^h(0)) = 0.$

(5) $\sum_{h \in H}(\bar{\theta}^h - \bar{\varphi}^h) = 0.$

When the set of assets J in the economy is very large, collinearity will render most assets redundant. In this case, there will be a set J^{CC}, containing only S assets, that can replace J as the set of actively traded assets without loss of generality. In this setting, a GEICC equilibrium will be a GEIC equilibrium in which the set of tradable assets contains J^{CC}; and a GEIRC equilibrium will be a GEIC equilibrium with an exogenously fixed set of collateral requirements. (The ending CC stands for complete collateral; the ending RC stands for regulated collateral.)

Araujo et al. (2012b) study how scarcity and an unequal distribution of durable goods with potential for collateral affect risk sharing and welfare. If the durable good is plentiful and satisfies the collateral constraints of the agents, the model is equivalent to a standard Arrow-Debreu model, and competitive equilibrium allocations are Pareto optimal.

In the presence of scarcity, however, most assets are not traded in equilibrium and markets are incomplete. The most interesting result—specially in light of recent regulatory trends—regards margin requirements and constrained efficiency. Araujo et al. (2012b) quantitatively address the question of whether government regulation can lead to welfare improvements if the good with potential for collateral is scarce. They provide a series of examples to illustrate their point.

In one particular numerical exercise, calibrated to match real-world data, Araujo et al. (2012b) study the role of subprime loans for risk sharing. They also investigate who gains and who loses in the economy through regulation. Their example has four states of nature and four types of agents with heterogeneous preferences and endowments calibrated to match income and wealth distribution in the United States. Agent 1 is considered to be rich; agents 2 and 3 are middle-class individuals; and agent 4 is poor. Endowments for nondurable goods are interpreted as income, and endowments for the durable goods are interpreted as wealth.

In this economy, what would be the consequences of regulating default and collateral? In other words, what welfare properties do equilibrium allocations in the regulated economies have, in comparison to unregulated economies?

In the benchmark GEICC equilibrium, two assets are traded. The rich agent 1 lends in the subprime asset and borrows in the safe asset. All other agents borrow exclusively subprime. Agents 2 and 3 (the middle-class agents) actually save some money in the safe mortgage.

Let us start by thinking what would happen if, for example, we banished default altogether, by ensuring than only assets with collateral large enough to ensure full delivery in all states were traded. In Araujo et al. (2012b), the equilibrium that emerges from this extreme regulation is called GEIRC3 and results in all agents being worse off compared to the benchmark equilibrium.

A less stringent regulation would be to forbid only trades in assets with very low collateral requirements (subprime loans). The equilibrium under this environment (called GEIRC2 by the authors) makes agents 1 and 4 worse off, but improves the situation of agents 2 and 3, through lending in the safe asset.

Finally, GEIRC1 corresponds to the equilibrium where there is full default for all traded assets. The rich agent, agent 1, benefits from more lending in the subprime asset (due to the higher interest rate). Agents 2 and 3 cannot be made better off through any regulation. Agents 1 and 4 gain simultaneously if only subprime borrowing is allowed.

Figure 5.7 illustrates the welfare implications for each equilibrium.

From a policy perspective, the main message of the paper is that it is not optimal to regulate subprime loan markets, a result that is a direct consequence of scarcity. The subprime market is populated by borrowers with few durable goods to post as collateral. Regulation would essentially act as a barrier to these borrowers, limiting risk sharing. Moreover, equilibria in regulated economies are often not Pareto ranked, although it is possible to benefit some agents by regulation.

5   Conclusion

In this chapter, we discuss two topics worth revisiting in the wake of the 2008 financial crisis: bankruptcy laws and collateral regulation.

Given the origin of the 2008 financial crisis, the interaction between personal bankruptcy laws and mortgage markets is one that merits further and deeper study. The level of exemptions in personal bankruptcy codes determines the amount of debt that can be discharged. In 2005, the Bankruptcy Abuse Prevention and Consumer Protection Act (BAPCPA) came into effect, reducing the amount of debt that could be discharged. Some economists argue that, by raising the costs of bankruptcy, BAPCPA effectively increased the relative attractiveness of mortgage default. The discussion in the preceding pages helps explain the relation between exemption levels and rate of default.

Bankruptcy laws can also play a role in alleviating crises. A large body of work focuses on ex post efficiency at the firm level, making the case for firm reorganization when there are imperfections in the credit market. When financial distress is correlated among firms, allowing for reorganization can also prevent fire sales and the loss of firm value, speeding economic recovery. Again, one must pay attention to the general equilibrium effects. Excessive lenience may reduce recovery rates and delay debt collection to a point at which creditors themselves would be facing difficulties. In times of crisis, bankruptcy laws that promote expedient recovery of credit are of particular importance to the financial sector.

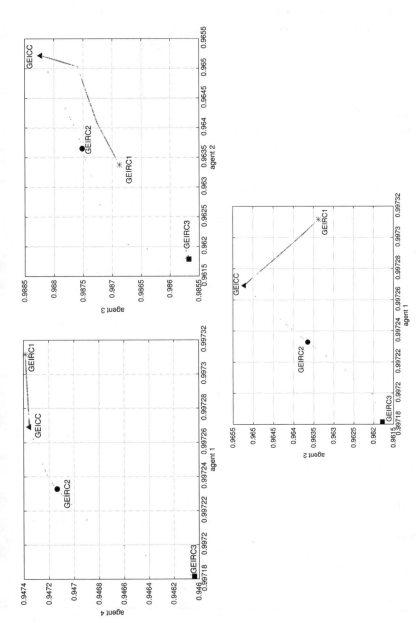

FIGURE 5.7. Welfare of agents under different environments. Regulation (GEIRC equilibria) never leads to Pareto improvement. Agents 1 (rich) and 4 (poor) gain simultaneously if only subprime is allowed (GEIRC1); agents 2 and 3 (both middle-class) cannot be made better off through any regulation. Source: Araujo et al. (2012b).

The results presented in Section 4 illustrate the trade-off faced by law-makers and regulators when attempting to avert future crises and can be used to evaluate the measures recently put in place to avert future crises. The most prominent of these measures is the Dodd-Frank Act. Among its main objectives is to hinder the fraudulent aspect of subprime loans. Certainly, a considerable amount of abuse occurred in the years that preceded the 2008 financial crisis. We should agree with the general idea of making banks reponsible for the misinformation that they have intentionally passed on to low-income home buyers. However, aside from this misconduct, subprime loans play an important role in the allocation of risk in the economy, particularly for low-income individuals. Moreover, collateral regulation does not look very promising in terms of welfare improvement.

We do not discuss in this paper the implications of quantitative easing, a policy undertaken by the Federal Reserve Board and several other central banks in an effort to mitigate the effects of the crisis. For a collateral model of the type discussed in Section 4 investigating the welfare implications of the massive Fed purchases of mortgage-backed securities, we refer the reader to Araujo et al. (2013).

Last but not least, in recent years, new ideas to improve bank regulation have appeared. Although we do not discuss such ideas as bank bail-in, living wills, bank bankruptcy laws, and convertible bonds in this paper, we do believe they are promising venues for future research and deserve more attention from the profession.

Notes

1. See Zame (1993).

2. See Araujo and Páscoa (2002) for a study of different distribution criteria in a GEI framework.

3. Araujo et al. (1998) generalize the result proving equilibrium existence with a continuum of states and without imposing any assumptions on ex post endowments.

4. These results are valid under certain conditions.

5. See, for example, "Downturn pushes more toward bankruptcy," *New York Times*, April 3, 2009.

6. A similar model applies to small businesses. Suppose that, instead of a two-period economy, there is only one time period in which the small firms' owners choose an amount B to invest in their project. The output $w_s B^\alpha$ is uncertain, since

it depends on the realization of the state of nature w_s. In this set-up, we reach the same results as those in the consumption model.

7. Townsend (1979) and Williamson (1986, 1987) show that the standard debt contract is the optimal contract for competitive financial markets. Ying Yan (1996) shows that the standard debt contract is the optimal debt contract for noncompetitive financial markets.

8. Moral hazard is relevant, because borrowers have a choice not to repay their debts.

9. La Porta et al. (1997, 1998) bring evidence of the key role of creditor protection and debt enforcement in supporting credit markets. They address the issue of actually measuring creditor protection and used the created measure to analyze 49 different countries with respect to the design of their commercial laws. Since then, a growing number of empirical studies has focused on the importance of certain aspects of the legal environment to promote financial development and growth, with a vast empirical literature bringing evidence of a positive correlation between creditor protection and credit market development.

10. See, e.g., Baird (1986) and Hart (2000).

11. See Bris et al. (2006).

12. Source: NBER-CES Manufacturing Industry Database, http://www.nber .org/nberces.

13. The Latin American and Caribbean block is composed of Argentina, Bolivia,Brazil, Chile, Colombia, Costa Rica, the Dominican Republic, Ecuador, El Salvador, Guatemala, Haiti, Honduras, Jamaica, Mexico, Nicaragua, Panama, Paraguay, Peru, Uruguay, and Venezuela.

14. See Araujo and Funchal (2005a).

15. See Araujo and Funchal (2005a) and Araujo et al. (2012a).

16. *Reorganização judicial*, in Portuguese.

17. Source: OECD (2012), Entrepreneurship at a Glance 2012, OECD Publishing.

18. See Araujo et al. (2002).

19. See, e.g., Geanakoplos and Zame (2014).

20. This model was introduced by Geanakoplos and Zame (2014).

21. See also Geanakoplos (1996).

References

Araujo, A., R. Ferreira, and B. Funchal (2012a). The Brazilian bankruptcy law experience. *Journal of Corporate Finance 18*(4), 994–1004.

Araujo, A., F. Kubler, and S. Schommer (2012b). Regulating collateral-requirements when markets are incomplete. *Journal of Economic Theory 142*(2), 457–476.

Araujo, A., and B. Funchal (2005a). Bankruptcy law in Latin America: Past and future. *Economia 6*(1), 149–216.

———. (2005b). How much debtors' punishment? *Ensaios Econômicos da EPGE.* Working Paper, Rio de Janeiro, Brazil.

———. (2009). A nova lei de falências brasileira: primeiros impactos. *Revista de Economia Política 29*(3), 191.

———. (2013). Bankruptcy law and credit market: A general-equilibrium approach. *FUCAPE Working Paper Series* (39). FUCAPE: Vitória, Brazil.

———. (2015). How much should debtors be punished in case of default? *Journal of Financial Services Research 47*(2), 229–245.

Araujo, A., and M. Páscoa (2002). Bankruptcy in a model of unsecured claims. *Economic Theory 20*(3), 455–481.

Araujo, A., P. Monteiro, and M. Páscoa (1998). Incomplete markets, continuum of states and default. *Economic Theory 11*(1), 205–213.

Araujo, A., M. Páscoa, and J. Torres-Martínez (2002). Collateral avoids ponzi schemes in incomplete markets. *Econometrica 70*(4), 1613–1638.

Araujo, A., S. Schommer, and M. Woodford (2013). Conventional and unconventional monetary policy with endogenous collateral constraints. NBER Working Paper 19711. Cambridge, MA: National Bureau of Economic Research.

Baird, D. (1986). The uneasy case for corporate reorganizations. *Journal of Legal Studies 15*(1), 127–147.

Bebchuk, L. (1988). A new approach to corporate reorganizations. *Harvard Law Review 101*(4), 775–804.

Bergoeing, R., P. Kehoe, T. Kehoe, and R. Soto (2002). A decade lost and found: Mexico and Chile in the 1980s. *Review of Economic Dynamics 5*(1), 166–205.

Berkovitch, E., and R. Israel (1999). Optimal bankruptcy laws across different economic systems. *Review of Financial Studies 12*(2), 347–377.

Berkovitch, E., R. Israel, and J. Zender (1997). Optimal bankruptcy law and firm-specific investments. *European Economic Review 41*(3), 487–497.

Bris, A., I. Welch, and N. Zhu (2006). The costs of bankruptcy: Chapter 7 liquidation versus Chapter 11 reorganization. *Journal of Finance 61*(3), 1253–1303.

Dobbie, W., and J. Song (2015). Debt relief and debtor outcomes: Measuring the effects of consumer bankruptcy protection. *American Economic Review 105*(3), 1272–1311.

Dubey, P., J. Geanakoplos, and M. Shubik (2005). Default and punishment in general equilibrium. *Econometrica 73*(1), 1–37.

Eberhart, A., and L. Senbet (1993). Absolute priority rule violations and risk incentives for financially distressed firms. *Financial Management 22*(3), 101–116.

Geanakoplos, J. (1996). Promises promises. *Cowles Foundation Discussion Papers.* New Haven, CT: Cowles Foundation.

Geanakoplos, J., and W. Zame (2014). Collateral equilibrium, I: A basic framework. *Economic Theory 56*(3), 443–492.

Hart, O. (2000). Different approaches to bankruptcy. NBER Working Paper 7921. Cambridge, MA: National Bureau of Economic Research.

Johnson, S., P. Boone, A. Breach, and E. Friedman (2000). Corporate governance in the Asian financial crisis. *Journal of Financial Economics* 58(1), 141–186.

La Porta, R., F. Lopez-de Silanes, A. Shleifer, and R. Vishny (1997). Legal determinants of external finance. *Journal of Finance* 52(3), 1131–1150.

———. (1998). Law and finance. *Journal of Political Economy* 106(6), 1113–1155.

Miller, M., and J. Stiglitz (2010). Leverage and asset bubbles: Averting armageddon with Chapter 11? *Economic Journal* 120(544), 500–518.

Morgan, D., B. Iverson, and M. Botsch (2009). Seismic effects of the bankruptcy reform. *Federal Reserve Bank of New York Staff Report* (358). New York: Federal Reserve Bank.

OECD (2012). *Entrepreneurship at a glance.* Paris, France: Organization for Economic Cooperation and Development.

Povel, P. (1999). Optimal "soft" or "tough" bankruptcy procedures. *Journal of Law, Economics, and Organization* 15(3), 659–684.

Townsend, R. (1979). Optimal contracts and competitive markets with costly state verification. *Journal of Economic Theory* 21(2), 265–293.

Williamson, S. (1986). Costly monitoring, financial intermediation, and equilibrium credit rationing. *Journal of Monetary Economics* 18(2), 159–179.

———. (1987). Costly monitoring, loan contracts, and equilibrium credit rationing. *Quarterly Journal of Economics* 102(1), 135–146.

Ying Yan, E. (1996). Credit rationing, bankruptcy cost, and optimal debt contract for small business. *Federal Reserve Bank of Cleveland mimeograph.* Cleveland, OH.

Zame, W. (1993). Efficiency and the role of default when security markets are incomplete. *American Economic Review* 83(5), 1142–1164.

Antes del Diluvio: The Spanish Banking System in the First Decade of the Euro

Tano Santos

1 Introduction

The Spanish banking crisis is one of the most salient chapters of the larger Eurozone crisis. It is, of course, associated with the boom and bust in the real estate sector, like many other banking crises, including the concurrent Irish crisis. It ended in the summer of 2012 when Spain's Eurozone partners put together a banking rescue package to assist the Spanish authorities with the recapitalization of distressed banks.[1] The changes in the Spanish financial system that the crisis has brought are enormous: the *cajas* sector, the notorious private savings and loans at the epicenter of the crisis, which at the peak comprised 50% of the Spanish credit market, is essentially no more. Just as the subprime crisis in the United States wiped out the U.S. investment banking industry by forcing its conversion into banks, the bust in the Spanish real estate sector wiped out the cajas, also by making them into banks. This paper provides a bird's-eye view of the evolution of the Spanish banking system, comprising both banks and the aforementioned cajas, in the years leading up to the crisis. I only briefly discuss the crisis itself and its handling by the Spanish authorities.

Figure 6.1 summarizes some striking macroeconomic trends during this period. Figure 6.1A shows the evolution of three variables: housing prices

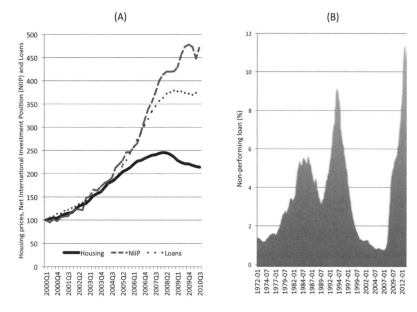

FIGURE 6.1. Panel A: Housing prices, absolute value of the Net International Investment Position (NIIP) and loan portfolio of credit institutions, all normalized by their corresponding values in 2000Q1 and multiplied by 100. The housing prices are in euro per square meter and correspond to assessment prices, not actual transactions data. Quarterly: 2000Q1–2013Q1. Panel B: Non-performing loan (in %) of credit institutions. Monthly: 1972:01–2013:05. Data source: Bank of Spain

in nominal terms, the (negative of the) net international investment position (NIIP) of Spain, and the loans to the private sector by Spanish credit institutions. All three variables are normalized by their values in the first quarter of 2000. The sample goes from 2000Q1 to 2010Q3; the vertical line denotes the peak of the real estate cycle. The initial years of the euro were associated with three events: strong current account deficits that resulted in large liabilities against the rest of the world, unprecedented growth in the loan portfolios of Spanish banks and cajas, and surging real estate prices. (Figure 6.2D shows real estate prices both in nominal as well as real terms.) The euro is at the heart of these trends, but why is a deeper question this paper does not attempt to address.

This paper is concerned with the behavior of Spanish credit institutions during the first decade of the euro. There are three types of credit institutions in Spain. First there are the commercial banks, which range from the large international bank (BBVA and Santander) to the purely

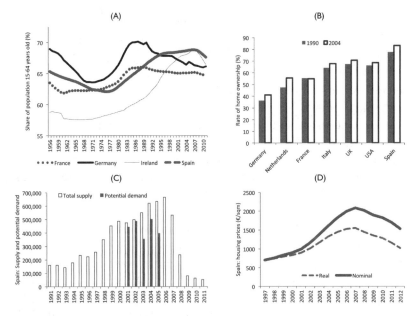

FIGURE 6.2. Panel A: Percentage of the population between 15 and 64 years of age. Annual: 1956–2011. Source: OECD. Panel B: Aggregate homeownership rates in selected OECD countries. Source: Andrews and Caldera (2011), Table 1. Panel C: Number of new housing starts for the years 1991–2011 and potential demand as estimated by García Montalvo (2007, Cuadro 2) for the years 2000 to 2005. Source for housing starts: Ministerio de Fomento. Panel D: Housing prices (euros (€) per square meter (sqm)) in nominal and in euros of 1997. Annual: 1997–2012. Source: Bank of Spain and IMF

national banks (Sabadell and Popular). The second class are the cajas, which were private savings and loans. As we shall see, the cajas had a peculiar governance structure that made them easy prey for the powerful regional political classes of Spain. Finally there are credit unions, which are so tiny compared to the commercial banks and cajas that I ignore them in what follows. Spanish commercial banks operate under regulations and norms similar to those in many other jurisdictions. All the main Spanish banks are publicly traded; certainly BBVA and Santander, the two behemoths of the Spanish financial system, are widely followed by analysts. In contrast, the cajas were not publicly traded and, though not unique to Spain, were the peculiarity of the Spanish financial system. They were, it is worth emphasizing, private institutions but were effectively controlled by the regional and municipal government sector, though supervised by the Bank of Spain. They were also the most dynamic part of the credit market during the two decades preceding the crisis, expanding aggressively to account for roughly 50% of loans and deposits on the eve of the crisis.

To gauge the enormity of the banking crisis, Figure 6.1B shows the nonperforming loan (NPL) ratio of Spanish credit institutions, that is, the percentage of delinquent loans. The Bank of Spain data, publicly available on its superb website, allows for the construction of this series dating back to the 1960s. The plot shows the monthly NPL ratio starting in 1972, the year the supervision of the cajas was transferred to the Bank of Spain, and ending in May of 2013. The plot summarizes well Spanish banking history over the past 40 years or so. The three Spanish banking crises are easy to spot. The first one, from the mid-1970s to the early 1980s, followed a period of liberalization and deregulation of the Spanish banking system; it was shaped by economic crisis induced by the oil shocks during that period. The second was associated with the severe recession of the first half of the 1990s. As in the case of the current one, the banking crisis then followed real estate boom. That crisis produced what was then the largest failure in Spanish banking, that of Banesto. The lessons of that crisis echo in the third one, which is the one currently raging. As can be seen, the NPL ratio has raced through its previous peak and has now become the most serious crisis in the past 40 years. It is a crisis like no other.

But what is perhaps most striking is the very low level of loan delinquency during the roughly first decade of the euro. It was during that first decade, between, say, 1998 and 2007, that all the bad real estate developer and construction loans as well as mortgages were granted. The bubble masked the serious credit quality problems developing in the banking system for many years. But more importantly it masked the serious design flaws in the governance structure of the cajas sector, which had become 50% of the Spanish financial system. This point has been made recently by Fernández-Villaverde et al. (2013): bubbles make for difficult inferences of the underlying governance structures of the economy subject to a speculative cycle and thus make it difficult to correct whatever imbalances are developing. The cajas are a case in point. The governance issues were well understood by many, but it was difficult to muster the evidence needed for reform when they were posting impressive profits; meanwhile their balance sheets were increasingly biased toward real estate risk and wholesale funding.

What was in need of reform? What were the governance problems in the cajas sector? The cajas had a peculiar status. They were private entities with ill-defined property rights that made them subject to political capture. The 1985 law that regulated the governance of the cajas enshrined the principle of local political representation, and both municipal and regional governments made their presence felt in the governing bodies of the cajas. Local governments, which are granted ample powers under the 1978 Spanish Constitution, were quick to regulate the cajas to further increase their control over them. Liberalization of the Spanish credit market and the loose monetary conditions that accompanied the introduction of the euro allowed them to grow and feed, and be fed by, the real estate bubble. They were attractive targets for political capture precisely because they were seen as the instrument to fund the many real estate projects that create the short-run prosperity that helps reelect local government officials. Thus, it is not surprising that many cajas were run at some point or another by prominent local politicians or even national ones and that most of them had to be restructured by the Bank of Spain during the crisis.

Interestingly, banks tracked the cajas quite closely. The cajas had traditionally more exposure to real estate than banks did, but banks also significantly increased the fraction of their loans going to real estate developers, construction companies, and mortgages during the first decade of the euro. In addition, the banks didn't slow down their lending or stop the securitization machine before the cajas did. So why did the banks fare better than the cajas? There are many possible reasons for this. One is that the banks were skimming the cream from the market, picking the best risks and leaving the worst ones for the cajas.[2] Bad governance may also have led to poorer management of the cajas, and this may have resulted in worse lending decisions. The combination of larger quantities and lower quality may have been enough to undo the sector. Finally, the cajas may have focused their lending on politically motivated projects, subject as they were to pressures by the local political elites, to which the banks were immune.

Bad governance is always a problem in any industry, but banks have additional safeguards against mismanagement in the form of bank supervisors. Thus, the Bank of Spain is another key element in this story. The Spanish central bank had the reputation of being a tough supervisor, both because of its handling of previous banking crisis and its supervisory innovations. It took an approach to supervision that emphasized economic realities rather than accounting rules, in an effort to exercise as much control as possible over the risks in the banking sector. Two examples attest to the unusual approach of the Bank of Spain to supervision. The first is the famous system of dynamic provisioning, which aims to build buffers over the cycle to smooth the flow of credit. This was met with much opposition from accountants, who prefer to recognize losses when they happen. The Bank of Spain instead stuck to the sound idea of forcing the banks to provision at the peak of the cycle, when banks typically grant loans of lower quality and can afford to provision for them, and not at the trough, when they only fund the safest credit and is very costly to provision.

The second supervisory tool had to do with the treatment of off-balance-sheet liabilities. Spain became the largest securitization market in the Eurozone and the second largest in Europe after the United Kingdom. Spanish securitization issues had the standard credit enhancements granted by the sponsors: whereas in other jurisdictions, such as the United States, securitization was seen as a way to spread assets and save on regulatory capital, the Bank of Spain forced consolidation of securitized assets whenever some of the risk was retained by the sponsor, forcing capital charges against those assets. This meant that in Spain, the shadow banking system was in plain sight. In this the Spanish experience is of some interest to students of banking, as it can inform current debates about supervision, as well as the efficacy of some of the tools being proposed to prevent banking crises.

Spain had a better supervisory framework than many other jurisdictions, but in retrospect it proved insufficient to prevent this enormous crisis. One lesson is perhaps that there is no substitute for judicious discretion: the problems were evident as they were happening and required action. Instead these tools may have led to an excessively complacent view of the ability of the Spanish banking system to absorb the shock when it came, as many expected it would. We will see that many inside the Bank of Spain saw and criticized this complacent attitude to no avail.

It is important to emphasize that the imbalances building in the Spanish economy were rather apparent and that policy makers and even the public were not blind to them. Indeed, a side aim of this paper is to change the view that some observers have that the bubble and the imbalances went unnoticed in Spain. Nothing could be further from the truth. The real estate bubble had been a topic of conversation in Spain since the early 2000s. Some academics, such as José García-Montalvo were, early on, vocal about the imbalances building in the Spanish real estate sector, and his warnings became more urgent as the bubble worsened. Jaime

Terceiro, both an academic of distinction and head of Caja Madrid until the mid-1990s, correctly diagnosed the governance issues plaguing the cajas and repeatedly pointed out the dangers associated with those governance flaws. Moreover, people who were going to have serious policy responsibilities had written extensively about the systemic dangers associated with the ongoing real estate boom. These include, for example, Miguel Sebastián, who became head of the economic office of the prime minister (a Council of Economic Advisors of sorts) in 2004 and Miguel Ángel Fernández Ordóñez, who was to become governor of the Bank of Spain in 2006. The list goes on, and their writings inform much of this paper. The point is that Spanish authorities were not caught sleeping at the wheel; rather, they saw the wall coming and decided not to steer the car away from it. This is important, because it furthers our understanding that speculative cycles are widely recognized but rarely acted on.

However, the source of exogenous variation that explains all these events is outside the scope of this paper. This is a period that saw real estate and public debt bubbles across many countries, including the United States, Ireland, Spain, and Greece, which suggests a common underlying factor for all of them. Overly loose monetary policies by the main central banks or the savings glut of exported economies are typically blamed for these global conditions. One possibility is that credit flows into some countries and not in others because their size allows them to absorb substantial amounts of this global credit glut. If these flows are intermediated by financial sectors with weak governance structures and plagued with agency problems, they may lead to poor capital allocation decisions and perhaps to speculative cycles supported by these large flows of credit. In globally integrated capital markets, weak governance banking systems may attract foreign, uninformed, capital in search of attractive yields. These capital inflows may in turn induce price appreciation dynamics that may mask the weak governance institutions underpinning the banking system in the first place. In addition, foreign investors have weak incentives to monitor as their investments are typically held in the form of debt. The cajas sector may have played that role in the Spanish situation: it was simply a weak link in a world with too much credit in search of high quality paper.

There are other questions that this paper does not address. As mentioned, it does not go further than 2009 and thus offers only brief comments about the crisis and how it was handled by the authorities. In addition, it does not present cross-sectional evidence beyond the distinction between cajas and banks. Current work by this author is directed toward a more comprehensive history of the Spanish banking system in the euro years, including the crisis. Finally, many aspects of the run up to the crisis deserve more focused research. There is, as we shall see, a lively debate among Spanish researchers about what factors explain the real estate bubble, and the dust is far from settled. All accounts of the Spanish banking crisis have a tentative aspect at this stage.

The paper proceeds as follows. Section 2 offers a brief survey of the real estate bubble in Spain, a necessary ingredient to understand the Spanish banking crisis. Section 3 describes the main actors in the Spanish banking crisis: the commercial banks, the cajas, and the Bank of Spain. Section 4 analyzes the evolution of the balance sheet of the Spanish banking system during the years preceding the crisis. Section 5 covers the early stages of the crisis, and Section 6 concludes.

2   The Real Estate Bubble

Spain grew at an average rate of 3.5% during the years 1999–2007, well above the rates for euro area (about 2%) and the United States (2.6%). Unemployment came from the dizzying heights of almost 16% in 1999 to slightly above 8% in 2007, the lowest unemployment rate in Spain since the late 1970s. This was accomplished in an environment where inflation was relatively low and stable, though higher than that of most trading partners, and public finances were being stabilized. Spain's gross debt to gross domestic product (GDP) ratio, a standard measure of fiscal probity, reached 36% in 2007. It is important to emphasize that all these positive trends preceded the introduction of the euro and had already been in place since the mid-1990s, when the economy was recovering from the recession in the first half of that decade and economic policy was dictated by the need to fulfill the requirements of euro membership.

It is in this benign environment that the real estate bubble began.[3] In the decade between 1997Q1 and the peak of the real estate bubble in 2008Q1, prices grew more than 200%, from 691 €/m^2 to 2,101 €/m^2.[4] In the same period, the consumer price index (CPI) went up by 40%, according to the Spanish Statistics Institute (INE). Figure 6.2D shows the housing prices in both nominal as well as real terms for the period 1997–2012. This plot underestimates the price appreciation in cities like Madrid or Barcelona, which saw much stronger booms.

2.1 Demographics and the Real Estate Bubble

Every bubble has an "honest origin," whether a technological innovation, a financial innovation that allows the extension of credit or risk sharing to a sector hitherto excluded from financial markets, or some unexpected demand shock that justifies the price increases. The Spanish housing bubble was no exception. Demography is the first place to look when it comes to housing.[5] The baby boom happened in Spain (and in Ireland) about a decade and half later than in other core countries in the Eurozone.[6] Figure 6.2A shows the proportion of the population between 15 and 64 years of age in four countries in the Eurozone. France and Germany had peaks on this metric in the mid-1980s, whereas Ireland and Spain had them in the mid-2000s. Clearly this peak has two opposing effects: there is an increase in the demand for housing and in the availability of labor supply for the construction sector to produce the new houses needed. Importantly, Spaniards access housing through ownership rather than rentals; thus, so the rather loose argument goes, demographic shocks can induce an increase in real estate prices. Indeed, Spain had one of the highest ownership rates among large economies on the eve of the euro, and it increased even more after the euro was launched (see Figure 6.2B).

In addition, Spain had very high levels of youth unemployment during the crisis in the first half of the 1990s, so the potential for household formation was certainly enormous.[7] New households are mostly driven by youngsters leaving their parents' homes, and some evidence suggests that the age at which these youngsters were purchasing their first home was dropping throughout the first half of the 2000s.[8] Other factors, such as household splits due to divorces, account for a small percentage of new households.

Spain also experienced strong immigration flows during the first decade of the euro. Of course the boom had a lot to do with immigration in the first place. As González and Ortega (2009) note, Spain topped international rankings in terms of immigration, both in absolute and relative terms. Between 2001 and 2006 the share of Spain's population that was foreign born more than doubled, from 4.8% to 10.8%. As before, immigration increases demand as well as supply of housing. To disentangle the many effects that confound the demand effects of the immigration flows on housing, González and Ortega (2009) use cross-sectional variation in immigration across the Spanish provinces and historical location patterns by country of origin. They estimate that immigration increased housing prices by about 50% and was responsible for 37% of the total construction of new housing units between 1998 and 2008.

2.2   Regulation and Taxation

Regulatory developments, or the lack thereof, as well as taxation also are typically mentioned as factors, though it is difficult to attribute the real estate boom to any single legal development. In particular, the supply of land is a constant topic of policy debate in Spain and has been blamed for the increase in housing prices.

Laws regulating the supply of land have always been rigid in Spain,[9] the efforts of successive governments notwithstanding, and thus it is difficult to claim that this factor was the main driver of the boom. But this was a constant theme in policy discussions as early as 1996 and 1997 and as a result of these debates, a new law was passed in 1998 to facilitate the supply of developable land and thus slow the increase in housing prices already taking place. Land prices obviously incorporate the expectations of housing appreciation, which were increasingly delinked from economic fundamentals.[10] It is indeed the case that land supply was certainly limited in the early stages of the real estate bubble. As García-Montalvo (2000, 85) showed using 1998 data, "urban land" was only 1.5% of total available land, lower than for other European countries.

The debate on whether restricted land supply was an important factor in the real estate bubble is still ongoing. For instance, García-Montalvo (2010) argues against it, claiming that land availability does not have any explanatory power for housing prices. In addition, he dismisses demographic factors as an explanation for the real estate bubble. Instead, Garriga (2010) builds a structural model and calibrates it to the Spanish economy circa 1995; in his calibration, fundamentals (demographics, interest rates, and land supply) can account for more than 80% of the real increase in housing prices. What is clear, though, is that the efforts to increase land supply did not make a significant dent in real estate prices, and it could be argued that they increased the misallocation of resources by making more land available for unwise real estate development projects.

One last issue concerns the fiscal treatment of ownership versus rental. As already mentioned, the rental market in Spain is essentially nonexistent and, once again, successive efforts to develop it have systematically failed. Many argue that the uncertainty surrounding the enforceability of rental contracts deters a more vigorous development of the rental market.[11] In addition, ownership has a very favorable tax treatment that makes renting unattractive. Traditionally, Spain has offered the standard mortgage interest rate deduction, though with caps, and between 1985 and 1989, this deduction was extended to second homes. This was key in a country where the ultimate dream is the weekend apartment near the coast. An interesting legal development that seems to add to the thesis that the timing of taxation changes bears some blame for the real estate boom is that the income tax code allowed for a deduction for rentals between 1992 and 1998, but this deduction was eliminated in 1999. In addition, there are several plans (Planes de Vivienda) offering direct subsidies to families seeking homeownership.[12]

2.3   Monetary Channels

Monetary channels may have played an important role as well in the Spanish real estate bubble. Indeed, the positive economic trends in Spain occurred while nominal interest rates, and spreads with respect to German bonds in the case of the European periphery, were dropping globally. The fall in inflation rates was not enough to compensate for the strong correction in nominal rates, and as a result, real interest rates also dropped. This drop was particularly pronounced in the case of Spain. The ex post three-month real interest rate was 5.31% between 1990 and 1998, whereas it was −.04% between 1999 and 2005. In the same periods the rates were 3.17% and 1.64%, respectively, in Germany and 2.21% and .72% in the United States. Evidence on the U.K. 10-year indexed bonds confirms this drop in real interest rates. Yields were 3.76% and 2.08% in the two periods considered.[13]

As many have argued, one possibility is that monetary policy was too loose, and the drop in interest rates produced a real estate appreciation that led to speculative dynamics. The argument is that had the European Central Bank (ECB) applied the appropriate Taylor rule *for Spain*, the real estate bubble would not have happened. It is indeed the case that if one applies a simple Taylor rule with standard weights to Spain and compares it with the actual rate, the Taylor residuals were negative.[14] There is a strong negative correlation between the average Taylor residuals in the first years of the euro and real house price changes in the same period.

In particular, Spain, Ireland, and Greece were countries with particularly strong negative average residuals and equally strong real housing price increases.[15]

In addition, the drop in nominal interest was bound to have a strong effect in Spain for two reasons. First, the fact that Spaniards access housing through ownership meant that any fluctuation in housing prices was destined to have widespread wealth effects.[16] Second, more than 80% of mortgages in Spain are adjustable rate mortgages, and thus monetary policy is transmitted directly to household balance sheets.[17] These wealth effects may have fueled in turn the housing price dynamics in Spain. Finally, strong competition among cajas for a significant share of the mortgage market, and the corresponding servicing fees, may have reduced mortgage rates further.

When evaluating these plausible explanations for the Spanish real estate boom, the reader should keep in mind that whatever the driving force behind the real estate bubble in Spain, supply responded dramatically. As Scheinkman (2014, 9) emphasizes, it is the signature of bubbles that they come accompanied by strong supply responses. It is difficult to assess what the gap was between supply and the actual and potential demand for housing, but estimates of excess supply run in the several hundreds of thousands. Figure 6.2C shows the total number of housing starts in Spain in the two decades from 1991 to 2011. Notice the enormous increase in housing starts during the years of the real estate boom. As mentioned, Spain saw some remarkable population growth during that period, so obviously the demand for housing grew with it. García-Montalvo (2007) estimates the potential housing demand using aggressive estimates on household formation in Spain during 2000–2005 in order to bias the estimate of the demand upward within reasonable bounds. In no year did housing demand exceed the number of housing starts, and the gap seems to increase as the boom progresses. These numbers have to be interpreted with great caution, as they hide great heterogeneity in both demand and supply. But it is the ultimate signature of a bubble that even in the presence of enormous supply effects, prices keep advancing to new heights. The strong supply response is not surprising. Spain has some very fine civil engineering and construction companies. These companies in addition gained enormous experience under the phenomenal cycle of public investments that had taken place in Spain since the 1980s, in a effort to bring up the quality of public facilities, highways, and airports and build a state-of-the-art high-speed train network. Perhaps the combination of sophisticated construction and civil engineering companies and the inflow of low-skilled workers is an important element in the construction boom.

Credit of course plays a critical role in this story, as in any real estate boom. We turn next to the funding side of the real estate boom.

3 The Spanish Financial Sector on the Eve of the Crisis

Many actors took part in the Spanish banking crisis. First are the households and corporations, both resident and nonresident, driving the demand for real estate. Second are the real estate developers and construction companies, supplying the apartments and commercial properties in unprecedented volumes. Third are the local and central government authorities in charge of the legal environment in which supply and demand meet, as well as on the demand side through, for example, the many infrastructure projects undertaken during this period. Finally, there is the banking system that is funding it all. A thorough account of the Spanish real estate bubble requires a proper understanding of the objectives and incentives of each of these actors as well as the restrictions under which they operated. Here I focus solely in the role played by the Spanish banking sector. I first offer an overview and brief history of the Spanish commercial banks. I then turn to the cajas sector. The Bank of Spain occupies the last section.

3.1 The Spanish Commercial Banks

On the eve of the euro, the Spanish credit market was dominated by two types of institutions: banks and the savings and loans, the notorious cajas. There are other credit institutions, but they are too small to matter and I ignore them in what follows (Table 6.1 shows the classification of the Spanish financial system used by the Bank of Spain for reporting purposes). This structure of the Spanish credit market was the result of a profound liberalization that spanned well over a decade, from the early 1970s to the late 1980s.[18] Prior to that the Spanish banking system was highly regulated: interest rates had to fluctuate within fixed floors and ceilings, and banks had limited flexibility on how to allocate loans, because they were required to favor investments in sectors officially targeted for development. In addition, branch expansion was restricted. Liberalization of

TABLE 6.1 **Financial institutions: Classification of financial institutions according to the Bank of Spain**

MFI[a]			
Bank of Spain			
OMFI[b]			
		Credit Institutions	
			Banks
			Saving banks (cajas)
			Credit co-operative banks
			Specialized credit institutions
			Other credit institutions
		Money market funds	
		Electronic money institutions	
Non-MFIs			
	Insurance Corp. and pension funds		
	Financial auxiliaries (brokers)		
	Other financial intermediaries		

[a]Monetary Financial Institutions
[b]Other Monetary Financial Institutions

the credit market, as is usually the case, immediately resulted in a banking crisis, as poorly managed banks were forced to compete for funding while shifting their portfolios toward riskier loans. The oil shocks aggravated an already serious situation by affecting corporate loan portfolios, and soon the crisis engulfed a large part of the entire banking system. Of the 110 banks operating in Spain in 1977, 51 had solvency issues between 1978 and 1983; only in that last year, the 20 banks of the Rumasa conglomerate were taken over by the authorities. These 51 entities made up 25% of the assets of the entire sector and 20% of its deposits.[19]

Unfortunately, the crisis caught the Bank of Spain with limited supervisory and restructuring tools. When the crisis started, Spain did not have either a deposit insurance mechanism or a formal receivership procedure. The Spanish authorities thus had to improvise to create the tools needed to handle an unprecedented systemic crisis, something that would be repeated in the most recent crisis. In 1977, The Spanish FDIC (called the *Fondo de Garantía de Depósitos en Establecimientos Bancarios*, or FGDEB) was created.[20] It was originally just a deposit insurance corporation without any resolution authority. This proved insufficient, given the magnitude of the crisis, and in 1980 the FGDEB was given resolution powers. It was only then that the slow process of resolving of the Spanish banking crisis can be said to have begun.[21] Simultaneously a similar deposit guarantee and resolution authority institution was created for the cajas, though they were largely free from the problems plaguing the Spanish banks.

This crisis, as banking crises always do, produced a more concentrated banking system. By 1986, shortly after Spain's entry in the European institutions and once the worst of the banking crisis was over, the Spanish credit market was dominated by seven large banks (Banesto, Central, Popular, Hispano, Santander, Bilbao, and Vizcaya) and the cajas, which were not then what they were to become. There was also a string of state-owned banks, of which the largest was Banco Exterior. Finally, and under the encouragement of the Bank of Spain, there was a small presence of foreign banks.

Entry in the European institutions, which took place in 1986, gave a renewed impetus to the liberalization of the Spanish economy.[22] The Second Banking Coordination Directive in 1988 established the creation of a Single Market for Financial Services on January 1, 1993. Spanish bankers, as well as authorities, were wary that the single market would produce the takeover of the main banks by foreign entities, so a second merger wave ensued. Banco de Bilbao and Banco de Vizcaya merged first, in 1988, to form BBV. The "A" of BBVA came afterward, when BBV merged with Argentaria, which was the entity created in 1991 to consolidate the state-owned banks.[23] Banco Central and Banco Hispanoamericano merged in 1991 to create the largest credit entity at the time, BCH. The recession that started in 1992 brought yet another virulent banking crisis, in this case affecting Banesto, which at the time was one of the largest banks in Spain. Banesto was put into receivership by the Bank of Spain in 1993 and sold to Santander in 1994. This sale is at the origin of Santader's growth, which continued in 1999 when it merged with BCH. The resulting entity was called Banco Santander Central Hispano (BSCH) until 2007, when the name was changed to Banco Santander.

Santander and BBVA continued their growth through a strategy of international expansion. BSCH went on to acquire Abbey National in 2004, and in 2007 a joint takeover of ABN AMRO landed Santander the Brazilian subsidiary of the Dutch bank, Banco Real, which was Santander's ultimate objective. The key international acquisition of BBVA occurred in 2000, when it took a majority stake in Bancomer to become a dominant player in the Mexican banking system (BBVA Bancomer).

3.2   The Cajas

DEFINITION AND HISTORICAL CONTEXT. The other half of of the Spanish deposit institutions are the cajas de ahorro (savings and loans), the epicenter of the current financial crisis in Spain. The cajas are private, deposit-taking institutions identical to banks except that their profits revert to a foundation that funds public-minded projects with these profits. These projects range from cultural activities to social assistance programs and research related activities. Roughly speaking, a caja is thus a commercial bank plus a foundation. There are two additional differences between the commercial banks and the cajas. First they had very different governance structures, and second, property rights were poorly defined in the case of the cajas.

The cajas have a long and venerable history, covering roughly four distinct periods. The first runs from their foundation, in the first half of the nineteenth century, to the advent of the Spanish Second Republic (1931). During that period, the cajas provided basic financial services to the poor and underprivileged. They remained small, local, and devoted to charitable activities. They were lightly regulated and from the very beginning, they were encouraged by the state as a means of providing much-needed stability in the financial sector. They were conservative financial institutions in that they were funded solely with deposits and lent only to the best available credit in their local area. The Second Republic and the Franco years introduced a period of progressive involvement by the state. Essentially the temptation to use the significant pool of savings in the cajas to fund public-sector deficits was too large to resist, and gradually the cajas were forced to have a substantial fraction of their assets in public debt or state-owned enterprises, measures that partially applied to banks as well.

The third phase starts when the operational equality between banks and cajas, on both sides of the balance sheet, was enshrined in law, with the passage of the RD 2290/1977. It is perhaps not coincidental that the law came precisely when Spanish banks were entering the aforementioned crisis, and the cajas, which had much healthier balance sheets, were seen as a readily available substitute for the ailing banks. Starting in 1977, the cajas, sheltered as they were from the causes of the banking crisis, were well positioned to compete with the debilitated banks in the Spanish credit market. In addition, the 1977 reform, in the spirit of the political times in Spain, democratized the cajas. In particular, the

"General Assembly" was to be the controlling body of the caja and was to be formed by representatives of depositors, founders, and local corporations. Still the governance structure was soon deemed to be inconsistent with the political development of Spain, which was devolving into a highly decentralized country dominated by powerful regions. As a result, the governance of the cajas was further reformed in 1985 with passage of the a new law aimed at providing the cajas with robust governance structures and ushering the fourth and last stage in the cajas history.[24] Because the governance of the cajas was a key ingredient in Spain's financial crisis, we turn to this issue next.

GOVERNANCE OF THE CAJAS.   To summarize, as the Spanish banks were entering their biggest crisis, the cajas were made operationally into banks. Tighter regulations and conservative management had left the cajas with healthier balance sheets and made them a viable alternative to the debilitated banking system. The regulatory changes brought about by the 1977 and 1985 reforms, discussed shortly, opened the door for the expansion of the cajas. However, the governance of the cajas had serious design flaws, which proved fatal once the credit bubble started. The cajas were not publicly traded institutions, but the 1985 law endowed them with governance institutions that mimicked those of publicly traded institutions. Unfortunately, form is no substitute for substance. The main flaws in the governance of the cajas were two.[25]

First, and as already mentioned, the cajas were private entities— roughly, banks owned by foundations. They operated and grew exclusively with retained earnings, well above the original capital supplied by their founders, who only had a minority interest in the cajas. Property rights were ill defined, something that would play a critical role in the early stages of the crisis. In particular, the cajas lacked shares, and thus shareholders. In addition, they lacked clear recapitalization mechanisms. Yes, something like a share existed (the *cuota participativa*), but it carried only cash flow and no control rights, rendering them unattractive as investment vehicles, given the serious governance concerns surrounding the cajas.[26]

A subtle consequence resulted from this lack of clear definition of property rights: since the cajas had no shares, they could not be acquired by banks, but the cajas could acquire banks. Thus, the takeover mechanism as a disciplining device was absent, which rendered the internal governance of the cajas all the more important. This key point was unappreciated at the time. The banks had undergone a process of international diversification both on the asset side of the balance sheet (as was the case for Santander and BBVA) and on the liability side. The euro had removed the exchange rate risk that had always impeded the flow of capital into Spain, and many foreigners rushed in to invest in the now-large Spanish commercial banks, bringing greater oversight and better governance practices. Nothing of the sort could happen to the cajas. Moreover, the fact that the cajas could own banks meant that they could "export" the bad governance to the banks they acquired. Indeed, the only bank to fail in this crisis, Banco de Valencia, was controlled by a caja, Bancaja, which was merged with Caja Madrid during the early stages of the crisis to form Bankia, the large behemoth that ended up nationalized in 2012.[27] Finally, because they were not publicly traded, there were no pricing signals to facilitate information aggregation and discovery; market participants had to rely on opaque primary markets for bank debt to learn the views of the market at large on the solvency of those institutions. It is important to note that the cajas filed regularly with the Spanish equivalent of Securities and Exchange Commission and were subject to standard auditing processes.

Second, these reforms, and the 1985 law in particular, ensured that the cajas were going to be controlled by the local political elites. Indeed, the 1985 law established that the cajas were to be governed by three institutions. First was the "general assembly," a shareholder meeting of sorts, which was to be the ultimate decision body of the caja. The law enshrined the percentage of the vote that the different stakeholders would have in this general assembly: depositors and workers would have 44% and 5% of the vote, respectively; the original founders of the cajas 11%; and a whooping 40% would go to the local political representatives of the municipalities were the cajas were operational. Second, the was "board" which was to be elected by the general assembly, each group represented in proportion to their voting power in this body. The board had two main responsibilities: oversight of the financial operations of the cajas, including disbursement of the profits for social projects, and appointment of the caja's "general director" or CEO. Finally, a "control board" was to be named, again in the same proportions as the board, to provide oversight of the board and review financial statements; this board was the key body in communication with the Bank of Spain.

It is important to understand that while other constituents were represented, the cajas were ultimately controlled by politicians. Depositors were represented in the general assembly but were easily captured by the local politicians. But this was in any case an anomaly; after all, what firm is controlled by its customers in a market economy?[28] The political control led to politically motivated investments. For instance, the Caja del Mediterráneo was effectively controlled by the local government of Valencia, the region of origin of this caja, as well as by the main municipalities of Valencia. Not surprisingly, it invested in every ruinous prestige project sponsored by the local government, such as the Ciudad de las Artes y las Ciencias, la Ciudad de la Luz, and the disastrous amusement park Terra Mítica.[29]

In addition, and almost simultaneously, governments of Spain's powerful regions[30] rushed in to regulate "their" cajas to align them with their local political objectives.[31] The central government, wary that these developments might deprive it of control in the all-important credit market, challenged these regional efforts before the Constitutional Court, the highest court in the land, only to see its case rebuffed in two landmark cases (48 and 49/1988). After this, the field was open for a complete takeover of the cajas sector by the local political elites. As noted by Fonseca and Rodríguez (2005, 397), these regional laws increased the representation of the local political elites in the general assembly at the expense of depositors.

Some specific examples may illustrate the extent to which the cajas were controlled by local political elites.[32] For instance, Caixa Catalunya was run by Narcis Serra, a prominent member of the Catalonian Socialist Party (PSC) who had a long and distinguished career as mayor of Barcelona in the early years of Spain's new democracy and as a congressman; he was also national minister of defense and deputy prime minister of the national government under prime minister Felipe González (of the Spanish socialist party, PSOE). He stepped down as congressman in 2004 and was named head of Caixa Catalunya in 2005, where he remained throughout the worst years of the real estate bubble; he was forced to resign and the Caja was nationalized after barely a year. in 2010. In Caja Madrid, the core of what was to become Bankia, Miguel Blesa, a lawyer by training, entered the board of this old caja in 1996 to become its head in lieu of Jaime Terceiro, a distinguished economist who had run the entity efficiently. According to press reports, Mr. Blesa's main qualification to run Caja Madrid was his close friendship with Prime Minister Aznar, of the conservative party (PP), which has controlled the region and city of Madrid for more than two decades.[33] To gain effective control of the

caja, the conservative party entered into a complex arrangement with
the main trade union represented on the board (Comisiones Obreras),
to gain the votes needed to displace Mr. Terceiro and place Mr. Blesa at
the helm of this centenary institution. The arrangement bound Mr. Blesa
in several directions, in particular, in matters concerning Caja Madrid's
investment policy. For instance, the agreement mentioned the need for
reactive relations with real estate developers. More importantly, the agre-
ment explicitly blocked any attempt to endow Caja Madrid with better
property rights and recapitalization mechanisms, which was to prove fatal
when the crisis came.[34]

Perhaps no case better exemplifies the incestuous relation between
local politics and the governance of the cajas than the case of the region
of Valencia. This prosperous region was one of the epicenters of the real
estate bubble and the Spanish banking crisis. It was home to three important financial institutions, Caja del Mediterráneo, Bancaja, and Banco
de Valencia, which was a century old bank controlled by Bancaja since
the mid-1990s. In 1997 the regional government took the fateful step
of changing the law regulating the cajas to increase the ceiling of political appointees that could serve in the governing bodies of the cajas.[35]
The law opened the possibility for the first time for the direct appointment by the local government of 28% of the board; this, together with
the municipal appointments (another 28%), ensured that the presence
of political appointees in the board well exceeded the 40% mandated
in the 1985 law (LORCA). In addition, the law transferred supervisory
responsibilities over the cajas to the Instituto Valenciano de Finanzas, a
body with no experience whatsoever in banking supervision. This reform
was supported both by the governing party at the time in the region (the
conservative party, or PP) and the opposition party (the socialist party,
or PSOE), which had engaged in similar maneuverings in the region of
Andalusia.[36] The 1997 law was sponsored by the then-economics minister of Valencia, José Luis Olivas, who in 2004, stepped down as president
of the region to head both Bancaja and Banco de Valencia until their
nationalization during the crisis. Mr. Olivas, a member of the conservative party (PP), which has controlled the rich region of Valencia for many
years, was a lawyer by training and had no experience in banking when
he became the head of these important institutions. These three financial
entities were eventually taken over and nationalized when the crisis hit.

With a few exceptions, these governance problems led to a scarcity
of managerial talent in the cajas sector. Cuñat and Garicano (2010) have

shown that on average, the human capital of managers in the cajas sector was low, particularly in the cajas where real estate lending and now nonperforming loans were most concentrated. Specifically, they found that a caja run by someone with postgraduate education, with previous banking experience, and with no previous political appointments, is likely to have significantly less real estate lending as a share of total lending, a larger share loans to individuals, a lower rate of nonperforming loans, and a lower probability of rating downgrades. The effects are quite large: those cajas led by chairs with graduate studies extended 7% more of their portfolio as loans to individuals and 5–7% less to real estate loans. Consistently with this, as of July 2009, they had significantly lower nonperforming loans, about 1% less. Given that the average in their sample was about 5%, this is a 20% drop just in this variable. Similarly, the role of banking experience was also highly significant: cajas led by those without banking experience had a 1% increase in nonperforming loans; this also partly reflects a larger portfolio allocation to real estate, of about 6% more. These two effects are cumulative; that is, compared to one who has graduate education and relevant experience, a chair without both increases current nonperforming loans in his or her caja by 2 percentage points. This is a large effect, of around 40% of nonperforming loans.

One last ingredient was added to this explosive cocktail of governance flaws. In 1988, the cajas, which until then had been restricted to operations in the regions where they were headquartered, were allowed to expand throughout the entire country.[37] Figure 6.3A shows the fraction of deposits issued by banks and cajas, and Figure 6.3B shows loans granted to the private sector as a fraction of the total. The cajas sector was able to gain significant market share at the expense of traditional commercial banks.[38]

In summary, the cajas (which operationally had been banks since 1977) had internal governance structures that were subject to capture by the local political elites, while at the same time they were insulated from market-disciplining mechanisms, like takeover threats by banks. Though many saw the potential for trouble, the Constitutional Court by 1988 had severely limited the ability of the central government to regulate the cajas. Relaxation of the geographic limitations of the cajas meant that these governance flaws could infect the larger Spanish economy, which was entering a period of considerable dynamism after Spain's entry into the European institutions. There was an additional change in the early 1970s relating to the cajas: in 1972, its supervisory body, the Instituto de Crédito

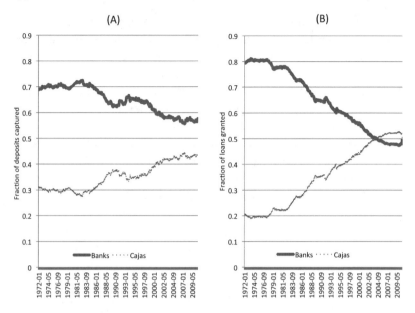

FIGURE 6.3. Panel A: Deposits of banks and cajas as a fraction of total deposits issued by both. Panel B: Loans granted to the private sector (households and firms) by banks and cajas as a fraction of total loans granted by both. Monthly: 1972:01–2010:09. Data source: Bank of Spain.

de las Cajas de Ahorros, was dissolved and its responsibilities transferred to the Bank of Spain.

3.3   The Bank of Spain

THE REPUTATION OF THE BANK OF SPAIN AS A TOUGH SUPERVISOR   The modern Bank of Spain came into being in 1962,[39] though by then it already had a long and distinguished history. Concerning banking supervision, though, the history of the Bank of Spain is quite recent As already mentioned, the banking crisis that started in the mid-1970s caught authorities without the necessary resolution framework to handle bank failures. In addition, the supervisory abilities of the Bank of Spain were rather limited when the crisis hit. The modern supervisory capabilities of the Bank of Spain are the result of that crisis.[40] Since then the Bank of Spain has built the reputation of a tough supervisor on three pillars.

First, the Spanish central bank acted decisively during the banking crisis of the early 1990s. In particular, its handling of the Banesto crisis in

1993, the largest banking failure in Spanish banking history at the time, was widely seen as effective and not onerous to the tax payer.[41] Second, while the aforementioned banking crisis was turning virulent, Spanish financial markets were undergoing a profound process of both liberalization and consolidation. Under the imposing shadow of Mariano Rubio, deputy governor between 1977 and 1984 and then governor between 1984 and 1992, the credit market was utterly transformed. His tenure coincided with a profound liberalization of the Spanish credit market, increased competition, and the entry of foreign banks into the traditionally closed Spanish market. In addition, during his years, the supervisory powers of the Bank of Spain were strengthened.

Finally, the Bank of Spain has proved willing to try what were at the time innovative macroprudential tools that alleviated some of the consequences of the banking crisis.[42] These tools, informed by sound economic reasoning, were met by resistance both by banks and cajas as well as observers at large, but, to its credit, the Bank of Spain stood up to the resistance. Two of these tools are discussed next.

The first tool, the dynamic provisioning system, was unique to the Bank of Spain. The origins of this institution date back to the banking crisis of the early 1990s, which had resulted in a severe contraction of credit. The Bank of Spain was concerned about the strong pro-cylicality of credit, which, in an economy strongly dependent on bank capital, was seen as deepening the business cycle. In addition, it was perceived that banking competition was producing aggressive loan pricing; as a result, it was felt that the level of provisions in the Spanish banking sector was too low (which was indeed the case compared to other OECD banking systems).[43] To protect bank capital over the cycle and produce a more stable flow of credit the Bank of Spain started to consider a new approach to provisioning. This new approach recognized that loan losses had to be provisioned at the peak of the business cycle, when the reckless loan is granted, not at the bottom, when bank lending is most conservative and loans are granted only to the safest credit. This how the Bank of Spain's notorious dynamic provisioning system came about. It is important to understand that the dynamic provisioning system did not come as an effort to prevent excessive credit creation during speculative cycles, which means that its effectiveness should not be judged along this dimension.[44] Dynamic provisioning is an ingredient—not the most important one—in the story of the Spanish banking crisis, but for reasons that are typically not fully appreciated and to which we shall return.

TABLE 6.2 **Dynamic provisioning: Weights for the different asset buckets**

i	Type of risk	$\alpha(\%)$	$\beta(\%)^a$
1	Cash and public sector securities and loans	0	0
2	Mortgages with LTV^b less than 80% and loans to corporates with $\geq$ A	.6	.11
3	Mortgages with LTV more than 80% and other collateralized loans	1.5	.44
4	Exposure to corporates with rating <A or non rated	1.8	.65
5	Consumer durable financing	2.0	1.1
6	Credit cards and overdrafts	2.5	1.64

^{a} α and β are the coefficients in the dynamic provisioning rule, see expression (1)
^{b} LTV, loan to value

Dynamic provisioning forces banks to hold provisions for losses according to the following formula:

(1)
$$G_t = \sum_{i=1}^{6} \alpha_i \Delta C_{i,t} + \sum_{i=1}^{6} \left(\beta_i - \frac{S_{i,t}}{C_{i,t}} \right) C_{i,t}.$$

In (1), G_t stands for generic provisions and $C_{i,t}$ for credit at time t in category i; $S_{i,t}$ stands for specific provisions; α_i is a parameter that determines how sensitive generic provisions are to credit growth in category i; and β_i is the average of specific provision over the business cycle. There were six categories of loans, which are reported in Table 6.2, together with their associated parameters.

The second tool was set up by the Bank of Spain that also proved prescient: the treatment of off-balance sheet liabilities and the capital charges that were applied to them. The issue was whether securitization and asset transfers to special purpose vehicles could lead to deconsolidation of the associated risks from the balance sheets of the sponsoring credit entities, whether banks and cajas. The issues are arcane from an accounting point of view but inform the Bank of Spain's reputation as a tough supervisor. In 2004, the Bank of Spain, which is the body responsible for the accounting standards of credit institutions, issued the necessary norms to implement the adoption of the International Financial Reporting Standards (IFRS) at the European Union level. The Bank of Spain interpreted IFRS criteria when it came to deconsolidation in a very restrictive manner, in a way that made off-balance sheet transactions rather unattractive. In particular, and judiciously, the Bank of Spain opted for an interpretation of IFRS's ambiguities in the accounting treatment of off-balance sheet transactions based on economic considerations rather than on the letter of the law. In addition (and to deal conservatively with the complexity of many of these arrangements), the Bank of Spain ordered that consolidation was required when it was difficult to assess whether a substantial risk transfer had occurred. In practice, any credit enhancement that the sponsoring entity would grant the off-balance sheet vehicle or any retention of subordinated liabilities would result in consolidation.[45] It is important to emphasize that all these actions did not prevent securitization from happening, and indeed, Spain became the largest securitization market in Europe after the United Kingdom, but for risk diversification rather than for regulatory capital arbitrage.[46]

THE BANK OF SPAIN AND THE REAL ESTATE BUBBLE. What was the attitude of the Bank of Spain to the imbalances building in the Spanish economy, particularly in its real estate sector? Did the Bank of Spain try to control the expansion of the cajas?

When considering these questions one must turn to the two governors at the head of the Bank of Spain during these critical years, Jaime Caruana and Miguel Ángel Fernández Ordóñez. The Bank of Spain is, by all accounts, a hierarchical organization, so the personalities of both the governor and the deputy governor play a critical role in the central bank's approach toward supervision. There were three issues that the Bank of Spain had to contend with. First was its role in the debate over whether Spain was experiencing a real estate bubble. Central bankers typically argue that they lack the instruments to identify and stop speculative cycles, which was certainly the case here, as monetary policy and interest rates were set in Frankfurt, not Madrid. The Bank of Spain could put more sand in the credit machine via dynamic provisioning, which can be seen as a macroprudential tool aimed at controlling the flow of credit to particular areas. Second, the serious flaws in the governance structure of the cajas meant that the Bank of Spain had to be particularly vigilant. Because the cajas were controlled by powerful local political elites, a particularly strong supervisory role was required. The Bank of Spain was going to be the key institution when the correction came, something widely expected in Spain since relatively early in the speculative cycle. Third, contingent planning and a clear path toward the likely restructuring of the Spanish credit market was among the Bank of Spain's responsibilities in anticipation of the crash.

Jaime Caruana, a telecommunications engineer by training,[47] arrived as governor in 2000 and served until 2006, when his term expired and he was replaced by Miguel Ángel Fernández Ordóñez, who served until 2012.[48] At the time of his selection, Mr. Caruana was the head of banking supervision inside the Bank of Spain. Before that he ran the Treasury Department under finance minister Rodrigo Rato, and in that capacity sat on the board of the Bank of Spain.

It was during Mr. Caruana's years that the real estate bubble got going in earnest. Contrary to the views expressed by some commentators, the real estate bubble was a constant feature in policy discussions and in the press, so much so that during the general election of 2004, it was the dominant theme of the economic policy debate. Interestingly, two debates with diametrically opposing policy implications were taking place simultaneously. First, was a popular debate centered around the issue of housing affordability. Politicians reacted to this concern by proposing measures directed toward the increase in the supply of housing but also by advancing proposals that reinforced speculation in the housing market.[49] A second debate was centered around the systemic implications of a potential housing crash.[50] Here observers and commentators proposed a transition to a more balanced growth model, one that emphasized productivity gains rather than overreliance on the construction sector.

The Bank of Spain featured prominently in these debates. In 2003, it produced two different studies arguing that real estate values were above their long-run values, somewhere between 8% and 20%, and that a correction was to be expected.[51] These studies were widely covered in the press.[52] The issue was politically charged, and the impact of these studies was such that both Spain's main economic authorities as well as leading bankers disagreed publicly with the findings of the research staff of the central bank.[53] In addition, the European Comission in its fall 2003 report emphasized the possibility that the Spanish real estate market was overheated.

Mr. Caruana had what can only be described as an ambivalent attitude toward the housing market. He explicitly denied the existence of a real estate bubble[54] but argued, on the contrary, for both strong fundamentals combined with mean-reverting speculative components as explanatory forces for the strong price appreciation taking place in the Spanish housing market at the time.[55] Clearly he was complacent about the ability of the financial sector to absorb the inevitable correction in housing.[56] Mr. Caruana's complacent attitude led, in an unprecedented gesture, the rank and file of the examiner body of the Bank of Spain to submit in 2006 a letter to the then–deputy prime minister and economics minister, Pedro

Solbes, alerting that the risks in the Spanish financial sector were much higher than what one could infer from Governor Caruana's speeches (see, for example, Caruana (2005).[57] The central bank examiners were brutal in their assessment of Mr. Caruana's tenure, pointing out that the relentless growth in credit was unsustainable and that the Bank of Spain had failed to enforce good risk management practices when instruments were available to do so. The letter, presciently, pointed out that the Spanish credit institutions were becoming overly dependent on wholesale short-term funding in euro markets; as a result, they were increasingly exposed to sudden changes in funding conditions. The letter, sadly, describes with an uncanny prescience the crisis that was to break in the Spanish credit market only three years later.

Mr. Caruana's six-year tenure ended shortly thereafter, and Miguel Ángel Fernández Ordóñez was named the new governor in 2006. He was to be the key character handling the biggest financial crisis in Spain's recent times. Mr. Fernández Ordóñez already had a long and distinguished career of public service. He had served under two administrations of the socialist party as a state secretary, a position just below the cabinet level, first as a state secretary for the economy and commerce under Prime Minister Felipe González and later as a state secretary for public finance under Prime Minister Rodríguez Zapatero. He also served as head of the Competition Court (an antitrust agency), where he encouraged a variety of liberalizing measures. Still, the appointment was seen as overly political by the conservative party, which was out of power after the 2004 elections. Traditionally the appointment of the governor of the Bank of Spain was reached by consensus between the two main political parties. This time it was not to be, something that would later have severe consequences for the handling of the banking crisis.[58]

4   The Accumulation of Risks in the Spanish Banks and Cajas

4.1   The Evolution of Balance Sheets up to 2010

Table 6.3 shows the aggregated balance sheet of the credit institutions as of November of 2010, once the first leg of the crisis had subsided and before the storms that were to occur in 2011 and 2012. The "size" of the Spanish credit institutions was around €3.3 trillion. The bulk of this balance sheet comprised loans to domestic residents other than the general government, which shows up under the rubric "Other resident sector."

TABLE 6.3 **Aggregate balance sheet of credit institutions (banks, cajas (S&L) and credit cooperatives) as of November 2010, in billions of euros**

Loans			Deposits		
	Credit system	230.5		Credit system	276.6
	General government	77.4		General Government	90.5
	Other resident sector	1,843.4		Other resident sector	1,444.4
	Commercial	*991.4*			
	Households	*810.0*			
	Other	*42*			
	Rest of the world	221.8		Rest of the world	471.1
Securities			Other Liabilities		
	Other than shares			Other than shares	435.0
	Domestic	319.3		Capital & Reserves	285.1
	Rest of the world	69.4		Social Security	3.4
	Shares			Accruals & sundry accounts	251.2
	Domestic	99.2			
	Rest of the world	76.9			
Cash		7.2			
Other		312.1			
Total		3,257.3	Total		3,257.3

Source: Bank of Spain

This entry comprises both loans to households, €810 billion, and firms, €991.4 billion. It is this portfolio where the real estate credit risk is concentrated, as we shall see shortly. A word is warranted about the securities in the credit institutions balance sheet. Roughly €420 billion of securities, both fixed income and equity, of domestic risk is held in this portfolio. Of this, €163.8 billion is held in government securities,[59] which represents a noticeable increase relative to the holdings at the beginning of the crisis, when they stood at about €100 billion in 2008. To this we have to add the loans made to the public sector in the loan portfolio to estimate the exposure of the Spanish credit institutions to this sector, which, as shown in Table 6.2, stood at €77 billion. The total exposure of the Spanish credit institutions to the public sector via loans and securities holding stood at about €240 billion. The public and the bank balance sheets already were beginning to get inextricably linked in 2010.

ASSETS. Strong patterns in the data show the changing risks in the asset and liability side of this balance sheet. Figure 6.4A shows an unheralded change in the evolution of finance in Spain—the explosion of household finance. Loans to households went from being 30% of total domestic private credit, defined as the sum of commercial and household loans,

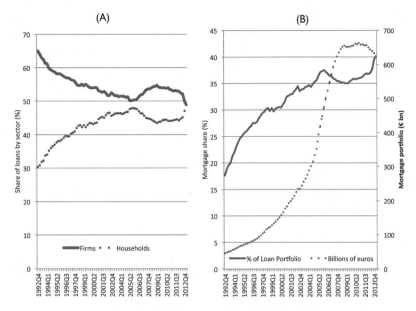

FIGURE 6.4. Panel A: Loans to nonfinancial firms and to consumers as a percentage of total credit to the private domestic sector. Panel B: Mortgages and loans for housing renovation as a percentage of total credit to the private domestic sector and nominal quantities in billions of euros. Quarterly: 1992Q4–2013Q1. Data source: Bank of Spain.

to almost 50% by 2006, roughly equal to the percentage that commercial loans represent of the overall loan portfolio.[60] Household loans are mostly mortgages and loans related to housing renovations. Indeed, Figure 6.4B, shows, mortgages went from 17% of the loan portfolio to a peak of 37.5% in 2006Q1 before the crisis hit.[61] Figure 6.4B also shows the nominal magnitude of the mortgage portfolio in the Spanish banking systems, which, as of 2013Q1, was about €625bn, an impressive 60% of GDP; in 2000Q1 barely one year after the euro was launched and as the real estate bubble got going, the mortgage portfolio was only 25% of GDP.

   In general, the balance sheets of credit institutions became heavily biased toward real estate. Figure 6.5A shows the percentage of commercial loans tied to the real estate sector, defined as the sum of loans to construction companies and real estate developers. At the peak of the cycle, almost 50% of the loans of credit institutions were going to one of these two categories. This percentage was considerably higher for the cajas, reaching an impressive 60.8% at the peak of the bubble in 2007Q2.

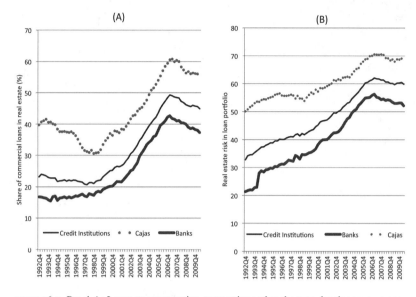

FIGURE 6.5. Panel A: Loans to construction companies and real estate developers as a percentage of loans to firms. Panel B: Real estate risk in the portfolios: Mortgages and loans for housing renovation, loans to construction companies and loans to real estate developers as a percentage of loans to households and firms. Quarterly. 1992Q4–2010Q2. Data source: Bank of Spain.

Banks, which also increased lending to construction companies and real estate developers, reached a 41% that same quarter, almost 20 percentage points below the cajas.

Finally, Figure 6.5B summarizes the real estate risk in the loan portfolios, defined as the percentage of the loan portfolio that is either a mortgage, a loan to a real estate developer, or a loan to the construction sector. At the beginning of the sample (1992Q4), credit institutions had an exposure to the real estate sector that accounted for 32.7% of the loan portfolio, whereas at the peak of the bubble, this number exceeded 62.0%. Concentration was worse for the cajas: on the eve of the crisis, 70% of their loan portfolio was either a mortgage, a loan to a real estate developer, or one to a construction company, compared to 55% for the banks.

These numbers probably underestimate the severity of the concentration problem in the loan portfolio of Spanish credit institutions for three reasons. First, the above definition excludes some categories, such as loans to hotels, that are closely related to real estate. Second, many of the banks and cajas had significant equity stakes in both construction companies and real estate developers. For instance, Bankia had significant stakes in large developers and construction companies, such as Metrovacesa and Realia. Third, some loans may have been misclassified in order to arbitrage the provisions that were required or simply to convey the impression of lower real estate concentration. The stress tests conducted by Oliver Wyman on the Spanish banking system in the summer of 2012 offers one of the few windows on this problem. For instance, Oliver Wyman (2012, 25) states that about 3% of the loans to small and medium enterprises should be reclassified as loans to real estate developers. As the report notes, this number is probably a lower bound on the misclassification problem, since by the summer of 2012, the financial institutions had gone through several asset quality review exercises and had been forced to recognize the real estate nature of many loans.

Throughout this discussion, it is important to remember that these aggregate numbers mask an enormous cross-sectional variation in exposure to real estate risk, in particular, exposure to real estate developer risk, as well as misclassification practices. Everything in a banking crisis is the tail of the distribution, and much is driven by the worse credit institutions. In addition, there is important variation within portfolios. For example, some institutions may have a larger fraction of their mortgage portfolio tied to first homes as opposed to second homes. The distinction is important, because risks and delinquency rates can differ dramatically across these two categories.

In summary, there was a substantial increase in portfolio concentration associated with the real estate bubble. Both banks and cajas considerably increased their exposure to real estate during this period, but the cajas were much more exposed than the banks. Much still needs to be done to understand the striking differential performance of cajas versus banks: quantities are not enough. For example, it would be interesting to know whether the banks cream skimmed the cajas of the best risks available. This is a sensible hypothesis, as it is likely that the human capital and risk management control of the cajas were inferior to that of the banks, as I argued in the previous section. If this is the case, the cajas would not only have *more* real estate risk in their books, it would also be *riskier*.

LIABILITIES.   How was it all funded? The right side of the balance sheet in Table 6.3 shows the structure of liabilities of the financial sector. As with

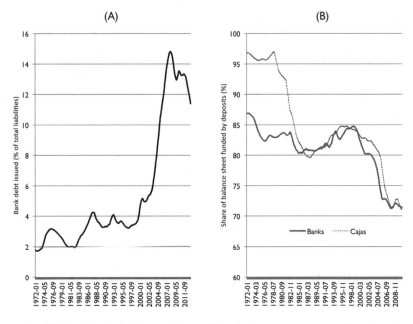

FIGURE 6.6. Panel A: Bank debt issued by credit institutions as a percentage of total assets. Monthly: 1972:01 to 2013:05. Smoothed with an MA-12. Panel B: Banks and cajas: Deposits as a percentage of total assets. Monthly: 1972:01 to 2010:09. Smoothed with an MA-12. Data source: Bank of Spain.

many other banking systems, deposits account for a significant fraction of the funding of Spanish banks and cajas as of 2010Q3. Still, the balance sheet masks significant changes in the nature of the funding during the decade from the introduction of the euro to the eve of the crisis.

Figure 6.6A offers a first glimpse of these changes. It shows bank debt issued by credit institutions. Panel B shows the percentage of the balance sheet that is funded by total deposits for both cajas and banks. These figures have to be interpreted with caution for two main reasons. First, there have been many institutional changes during this period, including accounting practices, that make comparison of magnitudes across such a long sample problematic. Second, as Table 6.3 shows, total deposit includes items that differ in their fragility; for instance, deposits from the rest of the world may be more jittery in a crisis than domestic deposits. In addition, deposits include a broad category of liabilities mixing, say, standard household deposits with liabilities linked to securitization vehicles. These data, though, are imperfect and as shown below, seriously underestimate the reliance on wholesale funding by part of Spanish credit institutions. Still, they are useful, because they allow for a comparison between the banks and the cajas.

Both plots suggest a similar story, namely, that banks and cajas dramatically increased their reliance on wholesale funding to finance the real estate bubble. Bank debt accounted for a small fraction of the balance sheet until the late 1990s but grew to 15% at the peak of the real estate cycle. Figure 6.6B shows that deposits were funding a lower percentage of the balance sheet for both cajas and banks and that there was a considerable drop in the first decade of the euro. In addition, the cajas took advantage of their operational equality with banks to converge to similar levels of deposit funding by the mid-1980s.

As mentioned, Figure 6.6B underestimates the reliance on wholesale funding by the Spanish banking system. The reason is that the category "deposits" includes a range of funding sources, including many securitization vehicles. To obtain a more disaggregated view of deposit funding, let us consider a slightly different data source. In doing so, we lose the ability to distinguish between cajas and banks, as the central bank itself does not report items on the liability side of the balance sheet by the nature of the credit entity.[62]

There are three broad entries in the definition of deposits, once one excludes the deposits of monetary financial institutions themselves (MFIs, including the Bank of Spain) and the public sector.[63] First there are deposits issued to households and nonfinancial corporations resident in Spain. Second, there are the deposits of other euro-area residents, including Spanish entities not classified under either households or nonfinancial corporations. Third, there are the liabilities against the rest of the world (non-euro-area residents) classified as deposits. Under the rubric of deposits of other euro residents are the asset securitization vehicles that the Spanish banks and cajas set up and that in 2005 they were forced by the Bank of Spain to consolidate, as discussed in the previous section. Deposits of pension and investment funds are also included under this heading.

Figure 6.7A plots the measure of total deposits as well as the deposits of Spanish households and nonfinancial corporations. As of June 2013, the deposits of residents and nonresidents, excluding deposits by the public sector as well as those of MFIs, amounted to €1.5 trillion. Of these, €950 billion corresponded to households and nonfinancial corporations, and €271 billion were deposits related to securitization vehicles

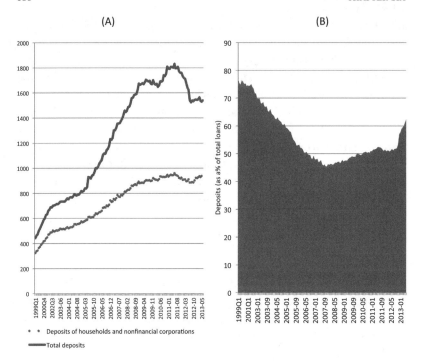

(A)   (B)

• • Deposits of households and nonfinancial corporations

▬▬Total deposits

FIGURE 6.7. Panel A: Total deposits of Other Monetary Financial Institutions (OMFI) and deposits of house-holds and nonfinancial corporations residents in Spain. Total deposits reproduces the measure of deposits in Table 1 in Martínez (2012) as follows. The starting point is the OMFI's Deposits of Other Resident Sectors in Spain and other euro member nations, from which we subtract the deposits of the public sector and add the deposits of other resident sectors from the rest of the world. The construction of the series is affected by the accounting changes discussed in Section 3, namely the fact that from June 2005 de-recognition of loans transferred to securitization vehicles after December 31, 2003 in which the sponsoring entity retained any risk was not allowed; higher deposits with these securitization vehicles were added on the liability side as a balancing item (see Martínez, Chart 1). The two vertical lines correspond to December 2003 and June 2005. Nominal; in billions of €. Panel B: Deposits of households and nonfinancial corporations residents in Spain as a percentage of the loans granted to other resident sectors resident in Spain, which are the same households and nonfinancial corporations, by credit institutions. Data is quarterly from 1991Q1 to 2002Q4 and monthly from 2003:01 to 2013:06. Data source: Bank of Spain.

resident in Spain;[64] deposits against the rest of the world were €45 billion. As can be seen in Figure 6.7A, total deposits grew considerably over the first decade of the euro and experienced a sudden stop about 2009, when, as we shall see, the securitization machine experienced a significant slowdown. Deposits of Spanish households and nonfinancial corporations grew as well but at a more moderate pace. The increasing

gap corresponds precisely to liabilities associated with securitization vehicles, over which the financial institutions retained some exposure.[65] The
two vertical lines in Figure 6.7A show the relevant dates for the accounting change discussed in the previous section. Notice that there is a
considerable jump in the series in June 2005. This is when securitized
assets (over which sponsoring entities retained risks) were reconsolidated
in the balance sheet, thereby producing an increase in deposits as a
balancing item.[66]

Figure 6.7B shows the percentage of the portfolio of loans and credits
to Spanish households and nonfinancial corporations that are funded by
deposits of those same households and nonfinancial corporations. As can
be seen, loans were funded by a decreasing fraction of deposits, reaching
a minimum of 45% in October 2007 near the peak of the real estate bubble. After that, a slow upward trend breaks in 2011, when a drop occurs
in the deposits of households and nonfinancial corporations. The strong
uptick at the very end of the sample is related to several policy initiatives
taken to tackle the Spanish banking crisis in the second half of the 2012;
specifically, during the first half of 2013, significant transfers were made
of real estate loans to the "bad bank" set up by the Spanish authorities to
assist with the restructuring of the Spanish banking sector.

In sum, Spanish entities clearly increased their reliance on wholesale
funding. A thorough examination of the deposits of financial institutions
reveals that a decreasing fraction of the loan portfolio was funded by
household or nonfinancial corporation deposits. Next we focus on a particular source of wholesale funding, the one that is linked to securitization
vehicles.

4.2   *The Spanish Securitization Machine*

Securitization was an important source of funding for the Spanish banking sector, to the extent that Spain was the second largest European
securitization market after the United Kingdom throughout this period.
Figure 6.8 shows the flows as well as outstanding securitization balances
by part of Spanish credit entities and the volume corresponding to banks
and cajas.[67] As the data in the previous section suggest, securitization is
a big part of the story of the Spanish real estate bubble and the evolution
of banking in Spain.

There are two distinct phases in the securitization cycle. From 2000 to
2006, the cajas accounted for a much larger fraction of the securitization

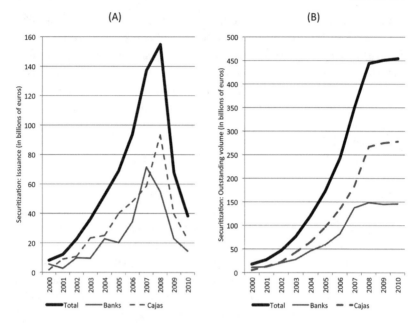

FIGURE 6.8. Panel A: Securitization issuance in billions of euros. Panel B: Outstanding stocks. Securitizations correspond to both asset as well as liability securitizations. In billions of €. Annual: 2000–2010. Data Source: Memoria de Supervisión Bancaria (2003–2010), Bank of Spain.

deals than did the banks. By 2006, the cajas were the sponsors of €134 billion of outstanding balances compared to €82.3 billion for the banks. Between 2006 and 2010, the banks accelerated their securitization deals. By 2010, Spanish banks accounted for €146 billion of the balances, whereas the cajas accounted for €278 billion. The numbers for the banks are slightly underestimated, as they exclude some securitization deals issued by the large bank holding companies that are classified under a different entry. There is a second important difference regarding the nature of the securitization deals.

Spanish institutions performed two types of securitizations.[68] The first is the traditional one: mortgages held in the balance sheet of the originator were transferred to an external vehicle, called *Fondo de Titulización Hipotecaria* (FTH), which funded the purchase of the loans through the issuance of securities with different cash-flow rights. The bulk of these securitizations were linked to mortgages.[69] The second is slightly more peculiar to Spain. In this case what is being securitized is effectively a liability, a single-certificate, privately placed covered bond (known in Spain as *cédulas hipotecarias singulares*). Banks and cajas both did a lot of the first type, but the second was overwhelmingly dominated by the cajas.[70] The probable reason for this stark pattern in securitization is that the single-certificate, privately placed covered bonds of the cajas were initially rather concentrated geographically. Thus it was advantegeous to pool the covered bonds of many cajas to gain some diversification as well as to reduce placement costs.[71]

An important caveat is that the evidence seems to suggest that a critical component of real estate risk remained on the balance sheet of credit institutions was linked to real estate developer loans. Unfortunately, the supervision reports of the Bank of Spain offer an incomplete series regarding securitization of this risk. From 2002 to 2008, which are the ones for which this entry is itemized in the reports, the outstanding balance peaked at €992 million in 2005 and then fell consistently. In 2008Q4, the outstanding balance of real estate developer loans was €318 billion, or 30% of Spain's GDP. Of those, €172 billion corresponded to the cajas and €132 billion to the banks.[72] A significant fraction of these real estate developer loans soon turned delinquent once the crisis came, much faster than any other item on the asset side of the balance sheet. This forced banks and cajas to provision for these losses. Thus, it seems that outside investors knew of the speculative nature of those loans and shied away from them, thereby leaving all the risk in the Spanish banking system.

In addition to real estate risk, the Spanish credit institutions soon started to securitize all sorts of risks. A market that grew rapidly was the securitization of loans to small and medium-sized entreprises (SMEs). In 2008, outstanding balances reached €33.8 billion, opening capital markets to this important segment of corporate Spain, which is skewed to smaller firms.

Securitization deals offer a glimpse into the role of foreigners in the Spanish real estate bubble: they gulped down the Spanish securitization issues. Figure 6.1 showed a strong correlation between the growth in the loan portfolio and the net international investment position of Spain. Figure 6.9 shows total securitization volumes as well as issues in the hands of foreigners. As before, the series available in the supervision reports is incomplete, but there is enough detail to quantify the significant fraction of the real estate risk that was flowing to foreigners. According to these reports, foreigners acquired a significant share of the paper issued by the Spanish securitization machine. Of the €356.8 billion outstanding in 2007,

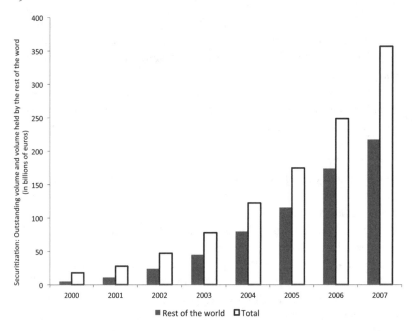

FIGURE 6.9. Spanish securitisation issues in the hands of the rest of the world and total out-standing. Nominal in billions of €. Annual: 2000–2010. Data Source: Memoria de Supervisión Bancaria (2003–2007), Bank of Spain.

€217.6 billion, or 60% of the total, was in the hands of foreigners. After 2007, the role of foreigners declined, because the appetite for more real estate risk in foreign portfolios was waning and Spanish credit entities were beginning to retain a large stake of their own securitization issues for rediscounting operations. The sudden stop that Spanish banks were to experience was not far off.

5   The Crisis Comes

When the funding crisis came, it did so from unexpected quarters—the U.S. subprime market. Though Spanish real estate prices peaked in 2008Q1, it was the dramatic events in the United States that grabbed all the attention. In the Eurozone, Ireland took the fateful decision to offer its famous guarantee on all bank debt, which was to determine so much of the path of the Eurozone banking crisis. In Spain, things didn't remain quiet. The spreads with the German bund rose well above the 100 basis points (bps) in 2008 and early 2009, when they reached a local peak of 155bps in March, compared to 40bps a year earlier. The spreads started drifting downward, and by the second half of 2009, they were again below 100bps, where they remained for a year, until the breakup of the Greek debt crisis. Quietly, in the fall of 2008 and in the context of some measures adopted at the Eurozone level, the Spanish government of Prime Minister Rodríguez Zapatero tried to ease the refinancing pressure some of the cajas were experiencing with a new bank debt guarantee program with a maximum insurable principal of €100bn. The program was to last for a year.[73] The names of the entities that took advantage of those programs now read like a who's who of problematic cajas: Caja Madrid, Bancaja, and Caja del Meditírraneo (CAM) to name a few. The program was renewed in 2009 and again in December 2011, as one the first measures of the newly elected cabinet. In 2009 the FROB, a special-purpose vehicle with capital from the public sector, was created to assist with the likely restructuring needs of the banking sector. It could, by law, leverage up its initial capital 10 to 1 for a total balance sheet of €100 billion. Slowly, Spain was setting up the institutions needed to tackle its banking crisis, in eerie similarity to the banking crisis of 1977–1983.

The global nature of the credit crisis was unfortunate, because it confounded the local causes of the adjustment already taking place in the Spanish economy in 2008 with the international factors. There certainly was widespread understanding of, and concern over, the dependence of Spanish credit institutions on foreign funding. But the fragility on the side of the Spanish economy was seen as springing from nervous global investors worried more about global credit conditions than about the solvency of Spanish credit institutions. The references to the strong solvency ratios of credit institutions in official documents are a constant throughout this period. Certainly, the dramatic phase of the banking crisis in 2011 and 2012 was clearly unanticipated. In addition, the public saw these events as being driven by external shocks that demanded external solutions, which made Spanish responses all the more challenging once, for instance, fiscal deficits started growing dramatically.

In March 2009, the first caja, Caja Castilla–La Mancha (CCM), was taken over by the Bank of Spain and immediately sold to another caja (Cajastur) with a generous asset protection scheme. This was the first significant intervention since the Banesto debacle in 1993. CCM was a relatively small entity, with about a €20bn balance sheet. It had been run since 1999 by a former congressman and prominent local politician from the region of Castilla La Mancha; an economist by training, he had no experience in banking when he became the head of CCM. CCM was involved in many ill-advised projects, such as the Ciudad Real Airport, a useless facility that became the poster child of the excesses of the real estate and infrastructure bubble. Its failure came as no surprise.[74] The initial injection by the Spanish equivalent of the FDIC (the FROB did not yet exist) wiped out a significant fraction of its funds. The total cost of the operation, between equity injections and the aforementioned asset protection scheme, was about €3.7 billion.[75]

As Prime Minister Rodríguez Zapatero as well as other officials repeated incessantly, the costs of the entire operation was a trifle for an economy the size of Spain's, but it was how the process was handled what sent troubling signals about the entire sector. Initially, the Bank of Spain approached other cajas to gauge whether there was any interest in taking over CCM. La Caixa, the largest of the Catalonian cajas and one the best run in the entire sector, declined. Unicaja, and Andalusian caja, decided to look into acquiring it and hired accounting firm Price Waterhouse Coopers (PWC) to review the books; when the due diligence uncovered a €3 billion hole in the 2008 numbers, the entire operation collapsed, casting doubts on the numbers of the rest of the system and on the Bank of Spain's grip on the entire cajas sector. It was the collapse of this merger that forced the Bank of Spain to intervene. This was a pattern that was to be repeated throughout the crisis: every time a caja was to be taken over by the supervisor, the nonperforming loan ratio would jump upward, and solvency issues were exposed. The opacity with which the sale to Cajastur took place baffled observers and only added to the suspicion that there were larger problems in the sector. Successive interventions (e.g., for Cajasur, CAM, and Bankia) also increased the concerns of increasingly worried analysts and European authorities.

Still, the situation had stabilized somewhat by the end of 2009 and 2010, which allowed the cabinet and the Bank of Spain to pursue a double strategy of mergers and aggressive loan loss provisioning in order to recapitalize the Spanish cajas and banks through retained earnings; all this was done with the occasional injection of capital, or hybrid forms of capital, by the FROB. Soon, of the 45 cajas or so that faced the crisis, the merger wave had produced 17. However, this accelerated process of consolidation only muddled things further. When more transparency was needed to facilitate the refinancing of good assets, mergers produced complex balance sheets that confounded the good with the bad assets. Unfunded stress tests did not help. Certainly one of the lessons of this crisis is that stress tests should be conducted only when there is a clearly funded recapitalization mechanism, with a generous public backstop, for the entities shown to have solvency challenges in adverse scenarios; otherwise, outsiders suspect that reported losses are fixed at what can be absorbed given the mechanism in place rather than at their real levels. This was never the case with the European Banking Authority tests, which further undermined the credibility of Spanish banking authorities.

In addition, the new bank debt guarantee program made sure that sovereign and banking balance sheets gradually would become inextricably linked. Since the worst cajas made the heaviest use of the debt guarantee program, they significantly increased the exposure of the Spanish taxpayer to the losses associated with the real estate boom, jeopardizing the credit quality of the sovereign. These debt guarantee programs not only transfer risk in the balance sheet of financial entities to the public balance sheet but also bias the actions of policy makers as the crisis deepens, increasing the risk that they may "gamble for resurrection," given the deep sovereign liabilities incurred through those guarantees.

The merger strategy and the aggressive loss provisioning strategy pursued by the government and the Bank of Spain, combined with the lack of strong equity injections, implicitly assumed the solvency of the entire system and of the cajas in particular, which is precisely what outside observers doubted. Moreover, the policy applied to the entire system—banks and cajas—regardless of the state of the portfolios of individual entities. This forced the good entities to provision when they didn't need to and the bad ones when they couldn't, which only increased incentives for evergreening, particularly in the most problematic side of the portfolio—the real estate developer loan book. Scant consideration was given to the implications of this approach for credit generation, or to the fact that the slow pace of the restructuring process was allowing for an increasing tangle between public and private banking balance sheets, through the provision of implicit and explicit guarantees as well as through the larger sovereign debt portfolios that the banks were building.

The merger strategy had another consequence that was to prove fatal. It created systemic entities where there were none. Such was the case with Bankia, the bank that resulted from the merger in December of 2010 of Caja Madrid, Bancaja, and five other smaller cajas. When founded, Bankia had a balance sheet of €328 billion, or 30% of Spain's GDP. Caja

Madrid and Bancaja had serious solvency issues, but Spanish authorities nonetheless encouraged the merger and then, incredibly, an IPO in 2011. Since there was no international institutional interest in the shares of this ill-fated bank, the majority of the shares were placed among uninformed retail investors (through the extensive branch network of the cajas that formed Bankia) and reluctant Spanish institutional investors. The Spanish SEC (the Comisión Nacional de Mercado de Valores) gave the green light. Understandably, many foreign observers saw this as a massive gamble for resurrection not just of a private entity but of the entire strategy pursued until then by the Spanish authorities. Before that, the previous CEO stepped down, and a nasty political and very public squabble took place between the president of the region of Madrid and the mayor of Madrid, two of the most prominent figures in the conservative party, for control of the entity. Eventually the party elder Rodrigo Rato, former IMF managing director, was named to head this behemoth. The political control of the cajas was there to the last.

In May 2012, less than two years after the IPO, Bankia requested a €19 billion bailout on top of the €4 billion it had already received from the FROB. The total bailout package for just this single entity thus amounted to 2% of Spain's GDP. When Mr. Rato and his team were forced to step down, the new team proceeded to restate the 2011 numbers: from a profit of €305 million to a €3 billion loss.

The Spanish banking crisis was entering its most acute phase, one that ends, to some extent, when Spain entered into a Memorandum of Understanding with its Eurozone partners. Spain was to receive a €100 billion credit line and conduct a serious stress test under the stern supervision of the ECB, the European Commission, and the IMF. The Memorandum of Understanding required Spain to entirely reform its supervision and resolution toolbox; in addition, it effectively terminated the cajas. The handling of the Spanish banking crisis had been transferred to a third, international, party. By then the lethal mix of politics and the cajas did not leave much room for any other alternative.

6   Conclusion

The purpose of this paper is to provide a bird's-eye account of the run-up to the Spanish banking crisis. It places the governance issues in the cajas sector at the center of the narrative. It argues that the credit bubble interacted with poor governance to produce a real estate bubble and the insolvency of a significant fraction of the Spanish banking system once the bubble burst. On the asset side of the balance sheet, there was a significant concentration of real estate risk, whereas on the liability side, there was increasing fragility. The fragility stemmed both from the maturity of these liabilities and from the nature of the holders of these liabilities. Though the Bank of Spain had proved prescient in implementing some novel macroprudential tools, these tools proved insufficient, and it showed little willingness to act more aggressively to prevent the excessive accumulation of real estate risk on the asset side of the balance sheet.

Plenty of evidence suggests that to some extent, the risks were well understood. The real estate bubble was a constant source of political commentary, prominent policy makers spoke publicly about the dangers of the bubble, and the research department of the Bank of Spain produced reports documenting the possible overvaluation in the housing sector as early as 2003. Though of course most observers are not privy to the internal debates inside the central bank regarding the imbalances building in the banking sector (and in the cajas in particular), it is clear that that as the examiners' letter to the economics minister attests, those debates were indeed taking place, and there was much disagreement about the proper course of action. Clearly the nature of the imbalances accumulating in the Spanish economy were understood, but the implications of those imbalances—in particular, in light of euro membership—were not fully internalized.

When it came, the banking crisis was to be a very different experience than the previous two banking crises for three reasons. First, it differed because a significant fraction of bank liabilities needed foreign capital to be refinanced; they were indeed liabilities denominated in Spain's national currency, the euro, but they were held by parties, which, when the crisis hit, were to distinguish between Spanish assets and otherwise identical assets issued by entities in other countries of the Eurozone. Second, it differed because the Bank of Spain could not act as the lender of last resort, and the management of the Spanish banking crisis was dependent on the actions of the ECB, which was to step into that role tentatively at best. Banking crisis management needs a mysterious combination of decisive actions when it comes to the discovery of the losses in the banking sector, ample liquidity, and strategic clarity. This is already difficult when all three tasks are concentrated in a single entity that combines supervisory responsibilities with the ability to provide liquidity. It is a herculean

task when supervision and liquidity provision are hosted in separate entities, the Bank of Spain and the ECB (and to a large extent, the strategic
direction of banking crisis management resided with the Eurogroup of
national finance ministers). Third and finally, the crisis centered around
the cajas and thus came with important political economy problems. The
cajas, which were private entities, were controlled by Spain's powerful
local political elites and thus from the very early stages of the crisis bank
resolution was inevitably seen as politically motivated. This time was
indeed different, and though the lessons of the past are always valuable,
the crisis required new modes of thinking from the Spanish authorities.

Many issues remain to be investigated more thoroughly. In particular, this paper does not attempt a more detailed comparative study of
the cajas. Not all the cajas were rotten, and one of them, La Caixa, not
only survived but has managed to become the third-largest Spanish bank,
Caixabank. Why did some of the cajas fare better than others?

Bank of Spain options during the years of the real estate boom need to
be studied as well. The Spanish central bank had had the vision to set
up unique institutions, such as dynamic provisioning, and took a very
conservative approach to off–balance sheet liabilities, rendering them
unattractive as a means of engaging in regulatory arbitrage. Though
things could have been worse without them, their efficacy has to be reeval-
uated in light of the Spanish experience. What should have been done to
prevent the imbalances building in the cajas' balance sheets?

Then there is the real estate bubble itself. A thorough account of it
has yet to be written. This paper argues that the bubble was recognized
in real time by many observers and policy makers. Why didn't they act
in a timely fashion? The huge size of the imbalances was not a mystery,
but the only response was to conduct a very restricted fiscal policy aimed
at countervailing the excessive leverage of the private sector. It resulted
in low levels of debt to GDP ratios and gave authorities to false sense of
comfort that there was always time to confront the Spanish banking crisis
with public funds if needed. The diabolic loop—the tangling of public
and private balance sheets that has dominated so much of the Eurozone
crisis—seems to have been far removed from the minds of Spain's leading
officials.

Finally, a full understanding of the Spanish banking crisis requires a
view that encompasses the Eurozone at large. The reason is that every
step, every crisis within the crisis, offered clues about the future direction
European authorities might take in the next one. The role of the ECB is

of critical importance. The balancing act between performing its duties as lender of last resort and providing adequate incentives for governments to continue the process of fiscal consolidation added an additional layer of complexity to the banking crises of Spain, Ireland, and other countries. The construction of the banking union in the Eurozone, and the pace at which is going to occur, is informed by the lessons that were drawn from the way national authorities handled their banking crises.

Notes

I thank Markus Brunnermeier, Ed Glaeser, Jesús Fernández-Villaverde, Ray Horton, Rafael Repullo, and Glen Weyl for their comments on an earlier draft of this paper. This paper was prepared for the Conference in honor of Jose A. Scheinkman and springs from innumerable conversations I had with him about these issues, over the past few years. As usual, his comments, questions, and views proved pertinent and prescient. He has been a mentor, a coauthor, and above all, a friend for over 20 years, and it is with deep gratitude that I dedicate this piece to him.

1. For a useful, up-to-date view of state injections into distressed Spanish institutions, visit the webpage of the FROB at http://www.frob.es.

2. For a model of cream skimming in financial markets, see Bolton et al. (2016).

3. In fact, the real estate boom that roughly covers the decade between 1999 and 2008 is the second boom in 20 years in Spain. The last one went from 1987 to 1991 and saw nominal prices grow 20% for three consecutive years. See García-Montalvo (2010, 84).

4. There are three sources of data for housing prices in Spain. The first is data based on appraisals computed for the purposes of requesting a mortgage. It is collected by the Ministerio de Fomento (Department of Public Works). A second source of data is collected by the Spanish Statistics Institute (INE), which uses prices collected in the public transactions registry. Both series have different problems. The appraisal data can be manipulated by the mortgage finance industry to produce desired outcomes. Values, for example, can be inflated to increase the probability of granting a mortgage. The second series has the problem that parties to real estate transactions have tax incentives to misreport transaction prices. Finally, there is a third source of data, which is the ask prices by homeowners offering their houses on real estate websites. For a lucid exposition of these issues and the consequences for our understanding of the correction in prices in the real estate market, see García-Montalvo and Raya (2012).

5. It is far from obvious that demographic shocks, which have long-anticipated effects, can produce the type of patterns observed in the Spanish real estate boom; frictions as well as behavioral biases are needed to prevent these shocks from being

fully incorporated into asset prices. Of course the classic reference here is Mankiw and Weil (1989). For a broader discussion of the issues surrounding demographics and asset prices, see DellaVigna and Pollet (2007). For a central banker perspective on demographic factors inducing real estate bubbles that includes some interesting international cross-sectional evidence, see Nishimura (2013).

6. The comparison between Ireland and Spain is a constant in accounts of the crisis. See Ahearne et al. (2008).

7. Vinuesa (2008) and García-Montalvo (2007) offer some treatment of the problem of household formation as well as household disappearance in Spain. Unfortunately it is difficult, with the existing data sources, to estimate with any precision the potential for household formation.

8. García-Montalvo (2007) offers some evidence that the median age of new homeowners decreased steadily between 2000 and 2005, from 35 years of age to 32.

9. Solé-Ollé and Viladecans-Marsal (2013, box 1) offer a succinct English summary of land regulation in Spain. Successive efforts by the central government to regulate land ownership have been met with stern judicial rulings from the Constitutional Court, which has reaffirmed the regional and municipal prerogatives in what concerns regulation of land ownership and rights.

10. See García-Montalvo (1999, 9). Land ownership and rights were regulated by Law 6/1998, which was rather controversial at the time and was met, successfully, with constitutional challenges. But this law did not take the political issues surrounding the legal underpinnings of land ownership from the table, and in 2002, Prime Minister Aznar offered the opposition party a grand bargain over this matter, one that would have to include municipal and regional parties. The stated purpose was to stop the strong housing inflation already taking place (see Carmen Parra and Anabel Díez, "Aznar ofrece un gran pacto para frenar el precio del suelo al que el PSOE pone condiciones," *El País*, November 21, 2002). Nothing came of it. A new law was passed in 2007 by the Socialist Party after its return to power in 2004.

11. In fact, one of the earliest legal measures in the crisis was Law 19/2009, which was aimed at removing some of the perceived elements blocking the development of the rental market. An additional reform was Law 37/2011, which was designed to expedite court procedures, in particular in all matters related to housing. See Mora-Sanguinetti (2012) for a thorough econometric study of the impact of judicial efficiency on home ownership and Mora-Sanguinetti (2011) for a brief discussion of issues surrounding the rental market in Spain.

12. For an early study on the effects of taxation on Spanish real estate prices, see López (2004). Incidentally, the motivating real estate bubble in López-García (2004) was the one that took place in the late 1980s, not the one in the first decade of the euro. Ortega et al. (2011) study the effects of different policies aimed at

eliminating tax biases in the real estate market in the context of a DSGE model calibrated to moments of the Spanish economy.

13. See Blanco and Restoy (2007, table 1).

14. See Dokko et al. (2009), who explicitly compute the Taylor residuals in a cross-section of European countries, which includes Spain. See, in particular, their figure A1.

15. See IMF (2009, figure 3.13, 108). For a more skeptical view of this channel, see Ayuso et al. (2006), who argue that the change in ex post real rates is likely to overestimate the drop in ex ante rates in the case of Spain.

16. Estimating the increase in wealth due to the real estate cycle is of course a daunting task. Uriel and Pérez (2012, 15) estimate that the value of the housing stock, which incorporates both quantity and price changes, has gone from €1 trillion in 1990 to €5 trillion in 2010, though the peak was reached in 2008, when they estimate the value of the housing stock at €5.3 trillion.

17. Garriga (2010, 8).

18. See Salas and Saurina (2003, table 1) for a list of relevant deregulation measures during this period as well as an empirical assessment of their impact on the market power of Spanish banks.

19. See Ontiveros and Valero (2013) for an informative account of this crisis. This crisis is the one featured as one of the "Big Five" in Carmen Reinhart and Kenneth Rogoff's research on financial crises. See, for example, Reinhart and Rogoff (2009, table 10.8).

20. RD 3048/1977 of November 11. RD stands for Royal Decree, a norm approved by the cabinet that goes immediately into effect but that ultimately has to be voted by parliament.

21. Fainé (2005) provides a lucid account of the origins of the FGDEB in the context of the banking crisis of those years. In particular, cuadro (table) 1 provides a comprehensive list of banks taken over by the FGDEB.

22. Rajan and Zingales (2003, 182–190) argue that once Spain entered the European institutions, increased competition in products markets made Spanish firms more reliant on outside finance. The prospect of cross-border capital flow following monetary integration made it difficult for governments to intervene in credit markets. These two effects created the constituency for financial liberalization and the breakup of the bank cartel.

23. Before adopting the name Argentaria, the consolidated state-owned bank was known as Corporación Bancaria de España. It merged Banco Exterior, Caja Postal de Ahorros, Banco Hipotecario de España, Banco de Crédito Local, Banco de Crédito Agricola, and Banco de Alicante.

24. This was the Ley 31/1985 of August 2, or LORCA (*Ley de Órganos Rectores de las Cajas de Ahorros*, or Law of governing bodies of the cajas); see also Ley 26/2003 of July 17.

25. See the prescient article by Terceiro (1995), who also provides a useful comparison with the regulation of similar institutions in other countries. Mr. Terceiro also published his views in the press; see, for example, "Problemas de la configuración jurídica de las cajas de ahorros," *Expansión*, October 2–3, 1995. Foreign observers of the Spanish financial system were not unaware of these governance problems; see, for instance, Mai (2004).

26. The cuota participativa was regulated during this period by the Real Decreto Ley 302/2004 of February 20, which in turn developed the relevant articles in the Ley 44/2002, which implemented a series of reforms in the financial sector.

27. Banco de Valencia was an old bank, founded in 1900, and at the peak of the real estate bubble was the sixth-largest bank in Spain. It had about €23 billion of total assets at the time of its nationalization, which occurred in November 2011.

28. This point has been forcefully made by Terceiro (2012, 20), who managed Caja Madrid for an extended time.

29. See Rosa Biot, "Lo peor de lo peor era la CAM," *El País*, June 25, 2012.

30. Spain's 1978 Constitution transformed the Spanish state from a centralized one to a highly decentralized one with 17 regions (including Catalonia, Madrid, Galicia, Andalusia, the Basque Country, Valencia,...), which were to develop their own financial legislative framework. The Constitution provides the minimum common framework, but the regions have substantial freedom to develop and adjust laws to their own local objectives.

31. Two regions rushed in to regulate the cajas at the same time that the central administration was developing the framework contained in the LORCA—Galicia and Catalonia. In particular, Galicia passed the Ley 7/1985 of July 17 and Catalonia the Ley de Parlamento de Cataluna 15/1985 of July 1, both imposing a local legislative framework on their cajas. The Galician cajas ended up being merged at the beginning of the crisis, but to no avail: the merged institution was nationalized in 2012. Of the two main cajas in Catalonia, one La Caixa went on to become the third-largest financial institution in Spain when forced to become a bank (Caixabank). The other one, Caixa Catalunya, failed was nationalized and eventually sold to BBVA.

32. Fonseca (2005, table 1) shows that more than 40% of the general assembly in the cases of Caja Castilla–La Mancha, Caja del Meditérraneo, Bancaja, Caja Madrid and Caixa Catalunya were political appointees. The Bank of Spain intervened in all those entities at different points during the crisis.

33. See, for example, Miguel Angel Noceda, "Quién es Miguel Blesa?" *El País*, June 17, 1996 or Íñigo de Barrón, "El amigo de Aznar que tocó el cielo financiero," *El País*, March 16, 2013.

34. This agreement was widely reported in the press though, incredibly, it was never submitted to the board of Caja Madrid for its consideration. See Terceiro (2012) and the news as reported in *El País*; "CCOO y PP rubrican su acuerdo

para que Blesa presida Cajamadrid" (September 7, 1996) and "El pacto entre el PP y CCOO para el control de Caja Madrid nunca fue aportado al Consejo" (September 21, 2003).

35. Law 4/97 of June 16. Until then the cajas from this region were governed by a 1990 regional law (Law 1/1990 of February 22), which assigned 35% of the representation to the municipalities but none to the regional government; this is what the 1997 law changed, increasing the representation of the regional government at the expense of the municipalities. The 1997 law was subsequently reformed in Law 10/2003 of April 3, bringing down the representation of the regional government and the municipalities to 25% each. All these legal changes did not alter the fundamental fact that the cajas were effectively controlled by the local political machines.

36. See Josep Torrent, "Presidente de la Ruina," *El País*, November 27, 2011.

37. Originally, the cajas were restricted to operations in the province (which are administrative subunits of the regions) where they were headquartered. In 1979 (Orden 20/12/1979), they were allowed to expand freely in the regions were they were headquartered. In 1988 (Real Decreto Ley 1582/1988 of December 29), the cajas were finally allowed to capture deposits throughout the entire country.

38. "Spanish banks" refers to the activities in Spain; thus, for BBVA and Santander, what gets computed in the statistics of the Bank of Spain are the Spanish operations of these large international banks.

39. Ley de Bases de Ordenación Bancaria of July 14, 1962.

40. This is not to say that there are no antecedents to bank supervision inside the Bank of Spain; for an absorbing account of this early history, see Moreno (2008). For the legal foundations of the central bank's supervision responsibilities at the beginning of the bubble years, see the Memoria de la Supervisión Bancaria en España en 2001 (recuadro II.1, 61), Banco de España, which is the annual report on banking supervision; chapter II provides a very clear survey of banking supervision in Spain; see also anexo I. The 2011 annual report in its anexo I also includes a more up-to-date picture as well as a useful organizational chart of the Bank of Spain.

41. For an account of the Banesto crisis, Ontiveros and Valero (2013) and the references therein.

42. In addition, the Bank of Spain has been instrumental in raising the level of economic research in Spain, both through its fellowship programs to fund PhD studies in the United States and its own research facilities.

43. See Saurina (2009, 13).

44. Saurina (2009) mentions, though, that moral suasion had stopped being effective when it came to convincing the banks to moderate the pace of lending, which suggests that putting sand in the loan origination machine may not have been far from the intentions of the Bank of Spain.

45. The relevant document here is the Bank of Spain's Circular 4/2004 of December 22, which is available in English at the Bank of Spain's website. For a brief summary of the issues concerning this document, the interested reader can consult the *Memoria de la Supervisión Bancaria 2004*, pages 114–118. See also Circular 3/2010 of June 29, which modifies Circular 4/2004. Thiemann (2011) provides a useful discussion of the issues as well as an insightful comparison across the different countries in the European Union. Obviously, the issue did not make it into the general press.

46. For empirical evidence on the rejection of credit risk transfer and regulatory capital arbitrage as a motive for securitization in Spain, see Cardone-Riportella et al. (2009).

47. Mr. Caruana is also a Técnico Comercial del Estado and Economista del Estado, which are civil service positions to which one only arrives after grueling public examinations. These civil servants typically become the economists that support the efforts of the different ministries, particularly the economics ministry and the public finance ministry.

48. Governors can only be appointed for one term of six years.

49. See, for example "Rato acepta que existen responsabilidades políticas en el encarecimiento de los pisos," *El País*, October 3, 2010, where Mr. Rato, at the time economics minister and deputy prime minister, was said to be proposing measures such as financial help for young couples, but also some to facilitate the increase in supply.

50. See, for instance, Miguel Sebastián, a future main economic advisor to Prime Minister Rodríguez Zapatero and industry minister, "El ladrillo y la burbuja," *El País*, June 22, 2003, and Miguel Ángel Fernández Ordóñez, the future governor of the Bank of Spain, "El Pinchazo de la burbuja de la construcción," *Cinco Días*, September 27, 2003. In addition, the research department of BBVA (the large Spanish bank) produced several pieces analyzing the real estate boom early in the cycle. See, for example, Balmaseda et al. (2002).

51. Martínez and Maza (2003) and Ayuso and Restoy (2006). These two pieces were summarized in Ayuso et al. (2003).

52. See, for example, C. Galindo, "El Banco de España avisa del riesgo de una ajuste brusco en la vivienda," *El País*, October 3, 2003.

53. "Rato anuncia la moderación de los precios de la vivienda y niega la existencia de burbuja inmobiliaria," *El Mundo*, November 4, 2003; "Montoro niega la existencia de la burbuja inmobiliaria," *El Mundo*, October 2, 2003; and "Botín niega que haya burbuja inmobiliaria y afirma que el informe del Banco de España se malinterpretó," *Cinco Días*, October 22, 2003. The opposition leader at the time, the future prime minister José Luis Rodríguez Zapatero, claimed that the bubble was a reality and that its burst would be disastrous for the Spanish economy; see Anabel Díez, "Zapatero culpa al gobierno de desoír sus avisos sobre el posible estallido de la vivienda," *El País*, October 4, 2003. *El País* (August 4,

2003), the leading Spanish newspaper, published a piece titled "Existe la burbuja inmobiliaria?" where they reported the views on the issue from a broad spectrum of leading economic agents. García-Montalvo (2008, apéndice) offers an impressive collection of statements by some authorities and business leaders on the topic of the real estate bubble.

54. Raquel Pascual, "Caruana niega que haya burbuja inmobiliaria y confía en un ajuste natural de los precios," *Cinco Días*, June 19, 2003.

55. For a window into Mr. Caruana's thinking at the time, see his speech on the occasion of the presentation of the Bank of Spain's 2002 *Annual Report* (Caruana 2003), page 17, in particular.

56. For instance in Caruana (2005, 15), he stated that Spanish credit institutions had solvency ratios as well as provisions that minimized the possibility of credit flow impairment in the presence of a correction in housing.

57. The letter was kept confidential until its existence was first reported by the daily *El Mundo*; see Carlos Segovia, "Los inspectores del Banco de España avisaron al Gobierno de la crisis en 2006," *El Mundo*, February 21, 2011. It can be found at http://estaticos.elmundo.es/documentos/2011/02/21/inspectores.pdf.

58. See Miguel Ángel Noceda, "Solbes elige a Fernández Ordóñez para futuro gobernador del Banco de España," *El País*, March 8, 2006.

59. These data appear in Table 4.4 (credit Institutions, Assets, Securities of the Statistics Bulletin of the Bank of Spain).

60. These two numbers do not add up to 1, because of a negligible percentage of unclassified loans.

61. After the crisis starts and particularly in 2012 and 2013, the data are much more difficult to interpret, because one needs to take into account transfers of real estate developer portfolio to the bad bank set up by the Spanish government at the end of 2013. These transfers result in a dramatic drop in the volume of real estate developer loans in the bank and cajas portfolios and a corresponding increase in the percentage of mortgages in the overall loan portfolio at the very end of the available sample.

62. Two main sources for data on deposits are available in the Bank of Spain website. Chapter 4 of the Statistics Bulletin, which is the data source used to construct the previous plots and tables, provides what is referred to as supervisory returns, data provided by the credit institutions to the Bank of Spain for supervision purposes. Chapter 8 provides what is referred to as European Monetary Union returns data, which are statements harmonized at the euro area level and that can also be found at the ECB website. There are many differences between these two data sets. For our purposes, it is enough to note that one can gain a deeper insight into the nature of wholesale funding by looking at EMU returns data and in particular, data on deposits, which is where a lot of the securitization vehicles are reported. The cost is that one looses the ability to distinguish between cajas and banks and instead is forced to consider the credit institutions as a whole.

In addition, chapter 8 is concerned with other monetary and financial institutions (OMFIs), which includes both credit institutions and money market mutual funds (MMMFs). MMMFs account for a small percentage of the aggregate balance sheet of OMFIs, so one can, when the data are not disaggregated by type of entity, proceed to draw inferences about credit institutions without much fear of biases. See also the notes to Figure 6.7. In addition, one could use alternative sources of data, such as the one available at the website of the CNMV, the Spanish equivalent of SEC, as well as the annual reports of both banks and cajas. For a first step in this direction, see Arce (2012).

63. Here I follow closely Martínez Pagés (2012), who provides an informative description of deposit construction for EMU returns.

64. There are securitization vehicles in other euro member states, but their aggregate size is a small fraction of that it those based in Spain.

65. The curious reader may be wondering why there is no plot showing the evolution of this entry. The reason is that table 8.26, series 6, which is where these deposits related to securitization vehicles are reported, only starts in June 2010.

66. Deposits in May of 2005 were €850 billion and jumped to €928 billion in June of that year.

67. Data for this plot is from the annual banking supervision reports from the Bank of Spain. These numbers differ considerably from numbers in private reports. For instance, the ESF Securitization Data Report corresponding to the summer of 2009Q2, using data from Bloomberg, puts the outstanding balance for Spanish collateral was €250.6 billion whereas the number at the end of 2008 in the aforementioned Bank of Spain report was €444.9 billion. Probably the difference is due to the nature of the securitization deals made by the cajas. Finally, the numbers reported in Figure 6.8 correspond to the securitization deals made by Spanish banks, not the entire consolidated sector.

68. Once again I follow Martínez Pagés's (2012, 4) lucid and concise description closely here.

69. Originally, only real estate risk could be securitized. Two legal developments are key in the Spanish securitization market. The Law 19/1992 of July 7 regulated the securitization of real estate risks, and the Royal Decree 926/1998 of May 14 effectively extends the possibility of securitizing other forms of collateral.

70. For instance, in 2009, of the outstanding balance of €368.8 billion of "asset securitizations," banks accounted for €229.1 billion and cajas for €115.2 billion. Of the €168 billion of "liability securitizations," banks accounted for only €8.5 billion, whereas cajas accounted for €156.2 billion.

71. See Bank of Spain, Memoria de Supervisión Bancaria 2003, p. 28.

72. The numbers do not ass up to 318 because some real-estate loans were issued by credit copperatives, special credit institutions, and other credit institutions. See table 6.1.

73. See RDL 6/2008 of October 13. Three days before, a law was passed to create a government-funded entity to acquire high credit quality assets issued

by both credit institutions as well as securitization vehicles (see RDL 6/2008 of October 10).

74. For an account of this case, see Íñigo de Barrón, "Caja Castilla-La Mancha, el aviso de una crisis que nadie quiso oír," *El País*, June 24, 2012.

75. This guarantee required an act of government (RDL 4/2009 of March 29), which had to meet during a weekend to approve the entire package.

References

Ahearne, A., J. Delgado and J. von Weisacker (2008). A Tail of Two Countries. *Brueghel Policy Brief.* Brussels, Belgium.

Ayuso, J., and F. Restoy (2006). House Prices and Rents: An Equilibrium Asset Pricing Approach. *Journal of Empirical Finance 13*(3), 371–388.

Ayuso, J., J. Martínez Pagés, L. Á. Maza, and F. Restoy, (2003). House prices in Spain. Economic Bulletin (October), 64–74.

Ayuso, J., R. Blanco, and F. Restoy (2006). House prices and real interest rates in Spain. Banco de España Research Paper. Madrid, Spain.

Balmaseda, M., I. San Martín and M. Sebastián (2002). Una aproximación cuantitativa a la burbuja inmobiliaria, *Situación Inmobiliaria, BBVA*. Bilbao, Spain.

Bolton, P., T. Santos, and J. Scheinkman (2016). Cream skimming in financial markets. *Journal of Finance 71*(2), 709–736.

Cardone-Riportella, C., R. Samaniego-Medina, and A. Trujillo-Ponce (2009). What do we know about banks securitisation? The Spanish experience. Working Paper, Universidad Carlos III de Madrid.

Caruana, J. (2003). Discurso de presentación del informe anual ante el consejo de gobierno del Banco de España. Madrid: Banco de España.

Cuñat, Vicente and Luis Garicano (2010). Did good Cajas extend bad loans? Governance, Human Capital and Loan Portfolios. In *The Crisis of the Spanish Economy*. Madrid, Spain: FEDEA.

DellaVigna, S., and J. Pollet (2007). Demographics and industry returns. *American Economic Review 97*(5), 1667–1702.

Dokko, J., B. Doyle, M. T. Kiley, J. Kim, S. Sherlund, J. Sim, and S. Van den Heuvel (2009). *Monetary Policy and the Housing Bubble*. Finance and Economics Discussion Series. Washington, DC: Federal Reserve Board.

Fainé Casas, I. (2005). La evolución del sistema bancario español desde la persepectiva de los fondos de garantía de depósitos. *Estabilidad Financiera* (8), 107–126.

Fernández-Villaverde, J., L. Garicano, and T. Santos (2013). Political credit cycles: The case of the Eurozone. Forthcoming, *Journal of Economic Perspectives*

Fonseca Díaz, A. R. (2005). El gobierno de las cajas de ahorros: influencia sobre la eficiencia y riesgo. *Universia Business Review—Actualidad Económica, Cuarto Trimestre 8*, 24–37.

Fonseca Díaz, A. R., and F. González (2005). Cambios en el Gobierno de las Cajas de Ahorros y Nivel de Riesgo. Efecto de las legislaciones autnomas. *Revista Espaola de Financiación y Contabilidad 34*(125), 395–422.

García-Montalvo, José (1999). El Precio del Suelo: La Polémica Interminable. Valencia, Spain: IVIE y Universitat de Valencia.

García-Montalvo, J. (2000). *El precio del suelo: la polémica interminable.* Barcelona, Spain: CREI y Universitat Pompeu Fabra.

———. (2007). Algunas consideraciones sobre el problema de la vivienda en España. *Papeles de Economía Española* 113, 138–153.

———. (2008). *De la quimera inmobiliaria al colapso financiero.* Barcelona: Antoni Bosch.

———. (2010). Land use regulation and house prices in Spain. *Moneda y Crédito* 230, 87–120.

Garriga, C. (2010). *The role of construction in the housing boom and bust in Spain.* Working Paper, FEDEA. Madrid, Spain.

González, L., and F. Ortega (2011). How do very open economies absorb large immigration flows? Recent evidence from Spanish regions. *Labour Economics 18*(1), 57–70.

———. (2009). Immigration and housing booms: Evidence from Spain. Discussion paper.

IMF (International Monetary Fund) (2009). *World Economic Outlook.* Washington, DC.

López-García, Miguel-Angel (2004). Housing prices and tax policy in Spain. *Spanish Economic Review 6*(1), 29–52.

Mai, H. (2004). Spain's cajas: Deregulated, but not depoliticised. *Deutsche Bank Research, EU Monitor, Financial Market Special* 20.

Mankiw, G., and D.N. Weil (1989). The baby boom, the baby bust and the housing market. *Regional Science and Urban Economics 19*, 235–258.

Martínez Pagés, Jorge. (2012). Analysis of recent changes in bank deposits in Spain. *Economic Bulletin* (September), 15–22. Madrid: Bank of Spain.

Martínez Pagés, J., and L. Á. Maza (2003). Análisis del Precio de la Vivienda en España. Documento de Trabajo, Banco de España, Madrid, Spain.

Matilde Mas, Francisco Pérez and Ezequiel Uriel (2011). El Stock y Los Servicios de Capital en España y su Distrubución Territorial y Sectoral (1964–2010). Bilbao, Spain: Documento de Trabajo, Fundación BBVA.

Mora-Sanguinetti, S. (2011). Algunas Consideraciones sobre el mercado de alquiler en España. *Boletín Económico, Noviembre, Banco de España* 80–91.

———. (2012). Is judicial inefficiency increasing the weight of the house property market in Spain? Evidence at the local level. *Journal of the Spanish Economic Association 3*(3), 339–365.

Moreno, F., Rafael (2008). Los Servicios de Inspección del Banco de España: Su origen histórico. *Estudios de Historia Económina* 53. Madrid: Banco de España.

Nishimura, K. (2013). Property bubbles and economic policy. Keynote speech delivered at the Special Panel on Property Markets, Financial Stability, and Macroprudential Policies, at the Allied Social Science Associations and the American Real Estate & Urban Economic Association Annual Meeting, San Diego, CA.

Oliver, Wyman. (2012). Asset quality review and bottom-up stress test exercise. Madrid: Bank of Spain.

Ontiveros, E., and J. Valero (2013). Las crisis bancarias en España, 1977–2012. *Revista de la Historia de la Economía y de la Empresa 7*, 277–317.

Ortega, E., M. Rubio, and C. Thomas, (2011). House purchases versus rental in Spain. *Moneda y Crédito 232*, 109–151.

Rajan, R., and L. Zingales. (2003). *Saving Capitalism from the Capitalists*, New York: Crown Business.

Reinhart, C. M., and K. S. Rogoff (2009). *This Time Is Different: Eight Centuries of Financial Folly*. Princeton, NJ: Princeton University Press.

Salas, V., and J. Saurina (2003). Deregulation, market power and risk behaviour in Spanish banks. *European Economic Review 47*(6), 1061–1075.

Saurina, J. (2009). Loan loss provision in Spain. A working macroprudential tool. *Estabilidad Financiera 00*(17), 9–26.

Scheinkman, J. (2014). Speculation, trading and bubbles. Economic Theory Center. New York: Columbia University Press.

Solé-Ollé, A., and E. Viladecans-Marsal (2013). *The influence wielded by land developer lobbies during the housing boom: Recent evidence from Spain.* CESifo DICE Report. *Journal for Institutional Comparisons 11*(2), 43–49.

Terceiro, J. (1995). Singularidades en el sistema financiero español: la situación de las cajas de ahorros. *Mercados Financieros, ICE* (748), 21–37.

———. (2012). Entorno Institutional Económmíco, Discurso. Madrid, Spain: Real Academia Españo.

Thiemann, M. (2011). Regulating the off-balance sheet exposure of banks: A comparison pre- and post-crisis. Brussels: Foundation for Progressive European Studies.

Vinuesa, J. (2007). Prospectiva demográfica y mercado de vivienda. Clm. Economía: Revista Económíca de Castillo La Manchu (11), 139–164.

CHAPTER SEVEN

Are Commodity Futures Prices Barometers of the Global Economy?

Conghui Hu and Wei Xiong

1 Introduction

Many commentators have argued that commodity futures prices are barometers of the global economy. Is this argument relevant in practice? Addressing this basic question helps evaluate the informational role of commodity futures prices. Due to the lack of centralized trading in spot markets for commodities, centralized futures markets serve as an important platform for aggregating dispersed information regarding supply and demand of commodities.

In this paper, we focus on analyzing whether prices of various commodity futures contracts traded in the United States reveal information that is relevant to stock prices of several East Asian economies, including China, Hong Kong, Japan, South Korea, and Taiwan. The U.S. commodity futures markets offer liquid futures contracts on a large set of commodities, which are heavily traded by traders from all over the world. Our analysis focuses on three key commodities, copper, soybeans, and crude oil, which represent three important commodity sectors—industrial metals, grain, and energy. East Asia is one of the most vibrant parts of the world economy. China and Japan are the second- and third-largest economies after the United States. In particular, as a result of its rapid economic growth in the past 20 years, China is widely recognized as a major engine of world economic growth. As a whole, East Asia has also imported a large fraction of the world's commodity output in recent years.

If U.S. commodity futures prices reveal useful information about the global economic strength, we expect East Asian stock prices to react to the commodity futures prices. The time zone difference between East Asia and the United States introduces asynchronous trading in the East Asian stock markets and the U.S. futures markets, which in turn allows us to analyze whether the lagged overnight returns of commodity futures traded in the United States predict East Asian stock prices. In our analysis, we also explicitly test whether the commodity futures prices reveal information beyond what is contained in the S&P 500 index futures price. We also control for commodity spot prices.

We find an evident change in the predictive power of U.S. commodity futures prices for East Asian stock prices beginning around the mid-2000s. There is little evidence of the commodity futures prices predicting stock prices in East Asian stock markets before 2005. In the latter period, significant evidence suggests that the lagged overnight futures returns of copper, soybeans, and crude oil positively predict index returns of all the East Asian stock markets. Interestingly, even after controlling for the S&P 500 index futures return, the predictive powers of copper and soybeans remain positive and significant, although that of crude oil becomes insignificant. By separately examining stock returns of a set of industries in China, Japan, and Hong Kong (ranging from supply industries that produce a given commodity, consumer industries that demand the commodity as an important production input, and other industries that are not directly related to the commodity) we also find consistently positive and significant predictive powers of the lagged futures returns of copper and soybeans for stock returns across all these industries, even after controlling for the S&P 500 index futures return.

The uniformly positive predictive powers of lagged futures returns for stock returns across these commodity-importing economies and across both commodity supply and consumer industries indicate that in recent years, commodity futures prices reveal information regarding the strength of the global economy, rather than commodity supply shocks or idiosyncratic demand shocks to the United States.

One might argue that the futures prices of copper and soybeans may simply reflect news that exogenously arrives at the markets during the hours the East Asian stock markets are closed and that East Asian stock prices would eventually incorporate the news regardless of the trading in the U.S. commodity futures markets. It is difficult to conclusively trace the information revealed by the futures prices of copper and soybeans directly to trading in these markets. Two features of our analysis nevertheless highlight that the information is special. First, the predictive powers of the lagged futures returns of copper and soybeans for stock returns of East Asian economies remain robust even after controlling for the lagged return of S&P 500 index futures. This suggests that the futures prices of copper and soybeans contain information beyond that in the S&P 500 index. One should not take this additional information for granted, as S&P 500 index futures price is a widely followed financial indicator of the U.S. stock market and the global economy. Second, the futures prices of copper and soybeans have stronger predictive powers for East Asian stock prices than their spot prices do, which indicates that the futures prices are more informative than the spot prices. Taken together, futures prices of copper and soybeans summarize information relevant to the East Asian economies, even if the information is also revealed by other sources.

From a conceptual perspective, our results are consistent with commodity futures markets serving the role of aggregating dispersed information among market participants across the world regarding the global supply and demand of commodities (e.g., Grossman, 1989). From an empirical perspective, our analysis echoes several existing empirical studies of the informational role of commodity futures prices. The classic study of Roll (1984) shows that the futures price of orange juice efficiently reflects information about temperature in central Florida, which produces most of the juice oranges in the United States. Garbade and Silber (1983) compare the roles of futures markets and spot markets in information discovery for a set of commodities and find that it is common for futures markets to play a more important role than spot markets.

In this light, our findings are perhaps not surprising at first glance, but they lead to several deeper questions. First, the large literature on the effects of oil price shocks on stock markets in the United States and other countries often yields contradictory results. For example, Jones and Kaul (1996), Nandha and Faff (2008), and Park and Ratti (2008) document that oil price increases have a negative impact on equity returns across different countries and different industries, although Huang et al. (1996) find little correlation between daily returns of oil futures and various stock indexes in the United States. To reconcile the difference in these findings, Kilian and Park (2009) highlight different impacts of supply and demand shocks to oil on stock prices by using a structural model to decompose oil price shocks. Building on this notion of oil supply and demand shocks having different impacts on stock prices, our finding of East Asian stock returns being negatively correlated with oil futures returns before 2005 but positively correlated after 2005 indicates a potential structural change in the composition of oil shocks in recent years. Similarly, our analysis also indicates a potential structural change in the composition of shocks to copper and soybeans, as their futures returns have a significant predictive power for East Asian stock returns after 2005 but not before.

What has caused this structural change? The change might be related to the quickly growing commodity demand from East Asian economies, in particular, China, reaching critical market share around the mid-2000s. This timing also overlaps with the large inflow of investment capital to the long side of commodity futures markets since the mid-2000s, which totaled more than $200 billion in 2008, according to an estimate of the report of U.S. Senate Permanent Subcommittee on Investigations (2009). This investment flow—largely attracted by the appeal that commodity futures returns are historically uncorrelated with U.S. stock returns and are instead driven by the growth of emerging economies—might have further tightened the link between commodity futures prices and East Asian stock prices. Precisely timing the structural break together with a systematic identification strategy would be helpful for uncovering its causes. We leave this analysis to future studies.

Our analysis is also related to the ongoing debate regarding whether speculation in commodity futures market in the form of indexed investment to commodity futures might have affected commodity prices.[1] In light of our finding that people across the world react to potential information in commodity futures prices, it is possible for commodity futures prices to influence the expectations of goods producers regarding the strength of the global economy and thus their decisions to acquire commodities as production inputs (a la Hayek 1945). Building on this informational channel, Sockin and Xiong (2015) develop a model to show that noise introduced by futures market trading can feed back to goods producers' commodity demand and spot prices.[2] This feedback mechanism is premised on commodity futures prices as barometers of the global economy. Did noise from futures market trading feed back to commodity demand and spot prices during the commodity price boom in 2007–2008? The question is key for systematically evaluating the role of futures market speculation, which we leave to future research.

This paper is organized as follows: Section 2 describes our empirical design, and Section 3 introduces the data. We report our findings in Section 4 and then conclude in Section 5.

2 Empirical Design

In this section, we first summarize commodity imports of East Asia. We then describe the approach we use to examine information flow from U.S. futures prices to East Asian stock prices and vice versa. Finally, we discuss how we interpret the information flow in light of demand, supply, and financial market shocks to commodity markets.

2.1 Commodity Imports of East Asia

Table 7.1 summarizes the imports of copper, soybeans, and crude oil by different regions in 2010. Mainland China contributed 28.9%, 59.5%, and 10.9%; Japan contributed 2.0%, 3.6%, and 7.9%; and South Korea contributed 3.9%, 1.3%, and 5.4% of the total world imports of copper, soybeans, and crude oil, respectively.

Figure 7.1 also plots the imports of these commodities across different regions in recent years. The rapid growth of imports by China in the past decade clearly stands out for all three commodities. For imports of copper, despite the contraction by the United States and Europe during the recent world economic recession from 2006 to 2009, China maintained a consistent, high growth rate except for a brief slowdown in 2008.

TABLE 7.1 **Commodity import in 2010, by regions**

	Unit	World	Mainland China	Japan	South Korea	Taiwan	U.S.	Europe
Copper	Billion USD	48.3	25.1	0.5	3.1		4.4	14.6
	% of World Import	100.0%	51.9%	1.0%	6.5%		9.0%	30.2%
Soybeans	Thousands of Metric Tons	95,869	57,000	3,450	1,260	2,500		14,000
	% of World Import	100.0%	59.5%	3.6%	1.3%	2.6%		14.6%
Crude oil	Thousand Barrels Per Day	43,677	4,754	3,472	2,372	886	9,213	
	% of World Import	100.0%	10.9%	7.9%	5.4%	2.0%	21.1%	

Notes: The data on copper are provided by the United Nations Commodity Trade Statistics Database, which records the dollar-denominated imported value of copper and articles by countries. The data on soybeans and crude oil are obtained from the *CRB Commodity Yearbook* 2011 and International Energy Statistics, respectively.

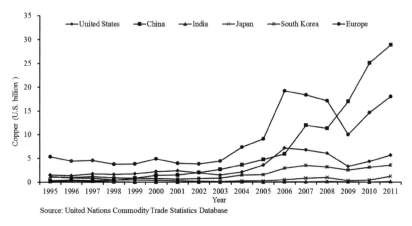

FIGURE 7.1A. Copper imports across regions. This figure plots the recent trends in imports of copper by various regions of the world. The data is provided by the United Nations Commodity Trade Statistics Database, which records the dollar-denominated imported value of copper and articles by countries.

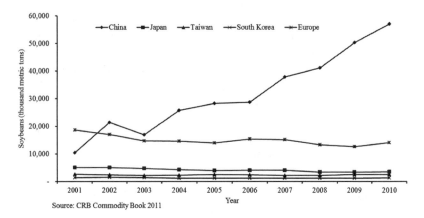

FIGURE 7.1B. Soybeans imports across regions. This figure plots the recent trends in imports of soybeans by various regions of the world. The data is obtained from the *CRB Commodity Yearbook* 2011.

For imports of soybeans, despite being the largest importer in the world, China had a steady growth after 2003 in sharp contrast to the flat curves of all other regions. For imports of crude oil, China also maintained a steady and rapid growth rate and eventually passed Japan in 2008 to become the second largest importer after the United States.

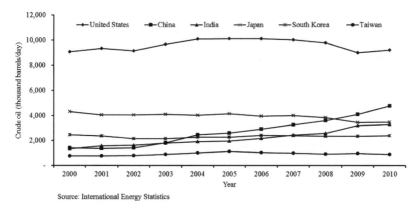

Source: International Energy Statistics

FIGURE 7.1C. Crude oil imports across regions. This figure plots the recent trends in imports of crude oil by various regions of the world. The data is obtained from International Energy Statistics.

Taken together, East Asian countries contribute a significant fraction of the world imports of copper, soybeans, and crude oil. Their large demands of these commodities make the interactions between their stock markets and commodity futures prices traded in the United States interesting subjects to examine.

2.2 Identification of Information Flow

Our empirical analysis focuses on examining how U.S. commodity futures price changes predict East Asian stock prices. We take advantage of the time zone difference between the United States and East Asia. As daytime in East Asia is nighttime in the United States, the predictive powers for East Asian stock prices by the return of U.S. commodity futures during the previous night reflect information flow from U.S. commodity futures prices to East Asian stock prices.

Figure 7.2A illustrates the regular trading hours of Chinese stock markets and U.S. futures markets. The Shanghai Stock Exchange opens at 9:30 a.m. (GMT + 8) and closes at 3:00 p.m. with a lunch break from 11:30 a.m. to 1:00 p.m., while the U.S. futures markets trade from 9:00 a.m. to 2:30 p.m. (GMT − 5). As the Shanghai time is 13 hours ahead of New York time (12 hours when the United States adopts daylight savings time), the trading in the Shanghai stock market closes even before it starts in the United States commodity futures markets.

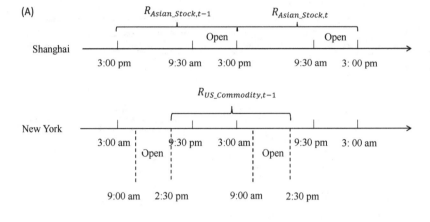

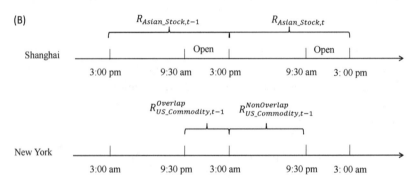

FIGURE 7.2. Trading hours. Panel A illustrates the regular trading hours of Chinese stock markets and U.S. futures markets. The Shanghai Stock Exchange opens at 9:30 a.m. (GMT + 8) and closes at 3:00 p.m. with a lunch break from 11:30 a.m. to 1:00 p.m., while the U.S. futures markets trade from 9:00 a.m. to 2:30 p.m. (GMT − 5). Panel B illustrates the overlapping trading hours and marks the division of the two sub-intervals.

To examine information flow from $R_{\text{US\_Commodity},t-1}$, the U.S. commodity futures return on day $t - 1$ (return from 2:30 p.m. of day $t - 2$ to 2:30 p.m. of day $t - 1$), to $R_{\text{Asian\_Stock},t}$, Asian stock return on day t (price change from 3 p.m. of day $t - 1$ to 3 p.m. of day t in Shanghai time), we run the following regression:

(1) $R_{\text{Asian\_Stock},t} = b_0 + b_1 R_{\text{US\_Commodity},t-1} + b_2 R_{\text{S\&P500},t-1}$

$$+ b_3 R_{\text{Asian\_Stock},t-1} + \varepsilon_t.$$

The term $b_1 R_{\text{US\_Commodity},t-1}$ measures the information transmitted from the U.S. commodity futures return during the U.S. trading hours to Asian stock prices after the Asian markets open the next day.

It is a relevant concern that the commodity futures prices may simply passively reflect exogenous news during the U.S. trading hours, and East Asian stock prices may eventually incorporate the news even without observing the commodity futures prices. Because we cannot find a counterfactual for how East Asian stock prices would fluctuate without the commodity futures markets, it is difficult to identify information actively acquired by traders in the commodity futures markets. Instead, we use two strategies to show that information revealed by the commodity futures prices is special. First, we include the overnight S&P stock index futures return $R_{\text{S\&P500},t-1}$ in regression (1) as a control. If the coefficient b_1 is still significant, it means that the information revealed by the commodity futures return is not subsumed by the information in the futures return of the S&P 500 index, a widely followed indicator for the strength of the U.S. and world economies. Second, we also include the spot return of the commodity during the previous night to control for information contained by the commodity's spot price.

Furthermore, to control for potential price momentum in East Asian stock markets, we also include the return of the Asian stock on the previous day, $R_{\text{Asian\_Stock},t-1}$.

A nuanced issue in our analysis is overnight trading in U.S. commodity futures markets. GLOBEX introduced overnight trading of commodity futures in 1994, and electronic trading systems further facilitated trading during night sessions, although futures trading during night sessions was light before 2005. With the introduction of overnight trading, U.S. commodity futures markets are open for almost 24 hours a day, which means trading in East Asian stock markets overlaps with night sessions of U.S. futures markets.

For the sample after 2005, tick-by-tick transaction data of U.S. commodity futures prices and S&P 500 index futures prices are available. We use this high-frequency data to construct returns of a commodity's futures and S&P 500 index futures during hours overlapping and nonoverlapping with each East Asian stock market in our sample. Specifically, we divide each day into two subintervals, one that overlaps with the trading hours of an East Asian stock market (e.g., the Shanghai stock market) and the other that does not overlap with the trading hours of the East Asian market. Note that the division of these subintervals may vary across different East Asian markets. Figure 7.2B illustrates the overlapping trading hours and marks the division of the two subintervals.

We then regress the return of the East Asian stock market on the commodity futures return and S&P 500 index futures return during the lagged nonoverlapping trading hours, $R_{\text{US\_Commodity},t-1}^{\text{NonOverlap}}$ and $R_{\text{S\&P500},t-1}^{\text{NonOverlap}}$, to examine information transmitted from these markets:

$$
\textbf{(2)} \qquad R_{\text{Asian}_{\text{Stock}},t} = b_0 + b_1 R_{\text{US\_Commodity},t-1}^{\text{NonOverlap}} + b_2 R_{\text{US\_spot},t-1}
$$

$$
+ b_3 R_{\text{S\&P500},t-1}^{\text{NonOverlap}} + b_4 R_{\text{Asian\_Stock},t-1} + \varepsilon_t.
$$

To control for information transmitted by the spot price of the commodity, we also add the lagged spot return from the previous day $R_{\text{US\_spot},t-1}$ to regression (2).

2.3   Interpretation of Information Content

To interpret information flow between U.S. commodity futures prices and East Asian stock prices, it is important to have a clear view of determinants of commodity futures prices. We can loosely classify determinants of commodity futures prices into several categories: supply shocks, demand shocks, and financial market shocks. These shocks originate from different sources and have different implications for commodity futures prices and their joint dynamics with stock prices. We briefly describe these shocks and summarize the extent to which the joint dynamics of East Asian stock prices and U.S. commodity futures prices reflect these shocks.

SUPPLY SHOCKS.   Economists have long recognized that shocks to oil supply are important drivers of oil price fluctuations, which in turn can have significant real effects on the economy. Hamilton (1983) shows that disruptions to oil supply and dramatic oil price increases preceded almost all U.S. recessions after World War II. Mork (1989) and Hamilton (2003) further document that the relation between oil price changes and GDP growth is nonlinear—oil price increases have much more important effects than do oil price decreases. Backus and Crucini (2000) provide evidence that oil price increases exacerbate international business cycles through the terms of trade between countries. Davis and Haltiwanger (2001) find that oil price increases significantly reduce U.S. manufacturing jobs, although oil price decreases do not lead to job creation in the same magnitude. More recently, by using a new measure of exogenous oil supply shocks, Kilian (2008a) shows that oil supply shocks have made little difference for the evolution of the U.S. economy since the 1970s, although they did matter for some historical episodes. Blanchard and Gali (2010) also emphasize that the real effects of oil shocks changed over time and were much smaller after 1984.

Suppose that a supply shock drives up the futures price of a commodity. The price increase raises commodity import costs to East Asian economies. As a result, the supply shock should push down the overall East Asian stock prices. The effect of the supply shock may vary across industries in that it hurts consumer industries that demand the commodity as production input but it benefits supply industries that produce the commodity.

DEMAND SHOCKS. Several recent studies highlight that demand shocks might also play an important role in driving oil prices. Kilian (2009) uses a global index of dry cargo freight rates to measure global economic activity and develops a structural VAR model for the dynamics of global oil production, global economic activity, and oil price. By decomposing the shocks in the economy to three orthogonal sources—an oil supply shock, an aggregate demand shock, and an oil specific demand shock based on certain identification restrictions—this study finds that the aggregate demand shock has a bigger impact on the oil market than previously thought. Furthermore, many economists argue that strong demand confronting stagnating world production was a major factor for the run-up of oil prices in 2007–2008 (e.g., Kilian 2008b; Hamilton 2009).

When discussing the effects of commodity demand shocks on East Asian stock prices, it is useful to differentiate between idiosyncratic demand shocks to the United States and global demand shocks. For example, the popularity of SUVs in the United States may increase U.S. oil consumption and thus oil futures prices. As this demand shock is associated with the U.S. economy, the subsequent oil price increase represents an increase in the cost of oil imports to East Asian economies. Like supply shocks, the local U.S. demand shock should drive down overall stock prices in East Asian industries, with a particularly strong effect on consumer industries that directly demand the commodity, although the shock would benefit supply industries that produce the commodity.

Global demand shocks have rather different effects. For example, the rapid economic expansion of emerging economies has led to growing demand for many commodities, such as oil, copper, iron ore, and soybeans. While growing global demand drives up the futures prices of these commodities, the booming global economy should lead to higher stock prices in East Asia despite the increased cost of commodity imports. In this case, we expect East Asian stock prices across all industries to rise with commodity futures prices.

FINANCIAL MARKET SHOCKS.   Due to the large inflow of investment capital into commodity futures markets during the past decade, commodity futures prices are now more exposed to financial market shocks. See Cheng and Xiong (2013) for a detailed review of specific economic mechanisms that allow financial market shocks to affect commodity futures markets.

Financial market shocks tend to induce positive correlations among prices of financial assets. For example, consider commodity index traders (CITs)—large portfolio investors who have invested hundreds of billions of dollars into commodity futures markets in recent years (e.g., Tang and Xiong, 2012). A positive shock to CITs' other asset holdings, such as U.S. stocks, would increase their portfolio values and risk capacities, and induce greater demands for investing in commodity futures. Such increased investment demands would in turn drive up commodity futures prices. To the extent that the shock may also induce CITs and other institutional investors to demand more East Asian stocks, the shock induces commodity futures prices to become positively correlated with East Asian stock prices. Basak and Pavlova (2016) develop a dynamic equilibrium model to describe such a mechanism through index investors' discount rate.

Two considerations allow us to isolate the effects of financial market shocks in our analysis. First, due to stringent capital controls that prevent capital from freely moving across the Chinese border, China's financial markets are largely segmented from world financial markets. Thus, we do not expect outside financial market shocks to directly impact Chinese stock prices through trading by CITs and other institutional investors. Second, we expect the return of the S&P 500 index to control for financial market shocks in our analysis of price reactions of other East Asian stocks.

In summary, different shocks to commodity futures prices have different implications for East Asian stock prices. In practice, neither market participants nor economic researchers like us observe the nature of shocks that drive commodity futures price fluctuations. Nevertheless, by analyzing the predictive powers of U.S. commodity futures prices for East Asian stock prices over a period of time, our study can uncover how participants of East Asian stock markets on average interpret information revealed by fluctuations of U.S. commodity futures prices. As the economic environment in the commodity markets and the global economy is likely to change over time, the composition of shocks to the economy might also change over time. As a result, we expect the information transmitted from the U.S. commodity futures markets to East Asian stock markets to vary over time as well.

3　Data

3.1　Commodity Prices

We obtain daily futures prices of copper, soybeans, and crude oil from the Global Financial Database (GFD). The GFD uses a rolling contract for its futures data. In most of the analysis, we use returns of rolling across the most actively traded futures contracts of these commodities. These contracts are typically front-month contracts.[3] For robustness, we also examine returns of more distant contracts. The results are similar to those obtained from front-month contracts.

Copper futures returns are measured as log changes of daily prices of the high-grade copper futures contracts traded in COMEX. Soybean futures returns are calculated as log changes of daily prices of soybean futures traded in CBOT. Crude oil futures returns are measured as log changes of daily prices of West Texas Intermediate (WTI) light crude oil futures contracts traded on NYMEX. For copper and soybeans, daily futures data start in January 1959, while crude oil futures data are only available after March 1983.

GLOBEX introduced overnight trading of commodity futures in 1994, and the emergence of electronic trading systems further facilitated trading during night sessions. For copper and crude oil, open outcry trading on NYMEX goes from 9:00 a.m. to 2:30 p.m. Eastern Time on weekdays.

Electronic trading starts at 6:00 p.m. Eastern Time on Sunday and closes at 5:15 p.m. on Friday. It stops trading from 5:15 p.m. to 6:00 p.m. each day. For soybeans, open outcry trading on CBOT goes from 9:30 a.m. to 2:00 p.m. Central Time. Electronic trading goes from 5:00 p.m. Central Time on Sunday to 2:00 p.m. on Friday with a daily break from 2:00 p.m. until 5:00 p.m.

As shown by Ulibarri (1998) and Lin and Tamvakis (2001), futures trading during night sessions was rather light in the early years. For the sample before 2005, we compute daily futures returns using closing prices of the most active contracts of each commodity during regular outcry sessions. For the sample after January 2005, Tick Data database gives intraday prices of copper, soybeans, and crude oil futures, as well as intraday prices of S&P 500 index futures. The data in this database are presented tick-by-tick and are delivered in compressed ASCII files with the TickWrite software, which allows clients to quickly and easily output time series data in ASCII format. TickWrite also makes it easy to create continuous futures data. We use the AutoRoll method recommended by TickWrite to roll futures contracts. AutoRoll computes daily tick volume for the most active and other contracts and rolls to a back contract when the daily tick volume of the back-month contract exceeds the daily tick volume of the current most-active month contract. As discussed in the previous section, we split the daily return of each commodity futures into overlapping and nonoverlapping parts in accordance with trading hours of each Asian stock market by using the tick-by-tick data.

We obtain metal bulletin copper high-grade cathode spot prices (MBCUUSHG) from Bloomberg. Daily spot prices of soybeans and crude oil are obtained from the GFD. The soybean spot prices are based on the closing prices in Southeast Iowa that are offered to producers as of 2:30 p.m. local time. This daily price report is prepared by the Marketing Bureau of Iowa Department of Agriculture and Land Stewardship. Spot prices of crude oil are closing prices for WTI crude oil offered at Cushing, Oklahoma, at 2:30 p.m. local time. The sample period starts in January 2005 and ends in September 2012.

3.2 East Asian Stock Prices

We obtain daily prices of East Asian stock indices from the GFD. We choose the most comprehensive and diversified stock index available for each market. For Japan, we use the Tokyo Price Index (TOPIX), which is a capitalization-weighted price index of all first-section stocks traded on the Tokyo Stock Exchange. Daily prices of TOPIX are available from 1959 on. The morning trading session of TOPIX runs from 9:00 a.m. to 11:00 a.m. Tokyo time (GMT + 9), and the afternoon session is from 12:30 p.m. to 3:00 p.m.

For Hong Kong, we use the Hang Seng Index, which includes the 33 largest firms in Hong Kong and represents about 75% of equity capitalization of the Stock Exchange of Hong Kong (SEHK). The Hang Seng Index is a value-weighted arithmetic index. Daily prices of the Hang Seng Index are available from 1972 on. The morning session of SEHK is from 10:00 a.m. to 12:30 p.m. and the afternoon session is from 2:30 p.m. to 4:00 p.m. (GMT + 8).[4]

The Korea Composite Stock Price Index is a capitalization-weighted price index including all stocks listed on the Seoul Stock Exchange. Daily prices of the Korea Composite Stock Price Index are available from 1962 on. The regular trading session of the Seoul Stock Exchange goes from 9:00 a.m. to 15:05 p.m. (GMT + 9) with a lunch break in the middle.

We use the Shanghai Market Index and the Taiwan Market Index to represent stocks traded in mainland China and Taiwan. Both indices are value-weighted arithmetic indices including all stocks traded in these markets. The data for the Taiwan Market Index starts in 1969, while the Shanghai Market Index became available only after 1991. In Shanghai, the morning session runs from 9:30 a.m. to 11:30 a.m. (GMT + 8) and the afternoon session is from 1:00 p.m. to 3:00 p.m. In Taiwan, the regular trading session goes from 9:00 a.m. to 1:30 p.m. (GMT + 8).

In Section 4.3, we also use returns of individual stocks to construct returns of a set of industries in the stock markets of Japan, Hong Kong, and mainland China.

4 Empirical Results

We first examine the weekly return correlations between the three commodity futures traded in the U.S. and East Asian stock indices. We then study the predictive powers of the lagged overnight return of each of the commodity futures for East Asian stock prices at both market and industry levels.

4.1   Weekly Return Correlation

To get an overall picture of the joint movements of U.S. commodity futures prices and East Asian stock prices, we plot correlations of weekly returns of the futures prices of copper, soybeans, and crude oil with index returns of the five East Asian stock markets in our sample based on two-year rolling windows. We choose correlations of weekly rather than daily returns to mitigate effects of asynchronous trading hours between U.S. markets and East Asian markets. For comparison, we also plot the weekly return correlations of the three commodity futures with the S&P 500 index futures.

The return correlations of copper, soybeans, and oil futures with the six stock market indices are depicted in Figure 7.3A, B, and C respectively. The starting year of each plot varies due to availability of data.

In the top-left plot of Figure 7.3A, the return correlation between copper futures and the S&P 500 index futures varies substantially over time. The correlation is particularly high in two periods, one in the late 1970s and early 1980s and the other in recent years—after the mid-2000s. It is well known that during the former period, stagflation caused both high inflation and slow economic growth in the U.S. and other advanced economies. The high return correlation between copper futures and S&P index futures reflects the stagflation of the time. The high correlation in the latter period, as pointed out by many commentators, may reflect the dependence of both copper prices and the U.S. economy on the rapid economic growth of emerging economies, such as China and India. The correlation in these two periods rises above 0.5, while outside these two periods, it is small and insignificantly different from zero.

The return correlations of copper futures with the stock indices of Japan and Hong Kong (Figure 7.3A top-middle and top-right plots) also have two peaks, one in the late 1970s and early 1980s and the other in recent years. The peak in the latter period was particularly high—higher than 0.5 and the previous peak. These two peaks likely reflect the same forces responsible for driving the correlation of copper futures with the S&P index, as discussed earlier. Outside these two periods, the correlation is small. The return correlations of copper futures with the stock indices of the Taiwan, South Korea, and Shanghai markets (Figure 7.3A bottom row) remain small and insignificant from zero until the mid-2000s, when they all experienced large increases and reached levels above 0.5. The absence of any pronounced correlation increase in late 1970s and early 1980s for these markets may reflect the fact that these countries' economies were in the early stages of development at the time. The economies of Taiwan and South Korea reached an advanced level and became well integrated into the world economy only in 1990s. China's economy reached this stage even later, as China did not have a stock market until the early 1990s. Despite the different stages of development of these East Asian economies, their stock markets all experienced the same large increases in correlations with copper futures in recent years. The focus of our analysis is to examine this common correlation increase.

Figure 7.3B depicts the return correlations of soybean futures with the six stock market indices. There are two notable points. First, the correlations of soybean futures with stock prices are more variable than the corresponding correlations of copper futures. Second, despite the greater variability, the correlations of soybeans futures with the stock market indices also experienced a common increase after the mid-2000s. This common increase resembles the increases in the correlations of copper futures with these stock market indices in the same period.

Figure 7.3C depicts return correlations of crude oil futures with the six stock market indices. As WTI crude oil futures started trading only in 1983, the correlation plots for all stock markets start in 1985, except the plot for China, which starts in 1995. There are also two notable episodes in these plots. First, in early 1990s, we observe large drops in the correlations of oil futures with the stock indices of the United States, Japan, Hong Kong, and South Korea to significantly negative levels. These drops were driven by the Gulf War, which caused oil prices to spike and stock markets across the world to decline. As widely recognized by the literature (e.g., Hamilton 2003), this episode reflects the effect of an oil supply shock. Second, since the early 2000s, there is a common increasing trend in the correlations of oil futures with these different stock market indices. In particular, at the peak in 2010, the correlations with the S&P 500, Hong Kong, and Taiwan indices have risen above 0.5. The increases in correlations with other market indices are more modest but nevertheless significant.

Taken together, the plots in Figure 7.3 demonstrate a clear pattern that—despite the large heterogeneity in the three commodities and the six stock markets—the return correlations between these commodity futures and stock market indices have all experienced large increases and have become significantly positive in recent years. These largely increased correlations are consistent with the finding of Tang and Xiong (2012) and

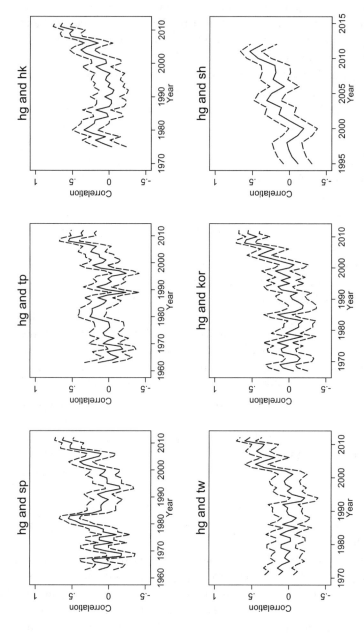

FIGURE 7.3A. Weekly return correlations between U.S. copper futures prices and stock indices. This figure depicts two-year rolling weekly return correlations of U.S. copper (hg) futures prices with the S&P 500 Index (sp), the Tokyo Price Index (tp), the Hang Seng Index (hk), the Taiwan Market Index (tw), the Korea Composite Stock Price Index (kor), and the Shanghai Market Index (sh).

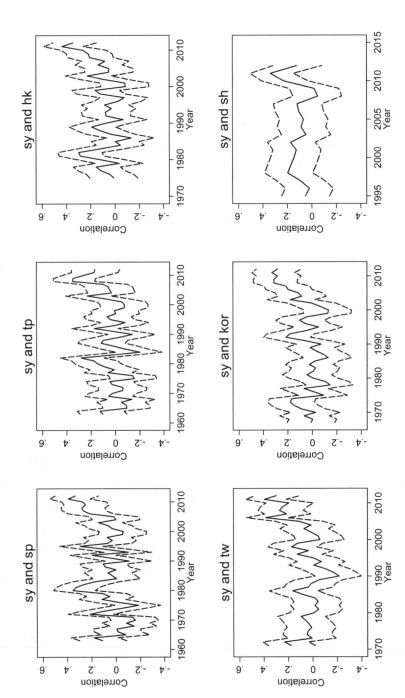

FIGURE 7.3B. Weekly return correlations between U.S. soybeans futures prices and stock indices. This figure depicts two-year rolling weekly return correlations of U.S. soybeans (sy) futures prices with the S&P 500 index (sp), the Tokyo Price Index (tp), the Hang Seng Index (hk), the Taiwan Market Index (tw), the Korea Composite Stock Price Index (kor), and the Shanghai Market Index (sh).

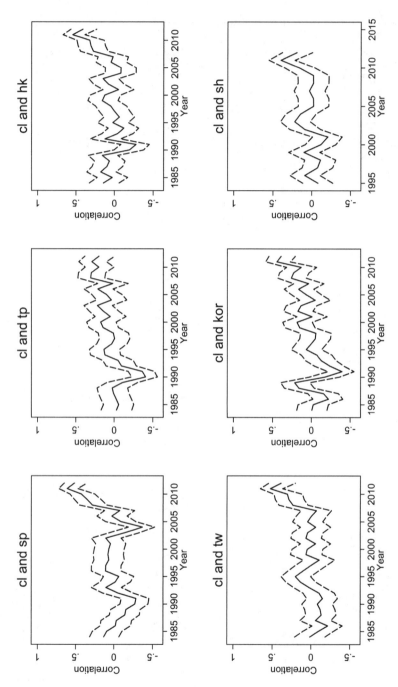

FIGURE 7.3C. Weekly return correlations between U.S. oil futures prices and stock indices. This figure depicts two-year rolling weekly return correlations of U.S. oil (cl) futures prices with the S&P 500 Index (sp), the Tokyo Price Index (tp), the Hang Seng Index (hk), the Taiwan Market Index (tw), the Korea Composite Stock Price Index (kor), and the Shanghai Market Index (sh).

Büyükşahin and Robe (2012), and they motivate our study of information flow between commodity future markets and stock markets.

4.2   Reactions of East Asian Market Indices to U.S. Commodity Futures Prices

We now analyze the predictive powers of U.S. commodity futures prices for East Asian stock prices. We first report results at the market index level in this subsection and then provide some additional results at the industry level in the next subsection.

Table 7.2 reports results from analyzing the regression specified in (1) of Section 2 for the sample before 2005, during which we have only daily data on commodity futures returns. Panel A summarizes the results from using the lagged copper futures return to predict the daily index return of each East Asian stock market. We find a significant predictive power of the copper futures return for East Asian stock indices without controlling for the S&P 500 index futures return. The estimate of the response coefficient b_1 is positive in each market and is statistically significant for Japan, Hong Kong, and South Korea. However, the estimate of b_1 becomes insignificant for all markets after including the lagged S&P 500 index futures return in the regression, indicating that before 2005, copper futures prices did not contain additional information beyond what is in the S&P 500 index. Furthermore, all East Asian stock market indices except the Shanghai Market Index respond positively and significantly to the lagged S&P 500 index return.

Panel B reports the results on the predictive power of the soybean futures return. We find little predictive power for these stock markets with the exception of Hong Kong, where the Hang Seng Index has a positive and marginally significant response to the lagged soybeans futures return without controlling for the lagged S&P 500 index futures return. Overall, there is little evidence before 2005 for the lagged futures returns of either copper or soybeans predicting East Asian stock prices after controlling for the lagged S&P 500 index futures return.

Panel C summarizes the predictive power of the crude oil futures return. In contrast to the responses to lagged copper and soybeans returns, the responses of the East Asian market indices to the lagged crude oil return are mostly negative except for the Shanghai Market Index. Without controlling for the lagged S&P 500 index futures return, the estimate of b_1 is significantly negative for Japan, Taiwan, and

TABLE 7.2 **Reactions of Asian stock indices to U.S. commodity futures prices before 2005**

Variables	(1)	(2)	(3)	(4)	(5)	(6)	(7)	(8)	(9)	(10)
	Japan		Hong Kong		Taiwan		South Korea		Shanghai	
					Panel A: Copper					
b_1	0.0119*	0.000170	0.0274**	0.00308	0.0159	0.00553	0.0162*	0.00749	0.00829	0.00653
	(1.80)	(0.03)	(2.16)	(0.26)	(1.58)	(0.55)	(1.91)	(0.88)	(0.31)	(0.24)
b_2		0.268***		0.458***		0.205***		0.181***		0.0262
		(10.08)		(14.25)		(9.39)		(7.05)		(0.78)
b_3	0.0836***	0.0615***	0.0100	−0.0127	0.0726***	0.0684***	0.0890***	0.0859***	0.0427	0.0428
	(3.60)	(3.01)	(0.41)	(−0.49)	(4.59)	(4.39)	(2.90)	(2.78)	(1.60)	(1.60)
Observations	9,999	9,976	6,980	6,979	8,770	8,748	9,849	9,830	3,092	3,091
Adj R^2	0.008	0.082	0.001	0.068	0.006	0.023	0.009	0.017	0.002	0.002
					Panel B: Soybeans					
b_1	0.00447	−0.00142	0.0293*	0.0189	0.0144	0.0110	0.00144	−0.00188	0.0340	0.0339
	(0.73)	(−0.25)	(1.93)	(1.26)	(1.48)	(1.14)	(0.14)	(−0.18)	(1.01)	(1.00)
b_2		0.266***		0.454***		0.204***		0.179***		0.0270
		(10.06)		(14.27)		(9.92)		(7.06)		(0.82)
b_3	0.0912***	0.0682***	0.0110	−0.0123	0.0718***	0.0661***	0.0909***	0.0875***	0.0434	0.0435
	(3.96)	(3.24)	(0.45)	(−0.48)	(4.54)	(4.24)	(2.98)	(2.83)	(1.63)	(1.63)
Observations	10,060	10,027	7,012	7,007	8,812	8,784	9,913	9,884	3,107	3,103
Adj R^2	0.009	0.081	0.001	0.067	0.006	0.023	0.009	0.017	0.002	0.002
					Panel C: Crude oil					
b_1	−0.0268***	−0.0168**	−0.00439	0.00938	−0.0442***	−0.0351***	−0.0229**	−0.0140	0.0117	0.0132
	(−3.56)	(−2.44)	(−0.46)	(1.03)	(−3.14)	(−2.70)	(−2.09)	(−1.33)	(0.73)	(0.83)
b_2		0.372***		0.500***		0.272***		0.296***		0.0315
		(10.23)		(13.09)		(9.95)		(10.18)		(0.96)
b_3	0.0649**	0.0280	−0.0383	−0.0728**	0.0922***	0.0873***	0.0587***	0.0469**	0.0443*	0.0444*
	(2.13)	(1.07)	(−1.21)	(−2.18)	(4.69)	(4.51)	(3.04)	(2.52)	(1.66)	(1.66)
Observations	4,591	4,590	4,507	4,506	5,089	5,089	5,078	5,077	3,094	3,093
Adj R^2	0.008	0.128	0.002	0.108	0.013	0.040	0.005	0.044	0.002	0.002

Notes: This table reports regression results on reactions of Asian stock indices to U.S. commodity futures prices using daily returns before 2005. For each pair of stock market index and commodity in our sample, we run the regression using equation (1). The sample period of each regression varies with the availability of data. Panels A, B and C display regression results with the futures return of copper, soybeans, and crude oil, respectively, as the predicting variable. In each panel, we report regression results without or with the control of the contemporaneous S&P 500 index return ($R_{S\&P\,500,t-1}$). The t-statistics adjusted for heteroskedasticity and serial correlations using the Newey-West method with five lags are reported in parentheses. We use *, **, *** to indicate significance at the 10%, 5%, and 1% levels, respectively.

South Korea. After controlling for the lagged S&P 500 index futures return, the estimate of b_1 remains significantly negative for Japan and Taiwan. In light of our discussion in Section 2.2, the negative responses indicate that crude oil futures returns reveal information regarding supply shocks of crude oil and that most Asian market indices react negatively to such information. This result is also consistent with the studies referenced in the introduction to this paper, which find that crude oil prices tend to have negative return correlations with stock prices across the world.

For the sample period 2005–2012, we are able to use tick-by-tick data to construct futures returns of the three commodities and S&P 500 index in two subintervals of each day, one for overlapping hours and the other for nonoverlapping hours with each East Asian stock market. In Table 7.3, we examine the reactions of the East Asian market indices to the lagged U.S. commodity futures return during the nonoverlapping hours by running the regression specified in (2) of Section 2. Panels A, B, and C report the reactions to the lagged return of copper, soybeans and crude oil, respectively.

In sharp contrast to the results before 2005, we find positive and significant responses for all East Asian market indices to the lagged returns of both copper and soybean futures even after controlling for the lagged return of S&P 500 index futures. The estimate of b_1 in each market with respect to the lagged futures return of either copper or soybeans is not only substantially larger in magnitude relative to the corresponding estimate reported in Table 7.2 for the pre-2005 sample but also statistically significant. Taken together, these results imply that after 2005, the futures prices of copper and soybeans contain information beyond what is revealed by the price of S&P 500 index futures and that East Asian stock markets respond significantly to price fluctuations of copper and soybeans futures. Given the tremendous popularity of S&P 500 index futures among financial institutions as a key indicator of the economic growth of the United States and the world, one would have expected S&P 500 index futures prices to serve as a sufficient statistic of information revealed by the commodity futures prices. Thus, it is rather striking to observe that the futures prices of copper and soybeans contain additional information.

While our main analysis uses rolling returns of the active futures contracts of the three commodities, we have also examined the predictive powers of returns of distant futures contracts of these commodities. The results are similar. This is not surprising, as it is well known that the prices

TABLE 7.3 **Reactions of Asian stock indices to U.S. commodity futures prices after 2005**

Variables	(1)	(2)	(3)	(4)	(5)	(6)	(7)	(8)	(9)	(10)
	Japan		Hong Kong		Taiwan		South Korea		Shanghai	
Panel A: Copper										
b_1	0.284***	0.0977***	0.327***	0.103***	0.195***	0.0393*	0.221***	0.0701***	0.176***	0.100***
	(11.23)	(4.23)	(10.40)	(3.53)	(7.91)	(1.75)	(6.88)	(2.58)	(6.84)	(3.40)
b_2		0.608***		0.679***		0.495***		0.460***		0.231***
		(17.46)		(15.18)		(13.27)		(9.62)		(4.41)
b_3	0.0347	0.0370	−0.0410	−0.0643	0.0458	0.0529*	0.112**	0.109**	0.00848	0.0130
	(0.87)	(0.99)	(−0.91)	(−1.38)	(1.64)	(1.93)	(2.47)	(2.49)	(0.30)	(0.46)
Observations	1,796	1,796	1,833	1,833	1,842	1,842	1,825	1,825	1,828	1,828
Adj R^2	0.135	0.372	0.124	0.326	0.072	0.242	0.080	0.196	0.028	0.047
Panel B: Soybeans										
b_1	0.188***	0.0600**	0.249***	0.0968**	0.151***	0.0552**	0.159***	0.0601*	0.188***	0.137***
	(5.41)	(2.35)	(5.86)	(2.53)	(5.95)	(2.34)	(4.69)	(1.91)	(5.72)	(3.81)
b_2		0.654***		0.720***		0.506***		0.489***		0.260***
		(19.68)		(16.90)		(14.50)		(10.59)		(5.44)
b_3	0.0126	0.0311	−0.0392	−0.0645	0.0420	0.0544**	0.113**	0.110**	0.0163	0.0199
	(0.29)	(0.82)	(−0.83)	(−1.41)	(1.52)	(1.98)	(2.49)	(2.52)	(0.56)	(0.69)
Observations	1,794	1,794	1,832	1,832	1,841	1,841	1,823	1,823	1,826	1,826
Adj R^2	0.040	0.364	0.052	0.324	0.030	0.244	0.037	0.194	0.023	0.052
Panel C: Crude oil										
b_1	0.173***	0.0280	0.188***	0.0114	0.125***	0.0105	0.122***	0.00317	0.0683***	0.000448
	(8.06)	(1.64)	(7.30)	(0.54)	(6.45)	(0.61)	(5.03)	(0.15)	(2.87)	(0.02)
b_2		0.654***		0.741***		0.514***		0.504***		0.297***
		(19.72)		(17.01)		(14.66)		(10.97)		(5.82)
b_3	0.00649	0.0286	−0.0594	−0.0686	0.0291	0.0507*	0.102**	0.107**	0.00487	0.0133
	(0.15)	(0.75)	(−1.21)	(−1.44)	(1.06)	(1.86)	(2.25)	(2.45)	(0.17)	(0.46)
Observations	1,796	1,796	1,833	1,833	1,842	1,842	1,825	1,825	1,828	1,828
Adj R^2	0.066	0.361	0.056	0.316	0.040	0.240	0.041	0.191	0.006	0.040

Notes: This table reports regression results on reactions of Asian stock indices to U.S. commodity futures prices from January 2005 to September 2012. For each pair of stock market index and commodity in our sample, we regress the Asian stock index return on the lagged non-overlapping return of the commodity futures using equation (3). Panels A, B and C display regression results with the returns of copper, soybeans, or crude oil as the predicting variable. In each panel, we report regression results without or with the control of the S&P 500 index return, which is contemporaneous to the commodity return. Due to the different trading hours of the Asian markets in our sample, the nonoverlapping subinterval for computing the returns of U.S. commodity futures and S&P 500 Index futures varies across different stock markets. The t-statistics adjusted for heteroskedasticity and serial correlations using the Newey-West method with five lags are reported in parentheses. We use *, **, *** to indicate significance at the 10%, 5%, and 1% levels, respectively.

of distant contracts move very closely with the front-month contracts. Our analysis suggests that distant contracts do not provide additional information relative to front-month contracts.

What kind of information is revealed by the futures prices of copper and soybeans? In Section 2.3, we classify four types of shocks to commodity futures prices: supply shocks, idiosyncratic demand shocks, global demand shocks, and financial market shocks. To the extent that commodity price increases driven by supply demands have adverse effects on commodity import economies, the positive reactions of East Asian market indices to futures prices of copper and soybeans cannot be explain by information regarding supply shocks of these commodities. Neither can the positive reactions be explained by information regarding idiosyncratic demand shocks of these commodities. This is because high commodity prices driven by idiosyncratic demand shocks in the United States would also boost commodity import costs of East Asian economies and should thus generate negative price reactions in East Asian stock markets.

It is possible for financial market shocks to cause a positive correlation between commodity futures return and Asian stock market returns. However, it is difficult for this mechanism to fully explain the positive predictability of copper and soybean futures returns for China's market return. As China's stock market is largely segmented from the outside world due to its capital controls, one would not expect trading by outside investors to directly affect the Shanghai Market Index. Furthermore, as we have controlled for the return of S&P 500 index, which would have captured financial market shocks, it is also difficult to attribute the positive responses of other East Asian stock markets.

The positive reactions of East Asian market indices to the lagged copper and soybean futures returns are likely to reflect information regarding global demand shocks to these commodities, which is ultimately related to the strength of the global economy. This is because a stronger global economy leads to higher stock prices in East Asian economies, despite their greater commodity import costs. In the next subsection, we further explore the stock price reactions of different industries to the lagged returns of commodity futures.

Panel C of Table 7.3 reports the predictive power of the lagged oil futures return for East Asian market indices. There is a dramatic change after 2005. Without controlling for the lagged S&P 500 index futures return, the responses of all East Asian market indices to the lagged oil futures return are positive and significant, as opposed to the negative reactions before 2005 shown in Table 7.2. These positive responses are broadly consistent with decreased effects of oil supply shocks documented by Blanchard and Gali (2010) and with the potentially more important effects of global oil demand shocks emphasized by Kilian (2009). However, after controlling for the lagged S&P 500 index futures return, the responses of all markets become insignificant. This indicates that information revealed by the oil futures return is subsumed by that in S&P 500 index futures return. As we discussed before, as one would have expected the S&P 500 index futures market to reflect most of the information about the global economy, this result is not so surprising. However, this result does make the significant amount of information revealed by copper and soybean futures prices even more striking.

One might argue that the information revealed by copper and soybean futures prices may simply reflect passive news that hits the public domain during the hours when the U.S. futures markets are open and the East Asian stock markets are closed. It is difficult to directly trace the information revealed by futures prices of copper and soybeans to active acquisition of traders in the U.S. futures markets. We can nevertheless compare the ability of futures and spot prices of these commodities to predict the East Asian stock prices. If the futures prices have stronger predictive powers, the information in the futures prices is superior to that in the spot prices and thus cannot be taken for granted.

In Table 7.4, we compare the information in the futures prices and spot prices of copper, soybeans, and crude oil in the post-2005 sample. Specifically, we run the regression specified in (2) of Section 2, which adds the lagged spot return of the commodity from the previous day. Due to the lack of high-frequency data on spot prices, we cannot construct spot returns during the nonoverlapping trading hours as we did for the futures return. The spot return from the previous day should nevertheless be sufficient to capture information contained in the spot prices.

Panel A of Table 7.4 reports the results from using both lagged futures and spot returns of copper to predict the return of each of the East Asian market indices. We find that if the lagged futures return is not included in the regression, the lagged spot return of copper is able to predict stock index returns of some markets, such as Japan and Taiwan. However, once the lagged futures return is included, the lagged spot return of copper becomes insignificant in all markets except Taiwan, while the lagged futures return is significant in Japan, Hong Kong, and Shanghai. It is clear

Variables	(1)	(2)	(3)	(4)	(5)	(6)	(7)	(8)	(9)	(10)
	Japan		Hong Kong		Taiwan		South Korea		Shanghai	
	Panel A: Copper									
b_1		0.0956***		0.142***		0.0267		0.0653*		0.155***
		(2.74)		(3.00)		(0.69)		(1.95)		(3.25)
b_2	0.107***	0.0916***	0.0623	0.401	0.0729***	0.0693**	0.0535	0.0440	−0.00720	−0.0259
	(3.32)	(2.98)	(1.23)	(0.86)	(2.84)	(2.19)	(1.27)	(1.10)	(−0.20)	(−0.73)
b_3	0.643***	0.581***	0.696***	0.600***	0.462***	0.444***	0.461***	0.418***	0.299***	0.197***
	(17.49)	(13.78)	(15.22)	(10.77)	(11.80)	(9.47)	(8.42)	(6.85)	(6.28)	(3.09)
b_4	−0.0305	−0.0107	−0.102	−0.0809	0.0118	0.0154	0.0579	0.0660	0.0188	0.0223
	(−0.58)	(−0.20)	(−1.51)	(−1.27)	(0.34)	(0.45)	(0.94)	(1.08)	(0.47)	(0.57)
Observations	1,024	1,024	1,048	1,048	1,067	1,067	1,051	1,051	1,043	1,043
Adj R^2	0.416	0.425	0.312	0.324	0.242	0.243	0.193	0.197	0.054	0.068
	Panel B: Soybeans									
b_1		0.0618**		0.110***		0.0684***		0.0801**		0.135***
		(2.26)		(2.96)		(2.61)		(2.47)		(3.53)
b_2	0.0128	−0.00970	0.00960	−0.0297	−0.00550	−0.0294	−0.0164	−0.0438*	0.0407	−0.00653
	(0.74)	(−0.53)	(0.32)	(−1.04)	(−0.31)	(−1.53)	(−0.65)	(−1.73)	(1.40)	(−0.22)
b_3	0.672***	0.657***	0.740***	0.713***	0.513***	0.498***	0.510***	0.490***	0.285***	0.254***
	(20.51)	(19.60)	(17.63)	(17.00)	(14.89)	(14.46)	(11.02)	(10.47)	(6.16)	(5.33)
B_4	0.0245	0.0312	−0.0733	−0.0638	0.0518*	0.0586**	0.107**	0.114***	0.00663	0.0146
	(0.63)	(0.79)	(−1.52)	(−1.42)	(1.91)	(2.15)	(2.43)	(2.60)	(0.23)	(0.51)
Observations	1,770	1,765	1,801	1,800	1,811	1,808	1,799	1,794	1,798	1,794
Adj R^2	0.362	0.365	0.315	0.323	0.236	0.241	0.192	0.196	0.040	0.049
	Panel C: Crude Oil									
b_1		0.0106		0.0252		−0.00199		0.0838**		0.0402
		(0.40)		(0.61)		(−0.07)		(2.33)		(1.02)
b_2	0.0241*	0.0168	0.00534	−0.0123	0.0118	0.0131	−0.0265	−0.0827**	−0.0108	−0.0372
	(1.67)	(0.75)	(0.25)	(−0.30)	(0.78)	(0.54)	(−1.41)	(−2.48)	(−0.51)	(−1.20)
b_3	0.656***	0.653***	0.735***	0.727***	0.506***	0.507***	0.511***	0.483***	0.293***	0.279***
	(19.77)	(19.73)	(17.02)	(17.31)	(14.69)	(14.55)	(10.97)	(10.52)	(6.20)	(5.51)
B_4	0.0205	0.0223	−0.0767	−0.0722	0.0449	0.0445	0.105**	0.118***	0.00557	0.00869
	(0.53)	(0.57)	(−1.61)	(−1.50)	(1.62)	(1.61)	(2.35)	(2.60)	(0.19)	(0.30)
Observations	1,752	1,752	1,793	1,793	1,798	1,798	1,784	1,784	1,784	1,784
Adj R^2	0.361	0.361	0.316	0.316	0.237	0.237	0.190	0.193	0.039	0.039

Notes: This table reports regression results for comparing the reactions of Asian stock indices to U.S. commodity futures and spot prices from January 2005 to September 2012. For each pair of commodity and East Asian market index, we run the regression using equation (4). Panels A, B, and C report regression results with the futures and spot returns of copper, soybeans, and crude oil, respectively, as the predicting variables. The t-statistics adjusted for heteroskedasticity and serial correlations using the Newey-West method with five lags are reported in parentheses. We use *, **, *** to indicate significance at the 10%, 5%, and 1% levels, respectively.

that the lagged futures return of copper has stronger predictive power than the lagged spot return.

Panel B of Table 7.4 reports the results from using both lagged futures and spot returns of soybeans to predict the return of each East Asian market index. The superior predictive power of the futures return of soybeans is even more evident. When lagged futures and spot returns are both included in the regression, the lagged futures return has significant predictive power in all markets, while the lagged spot return is insignificant in all markets. Taken together, Table 7.4 shows that futures prices of both copper and soybeans contain information superior to spot prices of these commodities.

4.3   Price Reactions of East Asian Stocks: An Industry-Level Analysis

Our analysis in the previous subsection shows significant and positive predictive powers of lagged futures returns of copper and soybeans for East Asian stock market indices after 2005. An analysis of the predictive powers for stock prices in different industries can further sharpen our understanding of the type of information revealed by the futures prices of copper and soybeans to East Asian stock prices. For example, price increases of copper futures driven by supply shocks should hurt industries that consume copper as a production input but benefit those that produce copper, whereas price increases driven by global demand shocks represent a stronger global economy and thus may boost stock prices of all industries, despite the increased copper consumption costs for consumer industries.

We use the Thomson Reuters Business Classification (TRBC) codes to classify firms into different industries. TRBC, which is owned and operated by Thomson Reuters, gives an industry classification of global companies.[5] We focus on a set of industries listed in Table 7.5 with the corresponding TRBC codes. We further group these industries into three categories: i) supply industries that directly profit from sales of a given commodity; ii) consumer industries that heavily rely on a given commodity as production input; and iii) other unrelated industries that are not directly connected to a given commodity in production and operation. To ensure that there are sufficient firms in each industry for our study, we perform the industry-level analysis only in the three largest stock markets in our sample: Japan, mainland China, and Hong Kong.

TABLE 7.5 **Industry categories and TRBC codes**

Names of Industries	TRBC Codes
Oil Production Related Industries	501020;501030
Diversified Metals & Mining	51201010;51201030;51201050
Electrical Components & Equipment	52102030;52102040
Consumer Electronics	53204020
Semiconductors	571010
Farming	54102010
Beverage	541010
Food	54102020
Chemicals	511010
Transportation	5240
Construction Materials	51202010
Steel	51201020
Industrial Machinery	52102010;52102020
Auto Parts & Equipment	531010
Real Estate Activities	554020
Food and Beverages	541010;54102020;543010
Healthcare	5610;5620
Software & IT Services	5720

Note: This table lists names and TRBC codes of different industries analyzed in this paper.

Table 7.6 reports results of the industry-level analysis, which uses the same regression specification as in Table 7.3. Panel A displays the results from using the lagged futures return of copper as the predicting variable. As expected, the price responses of supply industries in the stock markets of Japan, Hong Kong, and Shanghai are all positive and significant. Among consumer industries, such as electric equipment and electronics industries, we also observe positive and mostly significant stock price responses to the lagged copper futures return, although the estimate of the reaction coefficient b_1 is noticeably smaller than that of the supply industries. We also examine a set of other unrelated industries, ranging from cyclical industries (e.g., steel and real estate) to stable, noncyclical industries (e.g., telecoms or healthcare). Our regression result shows that even the stock prices of these industries—which are not directly related to either production or consumption of copper—have positive and significant responses to the lagged copper futures return. This pattern is stable and consistent across all three stock markets.

Taken together, our industry-level analysis of the predictive power of the lagged copper futures return for East Asian stock prices shows that our earlier result of significantly positive predictive power at the market

TABLE 7.6 **Reactions of Asian stocks to U.S. commodity futures prices: cross-industry analysis**

	Japan		Hong Kong		Shanghai	
	Coef	t-stat	Coef	t-stat	Coef	t-stat
Panel A: Copper						
Supply Industries						
Diversified Metals & Mining	0.118***	(4.66)	0.123***	(3.13)	0.392***	(7.89)
Consumer Industries						
Electrical Components & Equipment	0.113***	(4.71)	0.134***	(2.97)	0.0812**	(2.51)
Consumer Electronics	0.0724**	(2.05)	0.0571	(1.46)	0.0493	(1.25)
Semiconductors	0.0625***	(3.69)	0.0691**	(2.32)	0.0697*	(1.95)
Other Unrelated Industries						
Construction Materials	0.0929***	(4.03)	0.131***	(2.63)	0.0959***	(2.69)
Steel	0.152***	(4.75)	0.0984***	(2.72)	0.0619**	(1.97)
Industrial Machinery	0.096***	(4.14)	0.0490*	(1.73)	0.0813**	(2.34)
Auto Parts & Equipment	0.131***	(3.36)	0.0843***	(3.02)	0.0722***	(2.92)
Real Estate Activities	0.0587***	(2.74)	0.0656***	(2.69)	0.0454	(1.56)
Food and Beverage	0.0364***	(3.18)	0.0835**	(2.55)	0.0725**	(2.34)
Health Care	0.0451***	(2.63)	0.0664***	(2.77)	0.0562**	(2.31)
Software and IT Services	0.0411**	(2.19)	0.0500	(1.62)	0.0442	(1.58)
Panel B: Soybeans						
Supply Industries						
Farming	−0.0157	(−0.86)	0.0994***	(3.35)	0.217***	(3.60)
Consumer Industries						
Beverage	0.000881	(0.04)	0.0658	(1.58)	0.136***	(3.42)
Food Processing	−0.00632	(−0.35)	0.0988***	(4.24)	0.209***	(3.41)
Other Unrelated Industries						
Construction Materials	0.0389	(1.23)	0.0721	(1.23)	0.151***	(3.68)
Steel	0.0746**	(1.97)	0.0888**	(2.16)	0.138***	(3.00)
Industrial Machinery	0.0460	(1.48)	0.0661**	(2.16)	0.182***	(3.71)
Auto Parts & Equipment	0.0525*	(1.74)	0.0771***	(2.73)	0.151***	(3.26)
Real Estate Activities	0.0167	(0.54)	0.0824***	(3.30)	0.117**	(2.45)
Health Care	0.0236	(1.13)	0.0750***	(2.83)	0.153***	(3.42)
Software and IT Services	0.0259	(1.08)	0.0786***	(2.62)	0.133***	(3.19)
Panel C: Crude Oil						
Supply Industries						
Oil Production Related Industries	0.0709***	(4.39)	0.0669***	(3.16)	0.116***	(2.63)
Consumer Industries						
Chemicals	0.0265	(1.54)	0.0159	(0.86)	0.00506	(0.16)
Transportation	0.0114	(0.79)	0.0225	(1.07)	−0.0463	(−1.55)
Other Industries						
Construction Materials	0.0176	(1.00)	0.0525	(1.32)	−0.00263	(−0.27)
Steel	0.0632***	(2.82)	0.0506	(1.54)	−0.0214	(−0.59)
Industrial Machinery	0.0337*	(1.79)	0.0280	(1.32)	−0.0164	(−0.50)
Auto Parts & Equipment	0.0239	(1.32)	0.0248	(1.10)	−0.0466	(−1.45)
Real Estate Activities	0.0176	(0.90)	−0.0129	(−0.62)	−0.0363	(−1.10)
Food and Beverage	0.0172	(1.17)	−0.0241	(−1.09)	−0.00994	(−1.38)
Health Care	0.0100	(0.73)	0.0213	(1.14)	−0.0276	(−0.96)
Software and IT Services	0.00584	(0.36)	0.0364	(1.33)	−0.0264	(−0.94)

Notes: This table reports the regression results on reactions of Asian stocks to U.S. commodity futures prices using daily industry-level returns. We classify industries based on Thomson Reuters Business Classification (TRBC) codes described in Table 5. We then group industries into three categories: 1) supply industries; 2) consumer industries; and 3) other unrelated industries. The regression specification is the same as that used in Table 7.3. To save space, we only report the estimate of the coefficient b_1 for each industry return. Panels A, B, and C display regression results with the futures return of copper, soybeans, and crude oil, respectively, as the predicting variable. The t-statistics adjusted for heteroskedasticity and serial correlations using the Newey-West method with five lags are reported in parentheses. We use *, **, *** to indicate significance at the 10%, 5%, and 1% levels, respectively.

index level is robust and has consistent support across different industries. The fact that even consumer industries and other unrelated industries exhibit significantly positive stock price responses to the copper futures return underlines a clear message that East Asian stock markets consistently interpret futures prices of copper as a barometer of the global economy.

Panel B of Table 7.6 reports results from using the lagged futures return of soybeans as the predicting variable. Overall, the industry-level stock price responses to the lagged soybean futures return are consistently positive and significant across supply industries, consumer industries, and other industries in both Hong Kong and mainland China, similar to the responses to the lagged copper futures return. The industry-level results for Japan are somewhat weaker. We do not find significant price responses to the lagged soybean futures return in supply and consumer industries, although there are significantly positive responses in some other industries, such as those in steel and auto equipment. Perhaps this is because the Japanese economy is less involved in producing agricultural products, and Japanese investors do not pay as much attention to agricultural commodity prices as do investors in Hong Kong and mainland China.

Panel C of Table 7.6 reports results from using the lagged futures return of crude oil as the predicting variable. We only find significant price responses to the lagged crude oil futures return in supply industries. Supply industries in Japan, Hong Kong, and mainland China all exhibit significantly positive stock price responses to the lagged crude oil futures return. In contrast, across all three stock markets, consumer industries and other unrelated industries do not show any significant response, except the steel industry in Japan. The lack of price response outside supply industries is consistent with the weak market-level responses to the lagged crude oil futures return. These results show that oil futures prices do not transmit much information to East Asian stock prices.

5 Conclusion

This paper provides evidence of significant and positive predictive powers of the lagged overnight futures returns of copper and soybeans, albeit not crude oil, for stock prices across all East Asian economies and across a broad range of industries after the mid-2000s. Our findings highlight significant information flow from daily futures returns of copper and soybeans to East Asian stock markets and establish the futures prices of these commodities as barometers of the global economy.

Notes

We are grateful to Mark Aguiar, Ing-haw Cheng, Ed Glaeser, Lutz Kilian, Tano Santos, and José Scheinkman for helpful comments. Xiong acknowledges financial support from Smith Richardson Foundation grant #2011-8691.

1. See Cheng and Xiong (2013) for a review of this debate.

2. Interestingly, the European Central Bank (ECB) raised its key interest rate in July 2008—the eve of the most severe world economic recession since the Great Depression. According to reports released by the ECB, it interpreted the rising commodity prices as signals for strength of emerging economies and thus for strong inflation risk in the Eurozone. This interpretation demonstrates the possibility for commodity price fluctuations to feed back into the real economy through an informational channel.

3. An exception is copper. In recent years, COMEX expanded the set of copper contracts from the initial five contracts that mature in March, May, July, September, and December to 12 contracts maturing in each month of the year. Nevertheless, the newly added contracts remained inactive even when they were front-month contracts. In our analysis, we skip these contracts by rolling into the most active contracts based on trading volume.

4. On March 7, 2011, SEHK extended its trading hours in the first of two phases. The morning session was changed to run from 9:30 a.m. to 12:00 noon, followed by a 90-minute lunch break and an afternoon session from 1:30 p.m. to 4:00 p.m.. On March 5, 2012, the lunch break was cut to 60 minutes, with the afternoon session running from 1:00 p.m. to 4:00 p.m.

5. See http://thomsonreuters.com/products_services/financial/thomson_reuters _indices/trbc/ for more details.

References

Backus, D. K., and M. J. Crucini (2000). Oil prices and the terms of trade. *Journal of International Economics* 50(1), 185–213.

Basak, S., and A. Pavlova (2016). A model of financialization of commodities. *Journal of Finance* 71(4), 1511–1556.

Blanchard, O., and J. Gali (2010). Labor markets and monetary policy: A new Keynesian model with unemployment. *American Economic Journal—Macroeconomics* 2(2), 1–30.

Büyükşahin, B., and M. Robe (2012). Does paper oil matter? Energy markets' financialization and equity-commodity co-movements. Working paper, CFTC. Washington, DC.

Cheng, I.-H., and W. Xiong (2013). Commodity futures trading commission. *Annual Review of Financial Economics 6*, 419–441.

Davis, S. J., and J. Haltiwanger (2001). Sectoral job creation and destruction responses to oil price changes. *Journal of Monetary Economics 48*(3), 465–512.

Garbade, K., and W. L. Silber (1983). Price movements and price discovery in futures and cash markets. *Review of Economics and Statistics 65*(2), 289–297.

Grossman, S. (1989). *The Informational Role of Prices* (Wicksell Lectures). Cambridge, MA: MIT Press.

Hamilton, J. D. (1983). Oil and the macroeconomy since World War II. *Journal of Political Economy 91*(2), 228–248.

——. (2003). What is an oil shock? *Journal of Econometrics 113*(2), 363–398.

——. (2009). Causes and consequences of the oil shock of 2007–08. *Brookings Papers on Economic Activity* (Spring), 215–283.

Hayek, F. (1945). The use of knowledge in society. *American Economic Review 35*(4), 519–530.

Huang, R., R. Masulis, and H. Stoll (1996). Energy shocks and financial markets. *Journal of Futures Markets 16*(1), 1–27.

Jones, C. M., and G. Kaul (1996). Oil and the stock markets. *Journal of Finance 51*(2), 463–491.

Kilian, L. (2008a). Exogenous oil supply shocks: How big are they and how much do they matter for the US economy? *Review of Economics and Statistics 90*(2), 216–240.

——. (2008b). The economic effects of energy price shocks. *Journal of Economic Literature 46*(4), 871–909.

——. (2009). Not all oil price shocks are alike: Disentangling demand and supply shocks in the crude oil market. *American Economic Review 99*(3), 1053–1069.

Kilian, L., and C. Park (2009). The impact of oil price shocks on the US stock market. *International Economic Review 50*(4), 1267–1287.

Kyle, A., and W. Xiong (2001). Contagion as a wealth effect. *Journal of Finance 56*(4), 1401–1440.

Lin, S., and M. Tamvakis (2001). Spillover effects in energy futures markets. *Energy Economics 23*(1), 43–56.

Masters, M. (2008). Testimony before the Committee on Homeland Security and Governmental Affairs. U.S. Senate. May 20. www.hsgac.senate.gov/public /_files/052008Masters.pdf.

Mork, K. A. (1989). Oil and the macroeconomy when prices go up and down—an extension of Hamilton results. *Journal of Political Economy 97*(3), 740–744.

Nandha, M., and R. Faff (2008). Does oil move equity prices? A global view. *Energy Economics 30*(3), 986–997.

Park, J., and R. A. Ratti (2008). Oil price shocks and stock markets in the US and 13 European countries. *Energy Economics 30*, 2587–2608.

Roll, R. (1984). Orange juice and weather. *American Economic Review 74*, 861–880.

Singleton, K. (2012). Investor flows and the 2008 boom/bust in oil prices. *Management Science 60*(2), 300–318.

Sockin, M., and W. Xiong (2015). Informational Frictions and Commodity Markets. *Journal of Finance 70*(5), 2063–2098.

Tang, K., and W. Xiong (2012). Index investment and financialization of commodities. *Financial Analysts Journal 68*(6), 54–74.

Ulibarri, C. (1998). Is after-hours trading informative? *Journal of Futures Markets 18*(5), 563–579.

U.S. Senate Permanent Subcommittee on Investigations (2009). Excessive speculation in the wheat market. Committee on Homeland Security and Governmental Affairs, June 24. http://www.hsgac.senate.gov/subcommittees/investigat ions/hearings/excessive-speculation-in-the-wheat-market.

CHAPTER EIGHT

Social Learning, Credulous Bayesians, and Aggregation Reversals

Edward L. Glaeser and Bruce Sacerdote

1 Introduction

In the latter years of the past millennium, Internet stocks soared before crashing. Housing prices boomed between 2000 and 2006, even in areas where housing supply is essentially unconstrained, and then busted after 2007. The housing market collapse was associated with an even greater fall in the value of collateralized securities, which was associated with a worldwide banking crisis. Why did investors, from ordinary homebuyers in Las Vegas to the high fliers of Lehman Brothers, make such colossal mistakes?

These great asset-price convulsions persuaded many observers that investors are less than fully rational, and there has been at outpouring of research on behavioral finance (e.g., Scheinkman and Xiong 2003) aimed at understanding these events. Unfortunately, models of limited rationality suffers from Tolstoy's corollary—there is only one way to be perfectly rational but there are an infinite number of ways to be somewhat irrational—which means that the rigorous discipline that rational expectations placed on economic model building is largely lost in a world of limited rationality. Perhaps the best that can be done is to focus on modest deviations from rationality that generate far-ranging testable predictions.

In that spirit, this paper follows Glaeser and Sunstein (2009) and focuses on Credulous Bayesians. Credulous Bayesians are assumed to get everything about statistical inference right, except that they underestimate the magnitude of shared sources of error. If an individual appears whose views mirror their own, Credulous Bayesians are bolstered in their beliefs, even if that other individual's views were formed by the same sources of data that informed the Bayesian's original views. This error leads to the excess social influence documented by Asch (1955) and many others; it can explain the sizable fluctuations in asset prices that the world has recently experienced.

We illustrate that claim with a simple model in Section 2. When Credulous Bayesians have access to the signals that others receive, either directly because of communication or indirectly through the price mechanism, they become too confident in their beliefs. Scheinkman and Xiong (2003) show that this overconfidence, which springs from overestimating the novelty of others' sources of information, leads to extreme asset prices, where large busts follow large booms.

We make this point in Section 2 not as a contribution to the literature on behavioral asset pricing; variants of Credulous Bayesianism appear in many finance-related papers, such as DeMarzo et al. (2003). Our goal is to illustrate that a behavioral assumption that can justify the asset swings we observe also generates other testable predictions about behavior in other realms. For example, underweighting the common sources of shocks also implies that individuals will underestimate the connection between personal experience and error terms, which means that beliefs can be strongly correlated with observable characteristics. Perfectly rational Bayesians, conversely, should presumably correct for any correlation between signals and individual characteristics.

Credulous Bayesianism can also explain social multipliers, as discussed in Glaeser et al. (2003), when aggregate relationships are stronger than individual relationships. If characteristics influence information and information is shared, then an aggregate will reflect both private data and the data received by peers. This sharing process, as long as people fail to correct fully for the influence of characteristics on information, will lead the individual connection between observable variables and outcomes to be magnified at the aggregate level.

Credulous Bayesianism can also explain the more puzzling phenomenon of aggregation reversals, which occur when an aggregate relationship has the reverse sign of an individual relationship. Such reversals are rare but interesting, and three of them are the particular focus on this paper.

Richer people are more likely to vote Republican: Figure 8.1 shows this connection using 2000 data from the National Annenberg Election Survey. Figure 8.2 shows that richer states were more likely to vote Democratic in the 2000 election. Gelman (2008) provides a wonderfully detailed analysis of this phenomenon. People with more education attend church more regularly, as shown in Figure 8.3, but as Figure 8.4 shows, more educated denominations have far lower attendance rates (Glaeser and Sacerdote 2008). Figure 8.5 shows the positive individual-level relationship between income and service in the military; Figure 8.6 shows the negative state-level relationship between the same two variables.[1]

These three examples are aggregation reversals, in which a statistical relationship at the individual level is reversed at some level of aggregation, like the state or church denomination. On a statistical level, aggregation reversals illustrate the ecological fallacy that aggregate relationships easily inform us about individual-level parameters (e.g., King 1997). In this literature, aggregation reversals can result from an unusual distribution of omitted variables across units of aggregation. But this insight does not help us understand the economic causes of aggregation

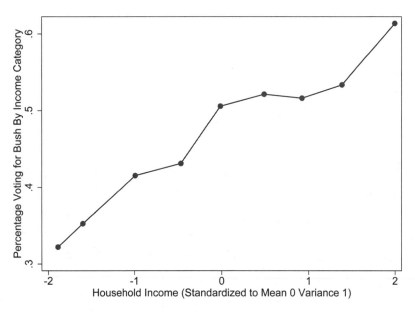

FIGURE 8.1. Voting for Bush and income: micro data

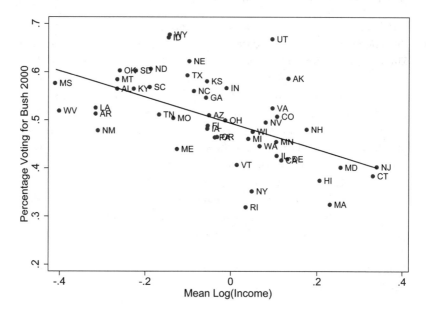

FIGURE 8.2. Voting for Bush and income: state data

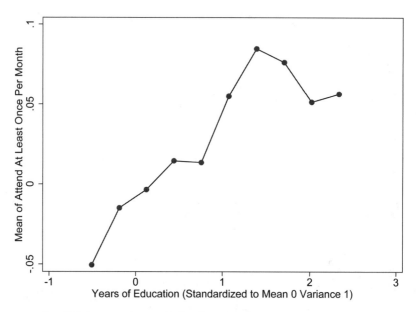

FIGURE 8.3. Religious attendance and education: micro data

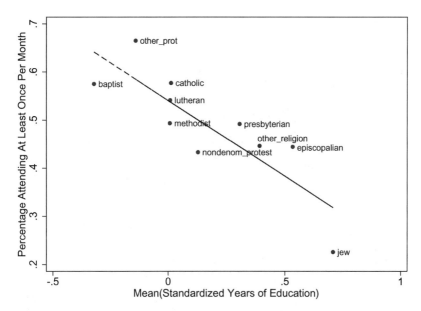

FIGURE 8.4. Religious attendance and education: denomination data

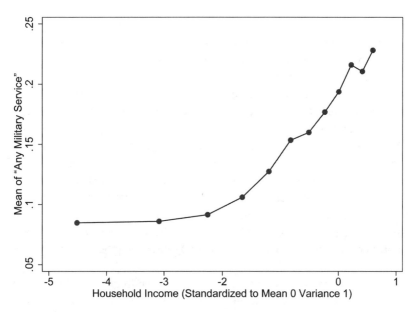

FIGURE 8.5. Military service and income at the individual level

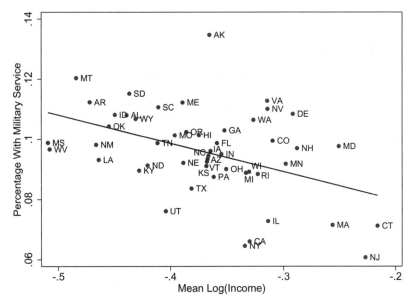

FIGURE 8.6. Military service and income at state level

reversals; knowing the economic causes could help us generate predictions about when these reversals might occur.[2]

The model of Credulous Bayesianism in Section 2 shows that social learning can create aggregation reversals only if the direct impact of the exogenous variable on behavior has the opposite sign of the impact of that variable on beliefs. For example, higher incomes might be associated both with a dislike for taxes and more liberal social beliefs. The dislike of taxes pushes richer people toward Republicanism; the liberal social views push them away from Republicanism. Moreover, there must be a social multiplier that operates on the indirect channel. In our belief model, this social multiplier exists because beliefs reflect social learning, which means that the aggregate relationship between beliefs and the exogenous variable is much stronger than the individual relationship between those two variables.

In Section 3, we present an empirical methodology to calibrate our model. We use individual-level relationships and the aggregate relationship between beliefs and the exogenous variable to predict the aggregate relationship between the exogenous variable and the outcome. The goal of this calibration is to show the plausibility of our model, not to reject alternative explanations for the aggregation reversal.

In Section 4, we look at the relationship between income and voting for George Bush in 2000. The rich were more likely to vote for Bush but less likely to agree with Republican social policies on prayer in schools or limits on abortion. The negative relationship between social policy views and income is much stronger at the state level than at the individual level, which suggests a sizable social multiplier. Finally, views on social policy are highly correlated with voting for Bush, which implies that these beliefs impact the outcome. Together, these facts predict an aggregation reversal that is larger than the one we empirically observe.

In Section 5, we return to the relationship between education and religion discussed by Glaeser and Sacerdote (2008). Education is positively associated with church attendance but negatively associated with belief in the devil or the literal truth of the Bible. The denominational correlation between education and these beliefs is much stronger than the individual correlation, which again suggests a large social multiplier. These beliefs are also highly correlated with attendance and seem to be important determinants of religious observance. Our parameter estimates again predict an aggregation reversal that is bigger than the one that we see in the data.

In Section 6, we examine the relationship between income and military service. Income is positively correlated with military service but negatively associated with pro-military beliefs. The income-belief relationship gets stronger at the state level, but the implied social multiplier is smaller than in our two other examples. The relationship between pro-military beliefs and military service is also weaker than the relationship between religious beliefs and religious attendance or social policy beliefs and voting Republican. Our results are mixed. Using one of our belief measures, we almost exactly predict the actual aggregation reversal. The other belief measure fails to predict any aggregation reversal. Section 7 concludes.

2   Credulous Bayesians: Excess Volatility, Social Mutlipliers, and Aggregation Reversals

In this section, we model the social formation of beliefs and examine the impact of these beliefs on social multipliers, aggregation reversals, and financial cascades. We assume that there is an unobserved state variable, denoted A, which may impact individual actions or the willingness to pay for a financial asset.

The expectation of A is based on a common prior, a private signal, and the communication of those signals within a community group. The common prior for A has mean zero and variance σ_A^2. Each individual receives a private signal S_i equal to $A + \kappa + \eta_i$, where η_i is an individual-specific, normally distributed error term with mean zero and variance σ_η^2. The term κ is meant to reflect common noise, which may be unknown but widely shared, or it may be a deterministic function of observable attributes.

In previous work (Glaeser and Sunstein 2009), one of us has followed DeMarzo et al. (2003) and investigated the impact of Credulous Bayesianism, in which individuals overweight the opinion of others, because they underweight the impact of common noise. In this paper, we examine two variants of this common belief. In the case where the common noise is stochastic and unknown, Credulous Bayesianism means that individuals underweight the variance of the unknown term. In the case where common noise is a deterministic function of observables, the Credulous Bayesians believe that the common noise term is smaller, and hence that the relationship between observables and beliefs is smaller.

Formally, Credulous Bayesians believe that the expectation of κ equals ρ_{CB} times the actual expectation of κ. When κ is unknown, with mean zero and variance σ_κ^2, then credulous Bayesians believe that the variance is $\rho_{CB}^2 \sigma_\kappa^2$, and we use the notation $\rho = \rho_{CB}^2$.

If $\kappa = cX_i$, where X_i represents a vector of known individual characteristics (with mean zero), then credulous Bayesians believe that $\kappa = \rho_{CB} cX_i$, and hence they underweight the true relationship between observables and common noise. In both cases, Credulous Bayesians tend to underestimate the common influences that shape beliefs. We first focus on the case in which the common noise is unobserved and unconnected with individual attributes; we then turn to the setting where individual characteristics shape beliefs.

One way of understanding the similarity between assuming that individuals underestimate the variance of κ and assuming that they understand the connection between κ and observables, is that if $\kappa = cX_i + \xi$, then the variance of κ across the population is $c^2 \text{Var}(X_i) + \text{Var}(\xi)$. Underestimating c is one way of underestimating the population variance. Another reason that underestimating the magnitude of these common errors leads to underestimating the connection between errors and observables is that if $\kappa = cX_i + \xi$, then the standard estimate of c is $\frac{\text{Cov}(X_i, S_i)}{\text{Var}(X_i)}$ and $\frac{\text{Var}(\kappa) - \text{Var}(\xi)}{c}$, which also suggests that individuals who underestimate the variance of common noise terms will tend to underestimate the impact of observables on beliefs.

Credulous Bayesianism is one way of modeling the observed tendency of subjects to overreact to the opinions of others. Asch (1955) pioneered a psychological literature showing that individuals base their stated beliefs on the statements of others, even about something so seemingly obvious as the length of a line. While some authors have suggested that Asch's results just show a tendency to conform in statements, not in beliefs, Berns et al. (2005) use brain scans to show that statements by peers about shapes cause activity in the parts of the brain associated with spatial analysis, not in the parts associated with social relations. Bandura (1977) is a classic text on the importance of social learning. In economics, Merlo and Schotter (2003) is just one of the many papers on the power of social learning in experimental settings.[3] There is abundant evidence on the importance of learning from people around us.

2.1   Communication and Excess Volatility

Here we assume that κ is unknown, with mean zero and variance σ_κ^2. Credulous Bayesianism is modeled by assuming that individuals believe that the variance of κ is equal to $\rho\sigma_\kappa^2$ and that the variance of η_z is $\sigma_\eta^2 + (1 - \rho)\sigma_\kappa^2$. Thus, individuals correctly understand the signal-to-noise ratio in any given message but incorrectly underestimate the common component of the noise.

Through communication, people learn the signals of a set of Z neighbors. The neighbors' signals are garbled in transmission, so that individual i learns $A + \kappa + \eta_z + \mu_z^i$ from individual z, where μ_z^i is the mean-zero garbling with variance σ_μ^2.

If individuals share their signals, then using the notation $\phi_\mu = \frac{\sigma_\mu^2}{\sigma_\eta^2 + (1-\rho)\sigma_\kappa^2}$, the signal extraction formula given these beliefs is

$$E(A) = \sigma_A^2 \frac{(1 + \phi_\mu) S_i + \sum_{j \neq i} S_j}{(\sigma_A^2 + \rho\sigma_\kappa^2)(Z + \phi_\mu) + \sigma_\eta^2 + (1 - \rho)\sigma_\kappa^2 + \sigma_\mu^2}.$$

As is emphasized by Glaeser and Sunstein (2009), the variance of ex post beliefs is declining with ρ. This basic point also appears in a simple asset pricing model, where individuals rationally interpret the meaning of prices but underestimate the variance of the shared noise term.

Assume that there are Z investors, all of whom have a common constant absolute risk aversion utility function that implies that if the individual buys Q units of the asset, his welfare is proportional to $(E(A) - P)Q - .5\varpi Q^2 \text{Var}(A - E(A))$, where ϖ is a parameter governing the degree of risk aversion. Each individual will buy the asset to the point where $Q = \frac{E(A)-P}{\varpi \text{Var}(A-E(A))}$. The quantity of the asset is in fixed supply Q_T. We consider a market setting where prices and order quantities reveal private signals. For example, assume that individuals make orders at a fixed price in consecutive order with some infinitesimal small probability that the market will end after each order has been placed. If order quantities are observed, then signals effectively will have been shared by the conclusion of the first round of bidding. Alternatively, we can just assume a rational expectations equilibrium in which prices and quantities essentially reveal everything.

In this case, the equilibrium price will equal

$$P = \frac{\sigma_A^2 \sum_z S_z}{\left(\sigma_A^2 + \rho\sigma_\kappa^2\right)Z + \sigma_\eta^2 + (1-\rho)\sigma_\kappa^2} - \varpi \text{Var}(A - E(A))Q_T/Z,$$

and the quantity held by each individual will be Q_T/Z.[4] The variance of prices falls with ρ, implying that Credulous Bayesianism will be associated with excess asset price volatility, because Credulous Bayesians overweight the opinions of others, and this means that common noise will excessively move markets, instead of being filtered out.

A somewhat more subtle effect is that the impact of asset price on supply will be weaker when individuals are Credulous Bayesians. Credulous Bayesians underestimate the variance of assets in their portfolios, and as a result, their willingness to pay drops less as the quantity of the asset increases. As a result, large inflows of new assets, created perhaps by a rise in securitization or an increase in the availability of Internet stocks, will have a more muted impact on prices than if buyers were completely rational.

This simple model mirrors the far more sophisticated approach of Scheinkman and Xiong (2003), who similarly address a setting where individuals become too confident about their beliefs. In that case, differences of opinion persist because of overconfidence, and trading occurs. In this case, the primary result of insufficient skepticism about the information of others is that prices become more volatile. In a sense, this links

Scheinkman's work on social interactions (Glaeser et al. 2003) with his later work on behavioral asset pricing.

2.2   Social Multipliers and Credulous Bayesianism

We now turn to beliefs and an action, where individuals base a choice, denoted Y_i, on net benefits (which are known) and benefits (which are assessed). Specifically, we assume total benefits of Y_i equal $(\gamma A + \beta X_i)Y_i$, where β is known, and A is estimated. Costs equals $.5Y_i^2$, so expected utility maximization implies $Y_i = \gamma E(A) + \beta X_i$. The variable X_i is meant to capture any variable, such as income or education, which might plausibly increase (or decrease) the benefits of the activity; β and γ are parameters that we normalize to be positive. By assumption, X_i has a direct impact on the choice of Y_i.

We know that $\kappa = cX_i$, but that Credulous Bayesians assume that $\kappa = \rho_{CB}cX_i$. In an earlier version of the paper, we demonstrated that similar results can occur if the observable operates by changing the variance of the noise terms, and in that case, aggregation reversals can be produced in a totally rational manner. However, here we assume that Credulous Bayesianism works by causing people to underestimate the impact that common experiences have on the signals that we receive. The values of X are known.

In the first case, standard signal extraction implies that the estimate of A equals

$$E(A) = \sigma_A^2 \frac{\left(\sigma_\eta^2 + \sigma_\mu^2\right)(S_i - \rho_{CB}cX_i) + \sigma_\eta^2 \sum_{j \neq i}\left(S_j - \rho_{CB}cX_j\right)}{\left(Z\sigma_A^2 + \sigma_\eta^2 + \sigma_\mu^2\right)\sigma_\eta^2 + \sigma_A^2\sigma_\mu^2},$$

which can be rewritten as

$$E(A) = K + \delta X_i + \lambda\delta\hat{X}_j + noise,$$

where $K = \dfrac{\left(Z\sigma_\eta^2 + \sigma_\mu^2\right)\sigma_A^2 A}{\left(Z\sigma_A^2 + \sigma_\eta^2 + \sigma_\mu^2\right)\sigma_\eta^2 + \sigma_A^2\sigma_\mu^2}$, $\delta = \dfrac{\sigma_A^2 c(1-\rho_{CB})\left(\sigma_\eta^2 + \sigma_\mu^2\right)}{\left(Z\sigma_A^2 + \sigma_\eta^2 + \sigma_\mu^2\right)\sigma_\eta^2 + \sigma_A^2\sigma_\mu^2}$, and $\lambda = \dfrac{Z\sigma_\eta^2}{\sigma_\eta^2 + \sigma_\mu^2}.5$.

The expected value of A equals a constant plus a slope parameter times the individual's own X characteristic plus a multiplier times that slope parameter times the average value of X in the individual's group. In a

previous draft, we also highlighted the possibility that individual characteristics would influence beliefs in a fully rational manner by impacting
the variance of noise terms. We are not discounting that possibility here,
but we instead focus on the alternative, simpler formulation, where
individuals have slightly incorrect beliefs.

While our signal-extraction description describes only one form of
social learning, the reduced-form relationship $E(A) = K + \delta X_i + \lambda \delta \hat{X}_j + \varepsilon_i$
captures the robust empirical relationships between many beliefs and
exogenous variables, such as the connections between education and
the belief in heaven or income and the belief that abortion is wrong.
Gentzkow and Shapiro (2004) show the relation between different forms
of education in the Islamic world and beliefs about who is responsible for
the September 11, 2001, attack on the World Trade Center. DiTella et al.
(2007) find that beliefs about capitalism are altered with an allocation of
property rights.

The relationship between observables and beliefs is something of a
challenge for conventional Bayesianism, since updating should presumably filter out the relationship between signals and observable characteristics. Credulous Bayesianism provides one justification for people failing
to filter fully. Credulous Bayesians underestimate the role that our backgrounds play in shaping our experiences, and hence there remains room
for our backgrounds to shape our beliefs.

This formula implies that average belief in community j equals $K + (1 + \lambda)\delta\hat{X}_j$ plus any noise that is not averaged away. The social learning
means that the impact of X on group-level beliefs will be stronger than
the impact of X on individual beliefs. The term $1 + \lambda$ is the ratio of the
impact of X on beliefs at the group level divided by the impact of X on
beliefs within groups, which we refer to as the social multiplier.

With this formulation of beliefs, individual outcomes satisfy

$$\textbf{(1)} \qquad Y_i = \gamma K + (\gamma\delta + \beta)X_i + \gamma\lambda\delta\hat{X}_j + \varepsilon_i,$$

and group outcomes equal $\hat{Y}_j = \gamma K + (\gamma\delta(1 + \lambda) + \beta)\hat{X}_j + \hat{\varepsilon}_j$. Table
8.1 lists the model's predictions about the coefficients when outcomes are
regressed on the exogenous variable.

The social multiplier that occurs when we compare within-group rela-
tionship to across-group relationship is $1 + \frac{\lambda\gamma\delta}{\gamma\delta+\beta}$. Since γ and β are always
positive, when δ is also positive, then the impact of social learning will
be to ensure that aggregate relationships are stronger than individual

TABLE 8.1 **Predictions of the model**

Marginal impacts of the exogenous variable on the outcome variable	Individual level	$\gamma\delta + \beta + \gamma\delta\lambda\mathrm{Cov}(X_i, \hat{X}_j)$
	Individual level within group	$\gamma\delta + \beta$
	Group level	$\gamma\delta(1 + \lambda) + \beta$
Variation in X explained by group-level dummies		$\mathrm{Cov}(X_i, \hat{X}_j)$
Marginal impact of the exogenous variable on proxies for belief	Individual level within group	$\psi_k\delta$
	Group level	$(1 + \lambda)\psi_k\delta$
Covariance of latent proxies for belief		ψ_k^2
Covariance of latent proxies for belief with latent outcome variable		$\psi_k\left(\gamma + \beta\delta + \beta\delta\lambda\mathrm{Cov}(X_i, \hat{X}_j)\right)$

relationships, as found in Glaeser et al. (2003). If econometricians lacked independent information on beliefs, then the size of the social multiplier would provide information about the value of λ, which in turn reflects $\frac{Z\sigma_\eta^2}{\sigma_\eta^2 + \sigma_\mu^2}$. Beliefs create a social multiplier where aggregate coefficients are bigger than individual coefficients. In that (probably more common) case, people with higher values of X choose higher levels of Y both because of the direct effect and the indirect effect through beliefs. The belief effect becomes larger at the aggregate level because of social learning, and this causes the aggregate coefficient to be larger than the individual coefficient.

2.3   Aggregation Reversals

As we discussed in the introduction to this paper, there are settings in which aggregation reversals occur, when a macrorelationship has the reverse sign of a microrelationship. The more interesting case that can explain aggregation reversals occurs when δ is negative and the indirect effect of X on Y that works through beliefs goes in the opposite direction of the direct effect of X on Y. An aggregation reversal requires the individual-level regression coefficient of Y on X to be positive, which means that $\beta > \gamma|\delta|\left(1 + \lambda\frac{\mathrm{Cov}(X_i, \hat{X}_j)}{\mathrm{Var}(X_i)}\right)$. An aggregation reversal also requires the aggregate regression coefficient of $\hat{Y}$ on $\hat{X}$ to be negative, which requires $\gamma|\delta|(1 + \lambda) > \beta$. Putting these conditions together implies that an aggregation reversal requires

$$1 + \lambda > \frac{\beta}{\gamma \, |\delta|} > 1 + \lambda \frac{\mathrm{Cov}(X_i, \hat{X}_j)}{\mathrm{Var}(X_i)}.$$

This inequality is closely analogous to (1) in the previous version of the model. Just as before, aggregation reversals require that the ratio of direct to indirect impact of X, $\frac{\beta}{\gamma |\delta|}$, must fall within a range. The upper bound on the range is again a social multiplier, but in this case, the social multiplier refers to the connection between the exogenous variable X and beliefs about A. The lower bound is again one plus a term that is small when $\frac{\mathrm{Cov}(X_i, \hat{X}_j)}{\mathrm{Var}(X_i)}$ is small. When $\frac{\mathrm{Cov}(X_i, \hat{X}_j)}{\mathrm{Var}(X_i)}$ is close to zero, then the inequality means that the ratio of direct to indirect effects must be greater than one and less than the social multiplier.

The model predicts when we should expect aggregation reversals. First, as we assumed above, there must be a correlation between the exogenous variable and beliefs that works in the opposite direction as the direct relationship between the exogenous variable and the outcome. Second, there must be a sizable social multiplier in the formation of beliefs, so that the relationship between beliefs and the exogenous variable is larger at the aggregate level than at the individual level. In the next section, we discuss our empirical strategy for estimating these parameters to assess whether the model can explain the aggregation reversals shown in Figures 8.1–8.6.

3 Discrete Outcomes and Empirical Implementation

In this section, we discuss an empirical approach to our model of aggregation reversals. Our approach is to estimate the key parameters using a set of empirical moments that excludes the aggregate relationship between exogenous variables and outcomes and then to see whether those parameters predict the aggregation reversal. This approach is certainly not an attempt to refute any alternative models of the observed aggregation reversals. Our goal is just to show that our model is at least a plausible explanation of these phenomena.

In keeping with the model, we continue to focus on one independent variable in each case, either income or education. The model is aimed at explaining an aggregation reversal of a univariate relationship, but we mean neither to suggest that other variables do not matter, nor to suggest that our coefficients are causal. In all cases, we are comfortable with the interpretation that the estimated univariate relationship reflects both the impact of the independent variable and other omitted variables that are correlated with that variable. The relationship between income and Republicanism that we examine surely reflects many things that are correlated with income. This is not a problem for the model, and we do not try to isolate any effects that reflect income alone.

We presented the model in a continuous formulation to make it more intuitive, but our examples will involve discrete outcomes and discrete beliefs. To move from the theory to the data, we assume that the observed outcome variable takes on a value of zero or one, which captures voting for Bush or attending church or owning a gun. We assume that individuals choose an outcome of one when $Y_i = \gamma K + (\gamma\delta + \beta)X_i + \gamma\lambda\delta\hat{X}_j + \varepsilon_i$ is positive. We assume that all relevant noise terms are normally distributed, and we let $F_z(\cdot)$ denote the cumulative distribution function and $f_z(\cdot)$ denote the density for a normal random variable z.

The expected share of people living in place j who choose the positive outcome will equal $F_{z_1}(\gamma K + (\gamma\delta(1+\lambda) + \beta)\hat{X}_j)$, where $z_1 = (\gamma\delta + \beta)(X_i - \hat{X}_j) + \varepsilon_i$. We assume that z_1 has the same distribution in each community. The average marginal effect of $\hat{X}_j$ on the share of the population that chooses one will equal $(\gamma\delta(1+\lambda) + \beta)\int_j f_{z_1}((\gamma K + (\gamma\delta(1+\lambda) + \beta)\hat{X}_j))\frac{1}{j}dj$, if there are measure J communities, so the average marginal effect of $\hat{X}_j$ on $\hat{Y}_j$ continues to be $\gamma\delta(1+\lambda) + \beta$, as shown in Table 8.1.

Within a community, for a given value of X, the share of people who choose one will equal $F_{\varepsilon_i}(\gamma K + (\gamma\delta + \beta)X_i + \gamma\lambda\delta\hat{X}_j)$. If the distribution of X within the community is characterized by a density function $g(X)$, the estimated marginal effect of X is $(\gamma\delta + \beta)\int_{x_i} f_{\varepsilon_i}(\gamma K + (\gamma\delta + \beta)x_i + \gamma\lambda\delta\hat{X}_j)g(x_i)dx_i$, so the average effect of x within communities is again $\gamma\delta + \beta$. We use the estimated within-group coefficient to provide us with an estimate of $\gamma\delta + \beta$.

The estimated marginal effect of X on Y across the entire population equals $\gamma\delta + \beta + \gamma\delta\lambda\frac{\partial E(\hat{X}_j)}{\partial X_i}$, and $\frac{\partial E(\hat{X}_j)}{\partial X_i}$ will again equal $\frac{\text{Cov}(X_i, \hat{X}_j)}{\text{Var}(X_i)}$. As such, the existence of discrete outcome variables does require probit estimation techniques, but it does not change the connection between the parameters of the model and relationship between exogenous variable and outcomes.

We assume that the X variable has mean zero and variance one, and we normalize our independent variables appropriately in the empirical work. The parameter $\frac{\text{Cov}(X_i, \hat{X}_j)}{\text{Var}(X_i)}$ can be measured directly from the data, as it reflects the share of variation in X that is across group rather than within group. This parameter can be estimated with the share of the variation in X that is explained by group dummies. We scale our X variables so that they have a mean of zero and a variance of one, so the missing parameter is just $\text{Cov}(X_i, \hat{X}_j)$.

We also assume that we do not measure beliefs directly but rather see several discrete measures of beliefs that take on values of one when $\psi_k E(A) + \xi_i^k$ is positive. For example, in the case of religious belief, we have questions on statements about belief in the devil and beliefs in the literal truth of the Bible. The parameter ψ_k reflects the relationship between the relevant beliefs and the particular discrete measure. The term ξ_i^k is an error term specific to the person and the measure of beliefs. By scaling δ and the error terms appropriately, we can always ensure that the latent belief variable has a variance of one. We also normalize $1 - \psi_k^2 = \text{Var}(\xi_i^k)$, so that the variance of the belief proxies also equals one. These assumptions are innocuous scaling assumptions about unobserved latent variables that drive the zero-one decision.

Within a given group, the share of the population that answers yes to belief question k is $F_{z_2}(\psi_k(K + (1 + \lambda)\delta \hat{X}_j))$, where $z_2 = \psi_k(\delta(X_i - \hat{X}_j) + \varepsilon_i) + \xi_i^k$. The estimated marginal effect of $\hat{X}_j$ will be $\psi_k \delta(1+\lambda) \int_j f_{z_2}(\psi_k(K + (1 + \lambda)\delta \hat{X}_j))\frac{1}{j}dj$ and the average effect will be $\psi_k \delta(1 + \lambda)$. Within groups, the estimated marginal effect of x on beliefs will be $\psi_k \delta$, so the ratio will again give us the social multiplier. As such, we use the within-group belief regressions to estimate $\psi_k \delta$ and the ratio of the coefficient on X from within-group and across-group regressions to estimate the social multiplier.

We estimate the parameter ψ_k by assuming that we have two potential proxies for the underlying beliefs. If ψ_k is the same for both these proxies, then covariance of the two underlying normal variables is equal to ψ_k^2. This covariance is empirically implied by the means and covariance of the two discrete measures of underlying beliefs. If the two values of ψ_k are not the same, then the potential range for ψ_k is between the underlying covariance and one, and we can consider this entire range for this variable.

Our final moment is the relationship between beliefs and outcomes. In both cases, we observe a discrete proxy for the relevant underlying variables Y_i and $\psi_k E(A) + \xi_i^k$. Again, we can use the means of the two discrete variables and their covariance to estimate the underlying covariance of the two normal variables. The model predicts that this underlying covariance will equal $\psi_k(\gamma + \beta\delta(1 + \lambda\text{Cov}(X_i, \hat{X}_j)))$.

Table 8.1 lists these set of predictions that we use to estimate the parameters. We need estimates of six parameters: β, γ, δ, λ, ψ_k and $\text{Cov}(X_i, \hat{X}_j)$. We use six moments to estimate these parameters: i) the within-group relationship between exogenous variable and outcome, ii) the amount of variation in the exogenous variable that is within group, iii) the within-group effect of the exogenous variable on the proxy for beliefs, iv) the across-group effect of the exogenous variable on the proxy for beliefs, v) the correlation of different proxies for beliefs, and vi) the individual-level covariance between the proxy for beliefs and the outcome variable. We will then see whether these parameters predict an aggregation reversal and whether they come close to predicting the observed aggregate relationship between the outcome and the exogenous variable.

The square root of the covariance of the latent belief variables provides our estimate of ψ_k. The share of variation in X that is explained by group dummies estimates $\text{Cov}(X_i, \hat{X}_j)$. The ratio of the aggregation relationship between the exogenous variable and the belief proxy and the within-group relationship between the exogenous variable and the belief proxy delivers $1 + \lambda$. The ratio of the within-group relationship between the exogenous variable and the belief proxy and the square root of the covariance of the latent belief variables delivers δ.

The value of β is found by subtracting δ/ψ_k times the estimated covariance of the latent belief proxy and the latent outcome from the estimated within-group marginal effect of the exogenous variable on the outcome and then dividing by $1 - \delta^2 - \delta^2 \lambda \text{Cov}(X_i, \hat{X}_j)$. The value of γ is found by subtracting this estimate of β from the estimated within-group effect of the exogenous variable on the outcome and then dividing by the estimate of δ.

4   Income and Republicanism

The aggregation reversal that occurs in the relationship between income and Republicanism is quite striking. At the individual level, there is a modest positive relationship between earnings and voting for President Bush in 2000. According to the National Annenberg Election Study of 2000, 55% of the top quintile of the income distribution voted for the Republican in 2000; 36% of the bottom quintile of the income distributed voted for him in the same year. This positive income–Republicanism relationship certainly corresponds with popular notions of Republicanism, but those notions are seemingly contradicted by the profoundly negative relationship between income and Republicanism at the state level shown in Figure 8.2. The correlation coefficient is −.57.

The model seems to have a reasonable chance of explaining this aggregation reversal because of the multiple aspects of Republicanism. In post-Reagan America, Republicanism has been associated with both lower taxes, which presumably appeal to the wealthy, and conservative social stances (Glaeser et al. 2007). Republicans have regularly championed school prayer and limits on abortion. The appeal of these social stances depends on conservative social beliefs that are not positively correlated with income. In the Annenberg data set, the correlation between income and the propensity to say that the government should not put limits on abortion is 10%. The combination of a direct relationship between income and the financial returns from low-tax Republican policies and an indirect relationship where income decreases conservative social beliefs (which decreases the support for Republicanism) suggests that our model may indeed explain the observed aggregation reversal.

To test this hypothesis, we use the Annenberg data to estimate the parameters of the model. We then see whether these estimated parameters predict an aggregation reversal and the coefficient seen in the aggregate data. We estimate an aggregate marginal effect of log income on the propensity to vote for Bush of −.274 using Federal Election Commission voting records and 2000 Census data on income, with a standard error of .058. This estimation is done using nonlinear least squares to fit the data to a cumulative normal function. This reflects our assumption that the underlying heterogeneity in political preferences is normally distributed. The ordinary least squares estimate is −.272 with a standard error of .057.

We have two different belief variables that we use in our estimation: survey responses to questions as to whether "the federal government should not put limits on abortion," and "the government should not support prayer in schools." In both cases, we have reduced the answers to these questions to taking on two values. The first column of Table 8.2 shows the results using the first question; the second column shows the results using the second question.

Two of our empirical moments are independent of the choice of belief variable. The marginal impact of income on voting for Bush, our estimate of $\gamma\delta + \beta$ is found using a probit equation with state fixed effects on the Annenberg data. As shown in the first row of Table 8.2, we estimate .079

TABLE 8.2 **Parameters for the relationship between income and voting for Bush in 2000**

Parameter	Abortion question	School prayer question
Within-state impact of income on voting for Bush $(\gamma\delta + \beta)$	.079 (.008)	.079 (.008)
Variation in income explained by states $\frac{\text{Cov}(X_i,\hat{X}_j)}{\text{Var}(X_i)}$	.023 (.004)	.023 (.004)
Implied covariance of latent beliefs ψ_k^2	.143 (.025)	.143 (.025)
Implied value of ψ_k	.378 (.034)	.378 (.034)
Marginal impact of income on belief within states $(\psi_k\delta)$	−.041 (.007)	−.079 (.013)
Implied value of δ	−.109 (.023)	−.210 (.039)
Marginal impact of income on belief across states $((1 + \lambda)\psi_j\delta)$	−.399 (.007)	−.477 (.010)
Implied value of λ	8.73 (1.714)	5.018 (.939)
Implied covariance of latent belief with latent outcome $\psi_k\left(\gamma + \beta\delta(1 + \lambda\text{Cov}(X_i,\hat{X}_j))\right)$	.219 (.015)	.148 (.027)
Implied value of γ	.598 (.070)	.432 (.082)
Implied value of β	.144 (.020)	.170 (.029)
Implied value of aggregate relationship $\gamma\delta(1 + \lambda) + \beta$	−.488 (.116)	−.377 (.112)
Estimated value of aggregate relationship $\gamma\delta(1 + \lambda) + \beta$	−.274 (.058)	−.274 (.058)

Note: Bootstrapped standard erross shown in parentheses.

for this coefficient. The estimate of $\frac{\text{Cov}(X_i,\hat{X}_j)}{\text{Var}(X_i)}$ is based on the amount of variation in income explained by state fixed effects. The second row of Table 8.2 shows our estimate of .023 for this parameter. We have also estimated this sorting parameter using the Census Individual Public Use Micro Samples and found a similar parameter estimate of .022.

As described above, we need the correlation between the two questions to form our estimate of ψ_k, which is based on the correlation of the two variables. The third row of Table 8.2 shows the estimated covariance of the latent belief variables of .143, which is our estimate of ψ_k^2.

The remaining rows in the table give estimates that differ between the two belief questions. In the fifth row, we show the estimated impact of income on beliefs within states, which is our estimate of $\psi_k\delta$. This estimate is $-.041$ in the case of support for limits on abortion and $-.079$ in the case of opposition to prayer in school. Income is more strongly negatively correlated with beliefs about prayer in school than with beliefs about limits on abortion. The sixth row shows the associated value of δ, which is found by dividing this estimate by our estimate of ψ_k. This parameter estimate is $-.109$ in the case of the abortion question and $-.210$ for the prayer question.

The seventh row gives the state-level marginal impact of the logarithm of income on the share of the population that answers yes to the two questions. In both cases, the estimated coefficient explodes. In the case of limits on abortion, the group-level coefficient rises to $-.399$, and in the case of school prayer, the group level coefficient rises to $-.477$. The much stronger aggregate relationship supports the hypothesis of a social multiplier, although sorting on omitted variables could explain some part of the observed group-level relationship.

In the eighth row, we report the value of λ implied by the ratio of group-level effects to individual effects. In the case of abortion, this parameter is 8.73. In the case of school prayer, it is 5.02. We also find evidence for social multipliers when we examine relationships at lower levels of aggregation. Perhaps it is surprising to estimate social multipliers that are this strong, but these findings are certainly in line with the social psychology literature, which argues that beliefs like these are very much the product of social interactions.

In the ninth row, we show the estimated covariance of the latent outcome variable (support for Bush) and the latent belief variable. There is a higher covariance in the case of the abortion question (.219) than in the case of the school prayer question (.148). This higher correlation reflects the stronger connection between Republicanism and views on abortion than between Republicanism and views on school prayer.

The tenth and eleventh rows give our estimates of γ and β, respectively—the impact of beliefs on voting for Bush and the direct effect of income on voting for Bush. In both cases, beliefs seem to have a much stronger impact on voting Republican than does income. We estimate γ coefficients of .598 and .432 for the abortion and prayer questions, respectively. When we use the abortion question, we estimate a direct effect of income (β) of .144. When we use the prayer question, we estimate a higher direct effect of income of .170.

The twelfth row gives the predicted group-level relationship between income and voting for Bush implied by these parameters. In both cases, the model predicts a healthy aggregation reversal. Using the abortion question, we predict a negative relationship of $-.488$; using the prayer relationship, we predict a negative relationship of $-.377$. This predicted relationship should be compared to the actual aggregate relationship of $-.274$ shown in the thirteenth row.

The predicted value found by using the school prayer question is reasonably close to the actual aggregate relationship; the prediction based on the abortion question is far too negative. Although given the imprecision of our estimates, it is not clear that we should make too much of these findings. We suspect that we are predicting too much of an aggregation reversal, because we are overestimating the size of the social multiplier in the case of the abortion question. For example, if we used the social multiplier estimated using the school prayer question but continued to use all the other moments of the abortion question, then our predicted aggregate relationship would be much closer to the actual aggregate relationship.

5   Religion and Education

We now revisit the connection between education and religion discussed in Glaeser and Sacerdote (2008). At the individual level, people with more education attend church more often. In the General Social Survey, 53% of college graduates attend church once per month or more, while 45% of high school dropouts attend that frequently. However, more-educated denominations are far less religious than less-educated denominations. Figure 8.4 shows the correlation between average years of education and church attendance across denominations.

As in the case of voting Republican, there are at least two different reasons to go to church. First, going to church is a conventional social activity that connects people in a community and provides certain type of services for children. Second, going to church is thought by some to yield otherworldly returns, such as going to heaven. Religious beliefs are surely based on social influences. Where else would most people come up with their views about the afterlife? These two different functions of church attendance—one of which is highly dependent on socially formed beliefs and one of which is not—suggest that our model can possibly explain the aggregation reversal.

Glaeser and Sacerdote (2008) provide evidence that education predicts participation in almost every formal social activity at the individual level. Education predicts membership in political clubs, fraternal clubs, hobbyist associations, and even sports clubs. In this light, it seems unsurprising that education also predicts membership in religious groups and attendance at church. There are several possible explanations of this fact. Group membership may be seen as a form of investment in social capital, and people who invest in human capital may also see returns to investing in social capital. Glaeser et al. (2007) argue that education includes heavy doses of socialization that increases the ability to interact effectively with others. If education directly increases the returns to social activity and if church going is a social activity, then this creates a direct effect, where education should increase the amount of church attendance.

Religion is, of course, not just another social club. Most religious groups also promise some forms of otherworldly returns to religious adherence. Yet education generally predicts less belief in the supernatural. For example, belief in heaven, the devil, and the literal truth of the Bible all decline strongly with years of education. There are several possible interpretations of this phenomenon. One view is that these phenomena are at odds with modern science, and more education naturally includes more of the science that disproves religious belief. An alternative view argues that secular education is often anticlerical, and the negative relation between education and religion reflects the impact of secularist indoctrination. We take no view in this debate, but simply note the robust negative relationship between years of schooling and religious beliefs.

Whatever negative effects exist between education and religious beliefs at the individual level, they do appear to be magnified at the denominational level. Figure 8.7 shows the negative relationship between average years of schooling in a denomination and belief in the devil. This magnification may well reflect the social formation of beliefs. Educated denominations contain people who are less likely to be strong believers and who speak those views regularly. The more-educated denominations are also more likely to have educated religious leaders who are less likely to be strong believers and who themselves determine the basic tenets of the denomination. More-educated denominations are more likely to have

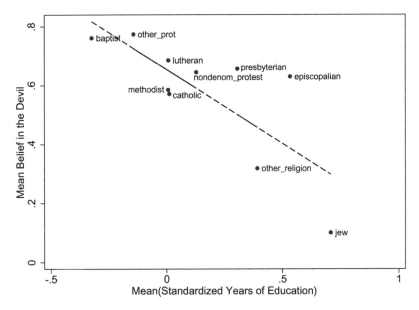

FIGURE 8.7. Belief in the devil by standardized education level

sermons discussing nuanced ethical issues rather than strong statements affirming the literal truth of the Bible or the damnation of nonbelievers.

We will use belief in the devil and in the literal truth of the Bible for our calibration. While these variables take on four and three values, respectively, in the General Social Survey, we reduce them to binary variables based on the mean response. Our calibrations appear in Table 8.3. In the first row, we describe the within-denomination relationship between education and attendance of .031. Education has been normalized to have a standard deviation of one, so this coefficient means that a one standard deviation increase in education is associated with a 3.1% increase in the probability that an individual will attend church regularly.

In the second row, we give the share of the variation in education that is explained by denomination fixed effects: 5.6%. Education is more closely linked to denomination than income is to states. The third row gives the correlation of latent belief variables implied by the correlation of our two proxies for beliefs, and the fourth row shows that this implies a value for ψ_j of .412.

The fifth row gives the marginal impact of education on belief within denominations. In both cases, more-educated people are less likely to

TABLE 8.3 **Parameters for the relationship between education and church attendance**

Belief question:	Bible is the literal truth	Belief in the devil
Within-state impact of on education on attendance $(\gamma\delta + \beta)$	.031 (.003)	.031 (.003)
Variation in education explained by denominations $\dfrac{\mathrm{Cov}(X_i, \hat{X}_j)}{\mathrm{Var}(X_i)}$	.056 (.002)	.056 (.002)
Implied covariance of latent beliefs ψ_k^2	.170 (.027)	.170 (.027)
Implied value of ψ_k	.412 (.033)	.412 (.033)
Marginal impact of income on belief within denominations $(\psi_k\delta)$	−.032 (.015)	−.118 (.010)
Implied value of δ	−.078 (.036)	−.287 (.036)
Marginal impact of income on belief across denominations $((1+\lambda)\psi_j\delta)$	−.602 (.004)	−.666 (.002)
Implied value of λ	17.731 (113.18)	4.628 (.517)
Implied covariance of latent belief with latent outcome $\psi_k\left(\gamma + \beta\delta(1 + \lambda\mathrm{Cov}(X_i, \hat{X}_j))\right)$	.148 (.026)	.130 (.021)
Implied value of γ	.369 (.070)	.365 (.068)
Implied value of β	.060 (.015)	.136 (.027)
Implied value of aggregate relationship $\gamma\delta(1+\lambda)+\beta$	−.479 (.128)	−.454 (.123)
Estimated value of aggregate relationship $\gamma\delta(1+\lambda)+\beta$	−.314 (.070)	−.314 (.070)

Note: Bootstrapped standard errors shown in parentheses.

have strong religious beliefs. A one standard deviation increase in education is associated with a 3.2% decrease in the propensity to say that the Bible is the literal truth and an 11.8% decrease in the propensity to believe in the devil. When we divide these values by our estimate of ψ_k in the sixth row, we estimate of δ to be −.078 and −.287 for the Bible and devil questions, respectively.

In the seventh and eighth rows, we show the results of the cross-denomination regressions of beliefs on education and the implied social multiplier. In the case of the Bible question, we estimate an aggregate coefficient of $-.6$ and a value for λ of 17.7. In the case of the devil question, somewhat appropriately, we estimate an aggregate coefficient of $-.666$ and estimate λ to be 4.6. The denomination-level coefficients are almost identical, and the difference in the social multiplier is driven primarily by the lower individual-level relationship between education and belief in the literal truth of the Bible.

The ninth row delivers the implied covariance between the latent belief variable and the latent attendance variable, which is .148 in the case of the Bible question and .13 in the case of the devil question. The ninth row shows that these covariances imply almost identical values of γ for the two belief questions: .369 and .365. In both cases, higher beliefs are strongly associated with greater propensity to attend church. The similar estimates of γ imply quite different estimated values for β: .06 for the Bible question and .139 for the devil question. The difference is driven by the much stronger correlation between education and belief in the devil than between education and belief in the literal truth of the Bible.

The twelfth and thirteenth rows give the predicted and actual aggregate relationships between education and religious attendance. In both cases, the parameters predict a robust aggregation reversal. With the Bible question, our parameters predict an aggregation reversal of $-.479$, and with the devil question, we predict an aggregation reversal of $-.454$. The actual aggregate relationship is $-.314$. We again predict too negative a relationship, although our standard errors are sufficiently big that these differences are only modestly statistically different.

There are many possible explanations for our overly negative predictions. In the case of the Bible question, we suspect that our estimate of the social multiplier is too high. In the case of the devil question, we may have overestimated the magnitude of δ, the connection between education and beliefs. As before, we think the lesson of this calibration is that the model is more effective at predicting the sign of the aggregate effect than at accurately predicting the actual size of the effect.

6   Income and the Military

We now turn to our final aggregation reversal: the relationship between income and military service. Figure 8.5 shows the positive relationship between veteran status, which is defined as having had some military service, and family income at the individual level. This relationship we show uses data from the General Social Survey, but the Census shows similar results. This relationship surely reflects some amount of both treatment and selection, but when we look at parental occupation status in the General Social Survey, we also find a −.02% correlation between higher-income occupations and entering into the Army. People from the lowest socioeconomic backgrounds tend not to join the army, either because they are not allowed in or because they choose not to join.

Figure 8.6 shows the relationship between income and military service at the state level using the 2000 Census. In this case, we look only at people born after 1950, which means that we are looking mostly at people who have volunteered. Alternative cutoff dates make little difference. People from lower-income states are much more likely to join the military than are people from higher-income states. The Northeast trio of Massachusetts, Connecticut, and New Jersey are particularly unlikely to have members in the military.

One explanation for this phenomenon that corresponds well with standard prejudices about red and blue states is that people in high-income areas are less likely to believe in military service. At the individual level, perhaps, relatively anti-war teachers perhaps tell students that fighting in the military is bad. And perhaps high levels of income correlate with a dislike of the self-sacrifice that military service entails.

We use two belief variables to look at enthusiasm for the Army. The first belief variable is a question about whether respondents think that the Army is a good experience for men. The second belief variable is whether respondents have confidence in the Army as an institution. In both cases, income and education are negatively correlated with the pro-military belief. In both cases, the correlations between income and beliefs at the state level are significantly stronger than the correlations between income and beliefs at the individual level.

Table 8.4 yields the parameter estimates for this example. The first row gives the within-state relationship between income and military service. A one standard deviation in log income is associated with a 5.9% increase in the probability of having a veteran in the household. The second row provides the variation in income explained by state dummies, which is the same parameter that appeared in our first example.

The third and fourth rows display the estimated covariance of the latent belief variables and the implied value of ψ_k: .335. These belief

TABLE 8.4 **Parameters for the relationship between military service and income**

	Military is a good experience	Confidence in the Army
Within-state correlation between income and military service ($\gamma\delta + \beta$)	.059 (.003)	.059 (.003)
Variation in income explained by states $\dfrac{\text{Cov}(X_i,\hat{X}_j)}{\text{Var}(X_i)}$	.026 (.002)	.026 (.002)
Implied covariance of latent beliefs ψ_k^2	.112 (.031)	.112 (.031)
Implied value of ψ_k	.335 (.047)	.335 (.047)
Marginal impact of income on belief within states ($\psi_k\delta$)	−.035 (.015)	−.027 (.003)
Implied value of δ	−.104 (.047)	−.082 (.016)
Marginal impact of income on belief across states ($(1+\lambda)\psi_j\delta$)	−.125 (.003)	−.190 (.002)
Implied value of λ	2.577 (23.04)	5.923 (.758)
Implied covariance of latent belief with latent outcome $\psi_k\left(\gamma + \beta\delta(1 + \lambda\text{Cov}(X_i,\hat{X}_j))\right)$	.191 (.023)	.011 (.009)
Implied value of γ	.583 (.109)	.037 (.028)
Implied value of β	.119 (.036)	.062 (.004)
Implied value of aggregate relationship $\gamma\delta(1+\lambda) + \beta$	−.098 (.065)	.041 (.015)
Estimated value of aggregate relationship $\gamma\delta(1+\lambda) + \beta$	−.092 (.028)	−.092 (.028)

Note: Bootstrapped standard errors shown in parentheses.

variables are less correlated than the belief variables in the previous examples. The fifth row shows the estimated impact of income on beliefs within states, and the sixth row shows the implied value of δ. We estimate that a one standard deviation increase in income is associated with a 10% decrease in pro-military beliefs, using the first question, and an 8% decrease in pro-military beliefs when we use the second question. In this case, the estimates of δ using the two different questions seem reasonably close.

The seventh and eighth rows give the estimated impact of income on pro-military beliefs across states and the implied values for λ. The implied values of λ are 2.6 and 5.9. The confidence in the army question appears to have a much stronger social multiplier.

The ninth row gives the implied covariance of the latent belief variable with the outcome. In the case of the question about the military being a good experience, the correlation is robust. The tenth row shows that this correlation implies that γ equals .58 for the question about the benefits of military service. The latent correlation between confidence in the army and military service is almost zero, and this implies a value of .037 for γ. This small connection between beliefs and outcomes makes an aggregation reversal unlikely.

In the eleventh row, we show the implied values of β which is .12 when we use the question about the military being a good experience and .06 when we use confidence in the army. These higher values in the case of the good experience come from a higher estimate of γ. When the impact of beliefs is estimated to be higher, then the direct effect of income must also be higher.

Finally, in the twelfth and thirteenth rows, we look at the predicted and actual aggregate relationship between income and military service. In the case of the good experience question, we predict an aggregate relationship of −.098, when the actual relationship is −.092. In the case of the confidence in the army question, our low estimate of γ means that we fail to estimate an aggregate reversal and predict an aggregate coefficient of .042.

7 Conclusion

This paper presents a model of aggregation reversals, where individual relationships have the opposite sign from group relationships. In the model, aggregation reversals occur when the exogenous variable impacts the outcomes through two channels. In one of the channels, there is a social multiplier, so the aggregate relationship between the exogenous variable and the outcome increases at higher levels of aggregation. We focus on the case where the exogenous variable is correlated with beliefs, because we believe social influence is a critical determinant of most beliefs. The model predicts that aggregation reversals will occur when the ratio of the direct effect of the exogenous variable on the outcome to the belief effect is negative and is somewhat greater in absolute value than one and is less than the social multiplier.

We applied the model to three examples of aggregation reversals. We did not try to rule out other alternative theories or identify causal parameters. Instead, we asked whether parameter values that were estimated from individual-level relationships and the aggregate relationship between beliefs and the exogenous variable would predict the aggregation reversal that we see in the data. Our work does not rule out alternative explanations but rather tries to establish some degree of plausibility for our theory.

We examined the relationship between income and voting for George Bush in 2000, the relationship between education and religious attendance, and the relationship between income and military service. We used two different belief variables for each aggregation reversal, yielding six different predictions about aggregate relationships. Our calibration exercise had successes and failures. In five out of six cases, the parameters did predict an aggregation reversal. Except for the one case, where we don't predict an aggregation reversal, we estimate a strong relationship between beliefs and outcomes and a large social multiplier in the formation of those beliefs. Together, these tend to predict an aggregation reversal. In many cases, we predict too much of a reversal, because our estimated social multiplier is quite large.

The paper suggests that the social formation of beliefs and the resulting social multipliers may be significant determinants of important aggregate phenomena. These three aggregation reversals are hardly the only such cases that exist. Figures 8.8 and 8.9 show the aggregation reversal in the relationship between gun ownership and income. In all of the cases we examined, we found substantial social multipliers in beliefs but also omitted variables that could be driving these findings. We hope that future empirical work will put more effort into more clearly identified estimates of the magnitude of social learning.

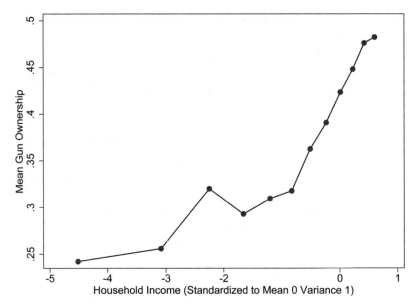

FIGURE 8.8. Gun ownership and income: micro data

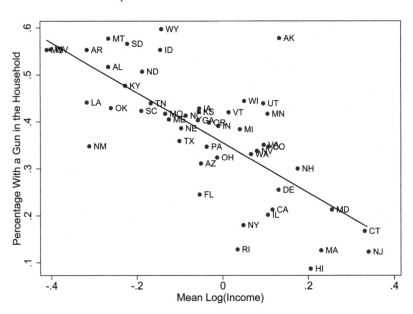

FIGURE 8.9. Gun ownership and income: state level

Appendix

Voting and Income: State-level voting results in 2000 are from the Federal Election Commission. State-level income for 2000 is calculated from the Individual Public Use Micro data available at ipums.org and uses the household income measure.

Microdata are from the National Annenberg Election Survey 2000. The data CDRom accompanies the volume Daniel Romer, Kate Kenski, Paul Waldman, Christopher Adasiewicz, and Kathleen Hall Jamieson (2004). *Capturing Campaign Dynamic.* New York: Oxford University Press. We use only the data collection waves that occurred after the election and code as voting for Bush all those who report voting for Bush. We code as zero those voting for Gore or some other candidate. The abortion variable is coded so that a one is given to those who respond that the Federal government should not restrict abortion. Those who respond that the Federal government should restrict are coded as zero. Those who say the Federal government should not allow school prayer are coded as one, and those who say the Federal government should allow school prayer are coded as zero.

Attendance and Education: We use the General Social Survey 2004 data. For attendance, we use the variable ATTEND and code as a one those who attend religious services once per month or more. For beliefs about the devil, we use the variable DEVIL and code as one those who say "yes definitely" or "yes probably" when asked whether they believe in the devil. Our recoded variable has a mean of 62%. For beliefs about the Bible, we code as one those who respond that "The Bible is the actual word of God and it is to be taken literally, word for word." Our recoded variable has a mean of 30%.

For denomination, we divide respondents into 10 denominations using the variables RELIG4 and DENOM. Our 10 denominations and frequencies are as follows:

Religion	Frequency	Percent	Cumulative
Baptist	9,547	20.64	20.64
Catholic	11,417	24.69	45.33
Episcopalian	1,103	2.38	47.71
Jew	973	2.10	49.82
Lutheran	3,127	6.76	56.58
Methodist	4,662	10.08	66.66
No religion	4,292	9.28	75.94
Nondenominational Protestant	1,965	4.25	80.19
Other Protestant	5,930	12.82	93.01
Other religion	1,340	2.90	95.91
Presbyterian	1,893	4.09	100.00
Total	46,249	100.00	—

Military Status and Income: We use the General Social Survey 2004 data. We use the inflation-adjusted income number from the variable REALINC. We use the variable VETYEARS to infer whether the respondent has any military experience. The mean of our variable for military service is 18.7%. For beliefs, we use MILOK and code as one anyone who believes that the military offers a good experience for men. The mean of our recoded variable is 62.4%. We also use CONARMY and code as one anyone who has "a great deal of confidence in the military." This variable has a mean of 62%.

Notes

Glaeser thanks the Taubman Center for State and Local Government for financial support; Sacerdote thanks the National Science Foundation. Gary King, José Scheinkman, and Glen Weyl provided helpful comments. Giacomo Ponzetto did heroic service discussing and improving the paper.

1. Data sources are described in the appendix to this paper.

2. One way of understanding the difference between our approach and the ecological inference literature is that this literature sees aggregate information as a means of inferring individual-level parameters, while we see aggregate relationships as intrinsically interesting.

3. There is also an extensive theoretical literature on social learning in economics following Kandori et al. (1993) and Ellison and Fudenberg (1993, 1995).

4. Credulous Bayesians believe $\mathrm{Var}(A - E(A))$ equals $\left(\rho\sigma_\kappa^2 + \frac{\sigma_\eta^2 + (1-\rho)\sigma_\kappa^2}{Z} \right) \times$ $\sigma_A^2 \Big/ \left(\sigma_A^2 + \rho\sigma_\kappa^2 + \frac{\sigma_\eta^2 + (1-\rho)\sigma_\kappa^2}{Z} \right)$.

5. Throughout the paper the symbol "$\wedge$" denotes an individual's estimate of a random variable.

References

Asch, S. E. (1955). Opinions and social pressure. *Scientific American 193*(5), 31–35.

Bandura, A. (1977). *Social Learning Theory.* New York: General Learning Press.

Berns, G., J. Chappelow, C. Zink, G. Pagnoni, M. Martin-Skurski, and J. Richards (2005). Neurobiological correlates of social conformity and independence during mental rotation. *Biological Psychiatry 58*(3), 245–253.

Demarzo, Peter, Dmitri Vayanos, and Jeffrey Zwiebel (2003). Persuasion bias, social influence and uni-dimensional opinions. *Quarterly Journal of Economic 118*(3), 909–968.

DiTella, R., S. F. Galiani, and E. S. Schargrodsky (2007). The formation of beliefs: Evidence from the allocation of land titles to squatters. *Quarterly Journal of Economics 122*(1): 209–241.

Ellison, G. and D. Fudenberg (1993). Rules of thumb for social learning. *Journal of Political Economy 101*(4), 612–643.

———. (1995). Word-of-mouth communication and social learning. *Quarterly Journal of Economics 110*(1), 93–125.

Gelman, A. (2008). Red State, Blue State, Rich State Poor State Princeton, NJ: Princeton University Press.

Gentzkow, M. A., and J. M. Shapiro (2004). Media, education and anti-Americanism in the Muslim world. *Journal of Economic Perspectives 18*(3), 117–133.

Glaeser, E. L., and B. I. Sacerdote (2008). Education and religions. NBER Working Paper 8080. *Journal of Human Capital 2*(2), 188–215.

Glaeser, E. L., B. Sacerdote, and J. Scheinkman (2003). The social multiplier. *Journal of the European Economic Association 1*(2), 345–353.

Glaeser, E. L. and C. R. Sunstein (2009). Extremism and social learning. Journal of Legal Analysis *1*(1), 263–329.

Glaeser, E. L., G. Ponzetto, and J. M. Shapiro (2005). Strategic extremism: Why Republicans and Democrats divide on religious values. *Quarterly Journal of Economics 120*(4), 1283–1330.

Glaeser, E. L., G. Ponzetto, and A. Shleifer (2007). Why does democracy need education? *Journal of Economic Growth 12*(3), 717–799.

Kandori, M., G. J. Mailath, and R. Rob (1993). Learning, mutation and long run equilibria in games. *Econometrica 61*(1), 29–56.

King, G. (1997). *A Solution to the Ecological Inference Problem.* Princeton, NJ: Princeton University Press.

Merlo, A. M., and A. Schotter (2003). Learning by not doing: An experimental investigation of observational learning. *Games and Economic Behavior 42*(1), 116–136.

Romer, D., K. Kenski, P. Waldman, C. Adasiewicz, and K. H. Jamieson (2004). *Capturing Campaign Dynamic*. New York: Oxford University Press.

Scheinkman, J. A., and W. Xiong (2003). Overconfidence and speculative bubbles. *Journal of Political Economy* (6), 1183–1219.

CHAPTER NINE

Finance and the Common Good

E. Glen Weyl

If you become an economist, your job will be to question why.
—José Scheinkman, personal conversation

I Introduction

B ecker (1976) famously observed that economists apply the theory of incentives to almost every aspect of human life—except for the economics profession itself. This chapter begins to fill this gap by considering how the economic environment influences the topics economists address in their research. I consider a simple decision of allocating attention either to normative, policy-oriented questions of final interest to governments and legal systems or to positive questions primarily of interest to private firms. Shifts in the regulatory environment and the economic cycle influence economists' allocation of time across these activities both directly (through consulting opportunities) and indirectly (through demand for teaching). I contrast two fields as a case study: finance and industrial organization (IO). Using a combination of hand coding of Internet searches and automated text analysis of articles, I show the bulk of both consulting and research in finance is on the positive side, whereas the bulk of both in IO is on the normative side. Although only loosely suggestive of the elasticity in which I am interested, these facts open an interesting line of research with implications for the design of regulations that hope to draw on economic expertise.[1]

Participants in each field can clearly see the consequences of the different foci of the fields. When financial economists discuss the "efficiency of markets," they are usually referring to *informational efficiency*, that is, whether predicting asset prices in a manner that would allow some form of "excess" profits over the risk-adjusted return on capital is possible. When most other economists discuss the "efficiency of markets," they are referring to notions such as Pareto efficiency, utilitarian social optimization, or social wealth-maximization à la Kaldor (1939) and Hicks (1939). Although informational efficiency of markets might superficially appear simply to be the component of allocative efficiency more broadly with which financial markets are concerned, we can easily see the two concepts are neither equivalent nor even closely aligned. Informational efficiency may arise simply from markets moving randomly (DeLong et al. 1990), with little relationship to underlying values, and even efforts to align market values more closely with fundamentals may harm the social allocation of risk (Weyl 2007; Simsek 2013a,b). Such efficiency may also be oversupplied relative to its cost of provision (Hirshleifer 1971). However, small amounts of predictability in prices may have limited allocative costs and may arise at any Pareto-optimal allocation (Grossman and Stiglitz 1980). Thus, a literature primarily concerned with informational efficiency is unlikely to produce insights to systematically aid in the development of public policies that promote allocative efficiency.[2] Although the question of informational efficiency may be of direct interest to investors attempting to profit in financial markets, it is at best of tangential interest to social planners attempting to maximize economic welfare.

I begin by documenting this pattern empirically in Section 2. Using automated text analysis calibrated by hand-coding articles as having positive or normative content, I show that IO has three times the number of articles with primarily normative content as finance does in its top three field journals.

Then in Section 3, I describe a model that accounts for the divergence between financial and industrial economics. Economics plays a crucial role in the rigorous scheme of competition policy in the United States and increasingly around the world. This role creates a demand from firms for economists and their students as consultants and expert witnesses for competition policy matters to defend their behavior on social welfare grounds or condemn that of their rivals or suppliers. This demand, in turn, creates further demand among economists who serve as teachers or consultants for academic research, providing tools and frameworks for analyzing these issues. In contrast, regulation of the financial sector has not been nearly as rigorous, either in terms of it stringency or, more importantly, its reliance on economics. This lack of rigor has reduced demand for economists and their students as consultants on allocative efficiency, and has stimulated demand for their assistance on financial engineering and profitable speculation. I discuss various pathways through which these external influences affect research in economics.

Of course, as I discuss below, these demand shifts were endogenous to the agenda of economics. The economic approach to antitrust law that I view as a demand shifter grew partially out of the Chicago School's advocacy, led by Aaron Director (Kitch 1983) and culminating with Posner's (1976) book on the subject, of an economic approach to antitrust law. In contrast, financial engineering grew out of Black and Scholes's (1973) and Merton's (1973) pioneering work on asset pricing, as documented by Bernstein (1992, 2007) and MacKenzie (2008). In ongoing research, conducted jointly with James Evans, we have collected a much more comprehensive data set to disentangle causation and economic structure in these relationships.

In the present work, I simply document, in Section 2, broad consulting patterns in the fields. First, I show that consulting plays an important role in the lives of many of the authors in my sample. Using relatively crude methods to translate publicly available data into income estimates, I estimate that approximately 40% of the income of authors in both fields comes from consulting activities, roughly consistent with self-reported income figures for the broader profession in the National Center for Education Statistics' *National Study of Postsecondary Faculty*. Second, I show that consulting activity in IO is primarily policy oriented, whereas consulting work in finance is primarily geared toward private interests. Together, these two facts weakly suggest material incentives are at least complementary with research focus.

Section 4 turns to the prospective (policy and predictive) implications of the model, in the case in which it is empirically valid. Responsiveness of academics to financial incentives implies that policy makers should not take the state of the economic art as a binding constraint on rigorous, economics-based financial regulation. Such responsiveness would mean that if a sufficiently rigorous regime with a focus on economic analysis is built, the economic research to populate the regime might come. Conversely, for those who are sympathetic to the general allocative efficiency of markets and believe that private parties are likely to capture research on allocative efficiency for distributive purposes, an additional cost of regulation would be the diversion of research away from what they would see as productive service of financial innovation and informational efficiency in the private sector. In either case, the model predicts the extensive rule makings under Dodd-Frank and the various sources of pressure for rigorous benefit-cost analysis of these regulations (Posner and Weyl 2014) will help reduce the demand for work on informational efficiency and increase the demand for work on allocative efficiency.

Section 5 concludes by discussing the role José Scheinkman's work may play in this shift. José's uniquely broad perspective in the community of financial economists provides inspiration for a move toward greater interest in the common good among financial economists. I relate a personal story in which José inspired me to decide to become an economist because such a path would allow me to consider the social value of activities in the financial sector.

2 Facts on Consulting and Research in Two Fields

To study the relationship between external economic conditions and research, I chose two fields in economics: finance and industrial organization (IO). I chose these two fields, because I know them both personally (having been trained in the former and working primarily in the latter), because they have significant potential to contribute both to social normative analysis and private profit maximization, and because they developed historically in similar periods. I also chose them because I believe they differ markedly in the consulting opportunities available in each.

My personal exposure, primarily through the activities of colleagues but also through my own career, suggested this difference. Most of my colleagues in finance have extensively consulted for private money managers on investment strategies, arbitrage activities, and/or capital and risk management. Most of my colleagues in IO, in contrast, have consulted for firms and governments in legal cases related to antitrust and other industrial regulations.

To verify my intuitions, I constructed a sample of articles in each field. On the basis of a subjective personal evaluation, I chose three leading field journals in each field. For finance, I chose the *Journal of Finance* (*JF*), *Journal of Financial Economics* (*JFE*), and *Review of Financial Studies* (*RFS*). For IO, I chose the *RAND Journal of Economics* (*RJE*),

International Journal of Industrial Organization (*IJIO*), and *Journal of Industrial Economics* (*JIE*). For each year since 1980 during which these journals existed, I randomly selected three articles from each to include in the sample.

For all authors of papers in this sample, I attempted to determine the extent and type of consulting in which they engaged. Because income from consulting is not publicly available, I used publicly available information as a proxy for the fraction of income individuals derived from consulting. I performed a Google search for the authors of every article, both separately and together with the key words "economics" and/or "consulting." Those authors who currently work in a private (hedge fund, consulting firm, etc.) or public sector (Federal Reserve, United States Department of Justice Antitrust Division Economic Analysis Group, etc.) consulting job received a score of 1, indicating all of their annual income comes from consulting. Those authors who are principals of, owners of, or are high-level executives of a consulting firm received a score of .75 (75% of income from consulting). Those individuals whose consulting involvement was significant enough to yield extensive mention outside of their personal websites (e.g., advertisement on the website of the firms they work with) received a score of .5. If none of the previous applies but the personal websites or curriculum vitae of individuals indicate that they are engaged in consulting activities at present, they received a score of .25. Otherwise, they received a score of 0. I dropped from the sample any author about whom I could locate no information. In addition, each author who did not receive a score of 0 was scored as doing consulting work primarily on policy, litigation, or other normative issues (scored as 1) or as doing consulting primarily on private business issues (scored as −1). Obviously, these quantities are extremely crude proxies for income and cannot be empirically calibrated at a detailed level to match income. Below, I discuss a broad, profession-wide calibration check on these magnitudes. However, these scores still provide a signal of the extent of involvement in consulting.

If consulting work appeared to be evenly split, the individual received a score of 0 in this type category. I formed a score for each individual as the product of the extent and type of her consulting activities; −1 indicates the strongest possible non-normative consulting activities, 1 indicates the strongest possible normative consulting activities, and 0 indicates mixed or no activities, with numbers in between representing corresponding degrees of focus in the two areas.

TABLE 9.1 **Descriptive statistics for authors' consulting activities**

Variable	Mean	Standard deviation	N	Standard Error (Mean)
		Finance		
Extent	.42	.32	265	.02
Type	−.40	.78	265	.05
Score	−.19	.42	265	.03
		Industrial organization		
Extent	.39	.29	262	.02
Type	.40	.80	262	.05
Score	.11	.42	262	.03

The 551 papers in my sample all had a first author, 319 of them had a second author, and 88 had a third author; authors beyond three were dropped. Of these 958 total authors, I dropped 82 because of a lack of sufficient information; these authors were primarily in European countries that did not have information easily accessible to English-language Google search. Thus, my sample should be thought of as primarily representing the American academy. Authors were clustered by articles; therefore, each observation corresponds to the average value of my variables for an article across all of its coauthors.

Table 9.1 reports some descriptive statistics. Two striking facts emerge immediately. First, consulting is an important source of income in both finance and IO, accounting for approximately 40% in both fields; the importance is slightly greater in finance than in IO, but the difference is not statistically significant.

Is this figure, based on my rough proxies for income shares, consistent with other information we have about the income of economists? The United States Department of Education's National Center for Education Statistics runs a National Survey of Postsecondary Faculty. In its 2004 wave, it asked individuals about their total individual income, their total income from outside their institution, including consulting, and the number of hours each week they spent on paid outside activities. Dividing means (raw data are not available to compute the statistic directly), on average, economics research faculty earn approximately 20% of their income from outside, and teaching faculty, approximately 28%. These percentages are 24% and 45%, respectively, for business faculty. These faculty report spending on average between 4 and 16 hours per week on outside paid activities, as one ranges across these groups. Given that finance and IO are exceptionally lucrative fields for consulting (fields like public finance or theory likely have very little consulting work), 40% of one's income coming from consulting does not seem unreasonable in these fields.

The second fact that immediately emerges, parallel to the observations in Section 1, is the dramatic difference between finance and IO. In IO, most consulting is policy related. In finance, most is not. Approximately 70% of consulting in each field falls into its dominant category, as can be seem by the fact that in each field, the average magnitude of the difference between activity in the dominant area minus that in the less dominant area is .4 and .7−.3 = .4. These differences are highly statistically significant. A similar pattern emerges in the consulting score, which is on average −.19 in finance and .11 in IO. Again, the difference is highly significant.

How does that finding compare to the research focus of the fields? I explored various methods classifying articles as normative/policy-oriented in focus or positive/profit-oriented, including automated text analysis based on either keywords or the whole text and the *Journal of Economic Literature* (*JEL*) codes.

First, a research assistant coded all the articles in the sample by hand based on whether the articles had significant normative or public policy content. I provide examples of these subjective codings and their justification in the appendix to this paper. My criteria for normative content were fairly broad: even if the paper does not derive formal normative statements, as long as a nonspecialist can clearly see the motivation of the piece and its implications are intended to be policy relevant in character, the piece was classified as normative.

Second, I used this dataset as a training set for various automated models for labeling articles in the two categories. The goal of this automated approach is to allow the dramatic expansion of my sample by roughly two orders of magnitude to encompass the full corpus of these journals since 1950 as well as articles in the top five general interest journals (the *American Economic Review*, *Econometrica*, *Journal of Political Economy*, *Quarterly Journal of Economics*, and *Review of Economic Studies*) with the *JEL* classification codes labeling them as financial economics or IO. I leave this for my work in progress with James Evans, but to make the coding as transparent as possible, results reported are based on the algorithm. The classification algorithm settled on used the frequency of occurrence of various key words, including "welfare," "social" or "socially," "antitrust," "regulation," and phrases related to "policy," such as "policy

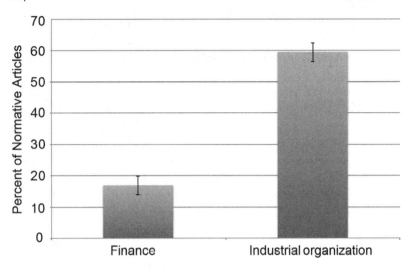

FIGURE 9.1. Percent normative articles by field, with confidence intervals in bars

recommendation." I describe the exact model in the appendix. The model achieved approximately 76% accuracy in cross-validation relative to the subjective evaluations, mostly erred by yielding false negatives, and had similar accuracy on both the IO and finance samples. However, the use of "antitrust" does make the algorithm somewhat more receptive to classifying IO articles as normative than it does finance articles, and thus biases the results somewhat in the direction of the results I find; subjective coding yielded similar but slightly less extreme results (54% to 21%, as opposed to 59% to 17%). I believe that the greater precision, transparency, replicability, and speed of the algorithmic results more than compensate for this potential bias.

I present the results of the analysis in Figure 9.1. The height of the graph represents the fraction of sampled articles in the two fields with normative content according to my classification scheme. I have grouped together all articles from finance journals and all from IO journals. I computed standard error bars assuming that each article is an independent observation. Clearly, the difference between the fields is highly statistically and economically significant. The clear majority of IO articles are classified as normative, whereas a small minority of finance articles are. IO is more than three times more normatively focused.

Thus, in both their research focus and consulting engagements, IO and finance lean roughly three quarters in their respective directions, though these directions are opposite in the two fields. Although these examples are only two case studies and the evidence is at best suggestive, the next section discusses a model in which these facts are linked causally.

3 Model of Economic Incentives and Research Priorities

Many of my colleagues in finance saw a major shift in their academic interests around the time they began consulting—shifts that retreated when they stopped consulting. These shifts were toward the sort of work on modeling asset prices that Section 2 argues is predominant in the field of financial economics. In contrast, many of my colleagues in IO were primarily game theorists, with a limited interest in applied policy work in IO and a greater focus on fundamental issues of equilibrium selection in games that were important in the field. Once they became interested in policy, their interest shifted much more to applied questions with direct policy relevance. Most have not shifted out of that interest, but those who have, also shifted back to their research interests. From my own introspection, I know my own private sector work, discussed below, above has affected my research trajectory, and in my case, the causation ran both ways: my shifting interests made me open to working with them, but my work with them has also shifted my interests.

In this section, I describe a model under which the respective market and regulatory environments governing financial and industrial policy shape the research priorities of economists. My account is somewhat analogous to the account provided by Fourcade (2009) for the divergent paths of the economics profession more broadly across various nations in the past century. However, it is more narrowly material (largely for simplicity of exposition) but relies somewhat more heavily on the institutional structure of the economics profession. I return at the end of the section to provide some nuances to the simple material account on which I focus.

In addition to their main academic work, many economists spend significant time and effort teaching graduate and undergraduate students, as well as on outside consulting opportunities, especially in fields such as industrial and financial economics, where such opportunities are well remunerated, as discussed in the Section 2. These obligations and outside opportunities are likely to shape the topics economists work on and are interested in through several pathways. In what follows, I analyze how outside consulting opportunities can shape economists' interests.

Some and perhaps most of these influences are filtered through teaching: if lucrative opportunities are available to those trained in a field, students will be interested in receiving training that helps them enter that field. Virtually any mechanism through which personally participating in consulting activities affects economists' research priorities will thus also affect the demands their students—and therefore the institutions (business schools and economics departments primarily) that employ them—will place on them.

However, this extra level of indirection adds little to the analysis, and thus I focus on pathways arising from personal participation in consulting, because these pathways are easier to explain and more readily empirically measurable, as I focused on in Section 2. The reader should keep in mind, though, that teaching may play a larger role than personal consulting engagements in shaping economists' research agendas, and thus my estimates below are likely an underestimate of the material influences on research agendas. Also, I use the term "consulting" to refer to all outside engagements taking place during a primarily academic career, whether they be during the academic year or during a leave of absence and whether they would typically be classified as consulting or as something else—management, serving as a principal or an advisor to an organization, a paid expert witness, and so on. I also classify among these activities the primary occupations of those publishing in academic journals but not pursuing academia as their primary employment. Clearly, the word "consulting" is too narrow to encompass this full range of activities, but it is useful for its brevity.

The most direct pathway through which outside consulting opportunities may influence economic research is through provision of an incentive for economists to develop models and tools that will make them more effective in these consulting jobs. Conversely, the consulting jobs provide economists access to information and data they could not otherwise access freely, changing the relative price of working on different projects. Here we can see clearly why such tools would also be useful in teaching students, who will eventually go on to participate in such consulting activities.

In addition, through these consulting projects, economists are exposed to, and become genuinely intellectually interested in, different topics than they otherwise would be. Such exposure and resulting interest is another complementary input to the production of research. The political science literature (Hall and Wayman 1990) has shown that a large part of the influence of those who make material contributions to political campaigns comes through access rather than literal quid pro quo. Analogously, the exposure that consulting projects give economists to relevant topics shifts their intellectual interests in that direction. Finally, academics may use publications on topics relevant to consulting projects to build a reputation that can be marketed to obtain consulting positions.

Although these mechanisms most directly affect economists who participate in the consulting work, they also filter through indirectly to other economists associated with or evaluated by them through several channels. First, consultants act as dissertation advisers to graduate students who may or may not go on to become consultants, helping shape what these students view as important or interesting questions. Second, consultants make decisions that affect whether their colleagues' articles will be published in top journals and whether their colleagues will receive job offers, tenure, prizes, and other professional accolades, and are likely to do so in line with what they consider to be important or valuable work. Third, in a number of informal settings, consultants play an informal advisory or evaluator role, such as workshops, paper discussions, and casual conversations that help set standards for what sorts of work is viewed as exciting or otherwise esteemed and what work is viewed as uninteresting or unrigorous.

These arguments all suggest why one would expect an upsurge of consulting opportunities in a particular area to shift economics research in the relevant field toward that area, regardless of what that area is. I now turn my attention to the nature of the topics that have prominently attracted economists' efforts in these two fields: finance and IO. The discussion below is anecdotal and based on my personal interactions with scholars in the field and knowledge of their extra-academic activities as a result of my having been trained as a financial economist but practicing primarily industrial economics since that time.

As I documented above, in IO, most consulting work available relates to antitrust legal cases brought by one of the major American, European, or Commonwealth antitrust agencies, or to other regulatory issues in one of these jurisdictions. Most top industrial economists have a close association with one or more of the largest consultancies on these issues, such as Bates-White, the Analysis Group, Compass Lexecon, or, in Europe, RBB Economics. Although I have thus far declined to engage in such relationships, I have repeatedly been asked to be involved, and many of my colleagues are involved in ways I have discussed with them at some length.[3]

These consultancies provide expertise to both private and public parties in legal cases. The demand for the consulting services these firms supply arose partly from regulatory and economic events (primarily the cases against AT&T and IBM during the 1970s) and partly from ideas such as the "economic turn" in antitrust law, beginning with the leadership of George Stigler and particularly Aaron Director at the University of Chicago Law School (Kitch 1983). The latter culminated, in the midst of the AT&T case, in Posner's (1976) argument that economic analysis should be used to determine the benefits and costs of different types of firm conduct, after which the influence of economics on antitrust law grew rapidly, as documented by Landes and Posner (1993). Government agencies' and courts' reliance on economic analysis has been increasingly formalized in the years since through a series of economics-based guidelines for the evaluation of firm conduct (in particular, the review of mergers) issued by antitrust agencies.[4]

Some consulting work in IO is driven more closely by the business demand of private firms. For example, Susan Athey, Patrick Bajari, Preston McAfee, and Hal Varian have taken on part- and in some cases full-time employment working primarily on business issues for private firms. I have myself pursued similar engagements; I am currently employed by Microsoft Research and have also worked with start-up companies Applico and Collective Decision Engines, which I cofounded. While some of my work at Microsoft relates to policy, most of my engagement at the company is around designing market mechanisms and pricing strategies. While these activities are rapidly growing in recent years, even now they remain a minority of consulting work performed by industrial economists and has largely been segregated into groups in business schools that have relatively limited communication with mainstream IO.

Matters are dramatically different in finance. If the epoch-defining work in IO was Posner's's economic approach to competition policy, the epoch-defining work in financial economics, and particularly asset pricing, was Black and Scholes's (1973) and Merton's (1973) arbitrage-based theory of derivative security pricing, as summarized by Duffie (2001). This theory, along with the other canonical "capital" ideas of asset pricing (Bernstein 1992, 2007), has generated substantial interest among applied money managers and has led many leading financial economists to establish relationships with such managers, especially of hedge funds. MacKenzie (2008) describes extensively how the ideas developed by economists have shaped modern financial markets. Perhaps the most (in)famous example of such a relationship was the role played by Robert Merton and Myron Scholes in the development of Long-Term Capital Management during the 1990s. Given the size of the boom in the financial sector during the period following the Black-Scholes-Merton work, as documented by Philippon (2015) and Greenwood and Scharfstein (2013), the growth in demand for financial economists' advice is unsurprising.[5]

Regardless, this strong demand for economic ideas in the operation of private financial markets has also had a powerful impact on demand for teaching. Take, for example, my alma mater, Princeton University. Since the late 1990s, Princeton, traditionally a robustly anti-professional university, has developed a terminal masters program in finance and a certificate program in finance for undergraduates. In sharp contrast to the courses offered in Princeton's economics department, virtually none of the courses offered in the finance masters program have any normative component, far less even than is reflected in the research agenda of the fields. Instead, the sequence is overwhelmingly focused on tools for asset pricing and financial modeling that are useful for firms. This change is one manifestation of the robust demand for teaching on topics useful to arbitrage and financial innovation activity that may help shape economists' research priorities, alongside the availability of outside consulting.

Whatever the reason, and in contrast to industrial economics, consulting work by financial economists on public policy and legal issues has been much more limited. Although some economists have played important roles in financial policy (e.g., Jeremy Stein recently at Treasury, Raghu Rajan's work with the International Monetary Fund and the Indian government, and Hyun Shin's work with the Korean government), most economists involved even in financial policy have been drawn from macroeconomics, public finance, or industrial and regulatory economics. Conversely—and again, this assertion is purely from my anecdotal experience—the representation of PhD economists in financial regulation is thin outside the Federal Reserve System, where most of the focus of the professional economists is on macroeconomic issues and to some extent the banking system, but little is on asset markets.

Why has the relative demand for economic expertise been so different in these two areas? The relative decline of traditional industry in the American economy may have played a role in this shift in private demand. The (exogenously) different regulatory environments in the two areas seem likely to have played a significant role as well. Competition enforcement, especially against mergers, is quite stringent in the United States, and firms are often asked to meet a high burden of economic proof to ensure their proposed mergers are welfare enhancing. Similarly high burdens in pharmaceutical pre-approvals by the Food and Drug Administration have stimulated extensive work on randomized trials of medical products. In contrast, financial regulation has generally and increasingly been lax in the United States and is based on rules with little grounding in the rhetoric of economics. Many of my finance colleagues, including many experts on financial regulation, have told me that litigation and policy consulting in finance never grew because firms always knew they could more easily get around rules than fight them in court. Some colleagues have told me they went into finance precisely because it was an arena where players were mostly wealthy grown-ups and externalities were contained, so that extensive regulation, at least based on economics (rather than accounting or transparency standards), was not crucial. Economic tools were thus rarely applied to establish or disprove the existence of burdens on regulated parties. As I discuss in Section 4, this fact began to change with the introduction of Basel II in the mid-2000s and has been changing increasingly rapidly following the fall-out of the the 2007–2009 financial crisis.

However, part of the difference is likely ideational, as emphasized by MacKenzie. Director and Posner's's calls for an economic foundation of antitrust law naturally led to demand among antitrust lawyers and judges for economic expertise, whereas the Black-Scholes-Merton framework suggested a natural role for financial economists in facilitating sophisticated arbitrage strategies. This reverse causality between academic ideas and financial incentives creates an obvious confound that motivates the next section of this paper.

4   Implications and Prospects for Change

In this section, I discuss two implications, the first normative/prescriptive and the second positive/predictive, of the model of the preceding two sections.

First, on the normative side, the theory implies that choices by policy makers influence academic priorities. Coates (2015) responded to my work with Eric Posner during the past few years calling for rigorous, quantitative, economics-based financial regulation (Posner and Weyl 2013a,b) with skepticism about the ability of existing economic tools to provide a foundation for such analysis. My findings here suggest this view may, in some sense, have things the wrong way around. The institution of antitrust standards based on economics may have stimulated the modern tools of IO-based antitrust analysis, rather than the other way around. If policy makers institute an important role for quantitative economic analysis in financial regulation, such a move is likely to stimulate the development of economic tools to carry out this analysis that may never be developed in the absence of such external stimulus. Thus, policy makers should not take the current state of economics research as fixed and its future state as exogenous to their activities, but instead should choose their actions in anticipation of the research these actions will stimulate, even in the absence of direct targeted grant making.

Precisely what policy makers should do based on such anticipation depends on their objectives and views of other economic and financial issues. A policy maker who believes that, at the margin, economics work on improving antitrust policy is largely wasted on rent-seeking by firms hoping to cut down their rivals and would better be invested in improving mechanisms firms use in their businesses, would be pushed to loosen antitrust regulations to redirect economics research in IO toward the private sector. I have some sympathy for this view; I believe that, on the margin, the recent work economists have been doing for private firms in IO has been more productive than policy work on antitrust. This view is obviously complementary to my own work private sector engagements, and the reader is left to judge the direction of causation.

If such a policy maker also believed that the efficacy of arbitrage and innovation in financial markets were more important than the likely ineffective regulation, they would oppose regulation all the more strongly for its incentive effects on economists. In contrast, a policy maker who, like me, believes that too little work in finance has considered issues of allocative efficiency, would view an important benefit of more stringent regulation to be the production of policy-relevant economics research it would likely induce. Researchers often argue that the asset-pricing literatures has only occasionally treated welfare, because welfare is "more difficult" to evaluate in financial markets than in product markets. My analysis makes me skeptical of that claim and leads me to believe that undeveloped demand rather than supply is the primary cause of the paucity of such work.

An alternative view to the one I put forward here is that public interest rather than material incentives is the primary external force. When climate change is in the news, economists work on climate change; when financial crises are in the news, economists turn their attention there. I believe this view has a lot of merit in many settings. Some of its implications are closely related to those discussed above. However, it suggests that, to shift economists' focus, bringing attention to a policy issue is more important than creating material incentives for studying that issue. These two means are not always aligned; much of the development of antitrust policy and the financial sector that created incentives for economists to work in these areas happened largely outside the eye of the general public.

Additionally, I do not believe this view can plausibly account for the divergence between finance and IO on which this paper focuses, namely, that one is interested in social welfare and the other in private profit. Arguing that private profit has risen and social welfare fallen in prominence in the public's mind in different areas, at least over the time spanned by my study, seems to be a stretch. Although public attention may well play an important role in guiding economists' work on public policy issues to those of greatest public interest at a given time, I doubt it plays an important role in guiding economists' work away from public policy altogether and toward maximizing the profits of private agents. However, I obviously cannot rule out the possibility that the more attention that is given to public policy in a sector, the more likely economists will be to work on it, even holding fixed material rewards.

In any case, turning to the positive side, we are in the midst of a natural experiment testing the relative importance of supply and demand for the production of normative work on finance. The financial crisis of 2007–2009 and the resulting Dodd-Frank Wall Street Reform and Consumer Protection Act have dramatically increased the demand for normative analysis by financial economists aimed at reducing the risks and costs of similar crises in the future, without obviously changing the degree of difficulty of resolving basic normative conundra in market trading. This increased demand coincided with substantial progress on these issues, at least anecdotally. For example, a long-standing "challenge" in evaluating welfare in financial markets was evaluating welfare in models where agents have heterogeneous prior beliefs, which many economists believe are important to explain positively the volume of trading observed in most financial markets. Until the crisis, this problem was open in the literature at least since the late 1970s. But following the crisis, several eminent economists, including Brunnermeier et al. (2014) and Gilboa et al. (2014), have take up this problem. More broadly, one can get a sense of the shift taking place by focusing on the part of the sample in Section 2 from the past five years. During this later period, I found that just over 27% of finance articles in 2008–2012 were normative. Although this percentage is higher than the average over the entire sample, the difference is not statistically significant. In the work with Evans, I hope to test this prediction more rigorously by increasing my sample size and by including articles from top general interest journals. However, because of the public nature of the events following the financial crisis, even a convincing test of this sort could not distinguish what part of increased interest in policy in finance is driven by publicity surrounding the crisis and what part is driven by changes in policy that attract limited public attention but shift financial incentives to economists. Establishing a longer time series will help identify historical events that can further test the theory.

5 The Role of José Scheinkman's Work and This Volume

As the incentives shaping research in finance change (and thus, perhaps, research itself changes), communication with other fields, such as IO and macroeconomics, with a more traditionally normative focus are likely to be instrumental in shaping a new path for financial research. In that process, the financial economist with the broadest experience and the widest range of interests throughout economics will naturally be the intellectual and personal inspiration for a new generation of researchers in finance. The most prominent and prototypical example of such a broad financial economist is José Alexandre Scheinkman.

I cannot think of any other primarily financial economist who has contributed to as broad a range of fields of economics as José has. From his early days as a mathematical economic theorist and macroeconomist, through his seminal work in IO, to his leadership in urban and social economics and his exploration of the boundaries between economics and other sciences such as physics, José's work shows a broader grasp of the big picture of economic science and the human intellectual project than any other financial economist I know. José's example and mentorship first led me to explore not just the role of finance in promoting the common good but also the interconnections of economics internally and with other fields more broadly. José's work on cities famously showed that a crucial reason for the economic success of urban centers was the cross-fertilization between different industries and thought patterns that cities permit. In that sense, José's work, his presence in workshops, his leadership at Princeton, where he was my adviser, and the circle of people he has drawn around him—so many of whom came for the conference on which this book is based—have played and continue to play the same catalytic role intellectually in finance that cities have so often played in economic development more broadly.

It is thus altogether fitting that the most powerful moment of catalysis in my academic life, the day I decided to become an economist, took place one evening in a restaurant in New York City with José. The summer between my sophomore and junior years of college, just after taking José's general equilibrium course at Princeton, I was an intern at a hedge fund in New York City. I was assigned to work on an arbitrage strategy between two markets that were crossed because of what my colleagues there called "technical reasons." In particular, individual investors in both America and Europe were holding securities with low returns and risk ill-suited to their personal situations, in opposite directions, because of heuristics that were popular on the two continents in evaluating securities. When the strategy succeeded and our firm did well out of it, I talked to two people about it.

The first was one of my superiors at the firm. I asked him what social service we had performed for which we had been rewarded so handsomely by the market economy. He initially said we had created liquidity in the markets, but I then followed up, questioning whether "liquidity" in this case meant more individual investors in the United States and Europe were able to hold inappropriate and exploitative investments. At that point, frustrated, he told me that "ours is not to reason why, ours is to do and die."

Still searching for an answer, I wrote to José who, only having known me in one half-semester's course, was nonetheless delighted to hear I was in New York for the summer, and took me out for the best Indian meal I had ever had. That evening, I recounted to him my experience at the fund that day. José, with his characteristically incisive brevity, told me, "If you become an economist, your job will be to reason why."

This paper argued that material incentives shape the behavior and priorities of academics. However, I am not a materialist-reductionist. Had you been walking the streets of Athens in the fourth century B.C.E. and asked an educated man what were the most important events happening, he most likely would have described the negotiations with Persia, the war with Sparta, and the success or failure of the most recent harvest. If you had asked him about a wandering man, asking questions in a marketplace, he might have scoffed that the society's ability to support such folks was an outgrowth of the Peace of Pericles and the commerce that filled the markets with people able to listen. And so it might have been. But the sands of time have buried the empire of Ozymandias, whereas the questions of Socrates have shaped Western Civilization and the way we think every day.

Thus, I believe that ideas, too, have their own logic and force. Although their seeds sprout slowly, they are rooted in deep and firm earth. I stand in wonder before what José Scheinkman has inspired in so many of us, how the forces that will shape our society's adaptation to one of the great crises of our time are inspired by his example, and how these ideas are but an early bud of José's branch on the tree that I know will grow stronger and more powerful with each year. In that wonder, I am grateful to be what José made me—one of the few whom the prosperity of our social system affords the right to spend my days questioning the foundations of that system, just as he has done so incisively for the past 40 years. I hope that in the smallest of ways, this final chapter is a tribute to that spirit, using the platform afforded me by the economics profession to prompt a rare bit of analysis and questioning of the driving forces of that profession.

Appendix

To provide a sense for how subjective evaluations that were used as the training set for determining a good automated algorithm were made, I chose articles uniformly at random from the set included in our corpus until I had one article labeled as normative and one labeled as non-normative in each of the two fields. Here is a brief description and justification of my labeling of those four articles.

- Finance, non-normative: Titman et al. (2004), in the *JF*, build a structural model of credit spreads, in the spirit of Merton's (1973), in a world of credit rationing and underinvestment in the spirit of Myers (1977) and Stiglitz and Weiss (1981). Whereas the latter papers are interested in the social underprovision of investment, Titman et al.'s focus is different; instead, they are interested, like Merton's, in the (theoretical and empirical) implications for asset pricing and only briefly mention social waste from underinvestment in the conclusion. Thus, the paper is primarily about valuing assets, not maximizing allocative efficiency, and thus was coded as non-normative.

- IO, non-normative: Saloner and Shepard (1995), in the *RJE*, test empirical hypotheses emerging from the literature on network goods by considering the correlation of adoption patterns of automated teller machines with bank network and deposit characteristics. They show that network size matters more than deposit size. Although such adoption patterns may have normative implications, the article does not explore them except as a direction for future research in the conclusion. The article is thus primarily about the choice patterns of firms rather than optimal policy and was thus coded as non-normative.

- Finance, normative: Bryant (1980), in the *JF*, considers whether nontransferable bonds are part of a socially optimal set of monetary instruments in a consumption-loans model in the spirit of Samuelson (1958). This focus is clearly an exercise in normative monetary theory and is classified as such.

- IO, normative: Seldon et al. (2000), in the *IJIO*, study the degree to which different media outlets are substitutes in generating sales for advertisers, and the extent to which declining returns to scale occur in advertising. Although fundamentally a positive analysis, the paper, beginning with the abstract and running throughout, constantly returns to the normative implications of the analysis for advertising bans, mergers, and the welfare impacts of advertising. The paper was thus classified as normative.

I used these subjective evaluations as a training set for simple tree-based, threshold-crossing models for labeling articles as positive or normative based on the occurrence of certain key words and phrases. I now describe the algorithm on which I settled. I assigned articles scores along each of five dimensions relating to different key words:

- *Welfare frequency* (W): frequency of occurrence of the word "welfare."
- *Social frequency* (S): frequency of occurrence of the words "social" or "socially."
- *Policy frequency* (P): frequency of occurrence of the phrases "policy recommendation(s)," "policy conclusion(s)," or "policy implication(s)."
- *Antitrust frequency* (A): frequency of occurrence of the word "antitrust."
- *Regulation frequency* (R): frequency of occurrence of the word "regulation(s)."

TABLE 9.2 **Score matrix for article coding**

	Score				
Score category	1	2	3	4	5
W	0	1	2–4	5–9	10+
S	0	1	2–3	4–7	8+
P	0	1	2	3	4+
A	0	1	2	3–5	6+
R	0	1	2	3–9	10+

Note: see text for explanations of table entries.

I then translated these frequencies nonlinearly into five scores, W, S, P, A, and R, according to Table 9.2. The score received in each of these dimensions is shown as the top row; each of the frequencies is shown as a row. Table entries are the range required for the relevant frequency to translate into the relevant score. Articles were then labeled normative if $2W + S + 3P + 2A + R > 12$. Several other algorithms, such as those based on simple averaging compared to a threshold or scores on any one individual threshold, yield similar results but were less precise. This algorithm yielded 82% correct labeling compared to subjective evaluations on the sample it was trained (and its parameters optimized) on, and 76% accuracy on the remaining half of the sample that was held out for cross-validation.

Notes

Microsoft Research New York City, New York, NY, and Department of Economics, Yale University, glenweyl@microsoft.com, http://www.glenweyl.com.

* I am grateful to the Marion Ewing Kauffman Foundation for supporting this research, and particularly for funding the excellent research assistance of Jacob Conway, Joe Mihm, Tim Rudnicki, Matt Solomon, and Daichi Ueda, without whom this project would have been impossible. I also appreciate the helpful comments of Dennis Carlton, James Evans, Gene Fama, Ed Glaeser, Bill Landes, Sam Peltzman, Dick Posner, Eric Schliesser, and participants at the conference of the same name as the volume in which this paper is published, as well as seminar participants at Duke University and the University of Chicago. I am particularly grateful for to my co-editors, Ed Glaeser and Tano Santos, for their detailed comments. All errors are my own.

1. Mirowski and Nik-Khah (2013) argue, in a view popularized in the 2010 hit film *Inside Job*, that economists working in the financial sector were led by material incentives to publicly defend (or, more often, refrain from critiquing)

market institutions that served their financial interests. In contrast, the view I put forward is not that financial economists defended the interests of the firms for which they worked in regulatory disputes; I believe IO economists, in contrast to financial economists, often did defend those interests. Instead, I suggest financial economists were simply not interested in such disputes and instead focused on aiding the private accumulation of wealth in markets rather than pushing public policy in one direction or the other. Although some examples of Mirowski and Nik-Khah's argument (they provide some) undoubtedly exist, I am skeptical that such evidence represents a widespread phenomenon, because in the case of IO, the most vocal critics of firms in academic work are often their most valuable defenders in consulting, and vice versa. I thus find that work defending firms is unlikely to systematically skew academic research in these firms' favor; in fact, such work might even have the opposite effect on average. Some evidence beyond Mirowski and Nik-Khah's anecdotes would be necessary to understand the broader validity of their argument. Hopefully, this article offers a first step down the path to answering questions of this sort, and my work with James Evans will allow Mirowski and Nik-Khah's hypothesis also to be tested.

2. Further, recent research by Azar et al. (2015) suggests the broad focus of financial economics on maximizing returns to capital may systematically undermine returns to other factors of production when diversification allows capitalists to collude and thus acquire market power.

3. In a single, very small exception, I consulted on a case for an hour with a Compass Lexecon economist. I have also extensively consulted with governments on antitrust matters, though almost all on policy rather than case matters.

4. See, e.g., United States Department of Justice and Federal Trade Commission (1982); United States Department of Justice and Federal Trade Commission (1992, 2010).

5. Of course, in parallel to this work on asset pricing, a separate but related literature on corporate finance arose that covered issues including financial regulation and corporate governance. In spirit, this literature is much closer to that of the policy-oriented IO literature. However, as the previous section shows, such policy-oriented work is quantitatively a smaller part of the finance literature than it is of the IO literature. This parallels how, quantitatively, the IO literature has some (but not much) work on the details of how firms should optimally price discriminate, optimize production, or gain competitive advantage over rivals. For those familiar with the respective literatures, comparing the Black and Scholes's (1973) and Merton's (1973) papers to perhaps the most prominent paper in the normative corporate finance literature, Diamond and Dybvig (1983) is useful. Despite this paper's enormous influence, it has a quarter fewer citations than does Merton's's paper and about one quarter those of Black and Scholes's (1973). Other comparisons make this quantitative contrast equally sharp. For example, Ross's

(1973) seminal work on agency theory has about half the citations of his work, 12 years later, on the term structure of interest rates (Cox et al. 1985). Although the field is diverse, as are all fields, the quantitative bulk of its focus is clear both anecdotally and formally from the evidence given in Section 2.

References

Azar, J., M. C. Schmalz, and I. Tecu (2015). Anti-competitive effects of common ownership. http://ssrn.com/abstract=2427345.

Becker, G. S. (1976). *The Economic Approach to Human Behavior*. Chicago: University of Chicago Press.

Bernstein, P. L. (1992). *Capital Ideas: The Improbable Origins of Modern Finance*. Hoboken, NJ: John Wiley & Sons.

———. (2007). *Capital Ideas Evolving*. Hoboken, NJ: John Wiley & Sons.

Black, F., and M. Scholes (1973). The pricing of options and corporate liabilities. *Journal of Political Economy 81*(3), 637–654.

Brunnermeier, M. K., A. Simsek, and W. Xiong (2014). A welfare criterion for models with distorted beliefs. *Quarterly Journal of Economics 129*(4), 1753–1797.

Bryant, J. (1980). Nontransferable interest-bearing national debt. *Journal of Finance 35*(4), 1027–1031.

Coates, III, J. C. (2015). Cost-benefit analysis of financial regulation: Case studies and implications. *Yale Law Journal 124*(4), 882–1011.

Cox, J. C., J. E. Ingersoll Jr., and S. A. Ross (1985). A theory of the term structure of interest rates. *Econometrica 53*(2), 385–407.

DeLong, J. B., A. Shleifer, L. H. Summers, and R. J. Waldmann (1990). Noise trader risk in financial markets. *Journal of Political Economy 98*(4), 703–738.

Diamond, D. W., and P. H. Dybvig (1983). Bank runs, deposit insurance, and liquidity. *Journal of Political Economy 91*(3), 401–419.

Duffie, D. (2001). *Dynamic Asset Pricing Theory*. Princeton, NJ, and Oxford: Princeton University Press.

Fourcade, M. (2009). *Economists and Societies: Discipline and Profession in the United States, Britain and France, 1890s to 1990s*. Princeton, NJ, and Oxford: Princeton University Press.

Gilboa, I., L. Samuelson, and D. Schmeidler (2014). No-betting Pareto dominance. *Econometrica 82*(4), 1405–1442.

Greenwood, R., and D. Scharfstein (2013). The growth of finance. *Journal of Economic Perspectives 27*(2), 3–28.

Grossman, S. J., and J. E. Stiglitz (1980). On the impossibility of informationally efficient markets. *American Economic Review 70*(3), 393–408.

Hall, R. L., and F. W. Wayman (1990). Buying time: Moneyed interests and the mobilization of bias in congressional committees. *American Political Science Review 84*(3), 797–820.

Hicks, J. R. (1939). The foundations of welfare economics. *Economic Journal 49*(196), 696–712.

Hirshleifer, J. (1971). The private and social value of information and the reward to inventive activity. *American Economic Review 61*(4), 561–574.

Kaldor, N. (1939). Welfare propositions in economics and interpersonal comparisons of utility. *Economic Journal 49*(145), 549–552.

Kitch, E. W. (1983). The fire of truth: A remembrance of law and economics at Chicago, 1932–1970. *Journal of Law and Economics 26*(1), 163–234.

Landes, W. M., and R. A. Posner (1993). The influence of economics on law: A quantitative study. *Journal of Law and Economics 36*(1), 385–424.

MacKenzie, D. (2008). *An Engine, Not a Camera: How Financial Models Shape Markets*. Cambridge, MA: MIT Press.

Merton, R. C. (1973). Theory of rational option pricing. *Bell Journal of Economics and Management Science 4*(1), 141–183.

Mirowski, P., and E. Nik-Khah (2013). Private intellectuals and public perplexity: The economics profession and the economic crisis. *History of Political Economy 45*(S1), 279–311.

Myers, S. C. (1977). Determinants of corporate borrowing. *Journal of Financial Economics 5*(2), 147–175.

Philippon, T. (2015). Has the us finance industry become less efficient? On the theory and measurement of financial intermediation. *American Economic Review 105*(4), 1408–1438.

Posner, E., and E. G. Weyl (2013a). Benefit-cost analysis for financial regulation. *American Economic Review Papers and Proceedings 103*(3), 393–397.

———. (2013b). An FDA for financial innovation: Applying the insurable interest doctrine to 21st century financial markets. *Northwestern University Law Review 107*(3), 1307–1358.

———. (2014). Benefit-cost paradigms in financial regulation. *Journal of Legal Studies 43*(S2), S1–S34.

Posner, R. A. (1976). *Antitrust Law: An Economic Approach*. Chicago: University of Chicago Press.

Ross, S. A. (1973). The economic theory of agency: The principal's problem. *American Economic Review 63*(2), 134–139.

Saloner, G., and A. Shepard (1995). Adoption of technologies with network effects: an empirical examination of the adoption of automated teller machines. *RAND Journal of Economics 26*(3), 479–501.

Samuelson, P. (1958). An exact consumption-loan model of interest with or without the social contrivance of money. *Journal of Political Economy 66*(6), 467–482.

Seldon, B. J., R. T. Jewell, and D. M. O'Brien (2000). Media substituion and economies of scale in advertising. *International Journal of Industrial Organization 18*(8), 1153–1180.

Simsek, A. (2013a). Financial innovation and portfolio risks. *American Economic Review Papers and Proceedings 103*(3), 398–401.

———. (2013b). Speculation and risk sharing with new financial assets. *Quarterly Journal of Economics 128*(3), 1365–1396.

Stiglitz, J. E., and A. M. Weiss (1981). Credit rationing in markets with imperfect information. *American Economic Review 71*(3), 393–410.

Titman, S., S. Tompaidis, and S. Tsyplakov (2004). Market imperfections, investment flexibility and default spreads. *Journal of Finance 49*(1), 165–205.

United States Department of Justice and Federal Trade Commission (1982). Horizontal merger guidelines. http://www.justice.gov/atr/hmerger/11248.htm.

———. (1992). Horizontal merger guidelines. http://www.justice.gov/atr/public /guidelines/hmg.pdf.

———. (2010). Horizontal merger guidelines. http://www.justice.gov/atr/public /guidelines/hmg-2010.html.

Weyl, E. G. (2007). Is arbitrage socially beneficial? http://papers.ssrn.com/sol3 /papers.cfm?abstract_id=1324423.

Acknowledgments

Many individuals played a role in making this book and the conference it is based on possible. Ephraim Gildor, Claudio Haddad, Pedro Morreira Salles, John Shepherd Reed, and William Janeway all provided financial support that was critical to enabling the conference where the papers in this volume were presented. Jessica Brucas was central to organizing the conference. Ye Li provided critical research assistance for the entire volume. Gerald Van Ravenswaay indexed this volume. We are especially grateful to Joseph Jackson, Holly Smith, and Jillian Tsui at the University of Chicago Press for guiding this volume through the publication process.

Contributors

Editors

EDWARD L. GLAESER is the Fred and Eleanor Glimp Professor of Economics at Harvard University.

TANO SANTOS is the David L. and Elsie M. Dodd Professor of Finance at the Columbia Business School.

E. GLEN WEYL is senior researcher at Microsoft Research.

Other authors

ALOISIO ARAUJO is professor of economics at the Getulio Vargas Foundation and the National Institute of Pure and Applied Mathematics in Rio de Janeiro, Brazil.

PATRICK BOLTON is the Barbara and David Zalaznick Professor of Business at the Columbia Business School.

RAFAEL FERREIRA is professor of Economics at the University of São Paulo, Brazil.

BRUNO FUNCHAL is professor at the FUCAPE Business School in Vitória, Brazil

LARS PETER HANSEN is the David Rockefeller Distinguished Service Professor in Economics, Statistics and the College at the University of Chicago.

CONGHUI HU is assistant professor in the Business School of the University of International Business and Economics in Beijing, China.

ALBERT S. KYLE is the Charles E. Smith Chair Professor of Finance at the Robert H. Smith School of Business at the University of Maryland.

BRUCE SACERDOTE is professor of economics at Dartmouth College.

JOSÉ A. SCHEINKMAN is the Charles and Lynn Zhang Professor of Economics at Columbia University.

WEI XIONG is the Hugh Lander and Mary Trumbull Adams Professor of Finance at Princeton University.

Index

Note: Page numbers followed by "f" or "t" refer to figures or tables respectively.